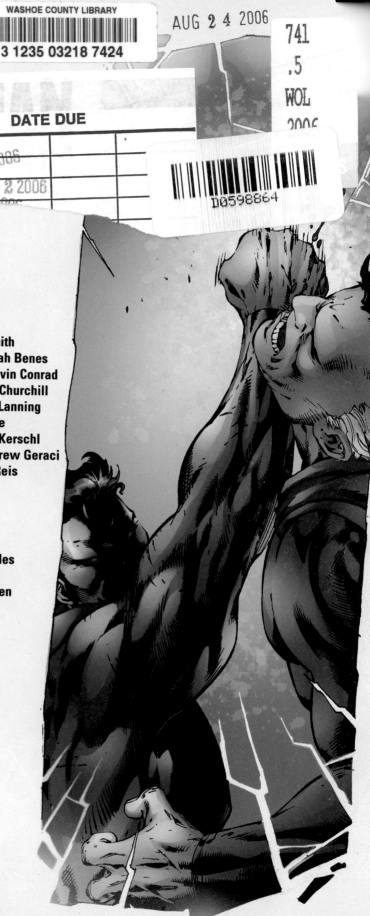

SUPERMAN
INFINITE

**Marv Wolfman   Joe Kelly   Geoff Johns
with Jeph Loeb**
WRITERS

**Dan Jurgens   Jerry Ordway   Cam Smith
Art Thibert   Nelson   Ed Benes   Mariah Benes
Howard Chaykin   Renato Guedes   Kevin Conrad
Dick Giordano   Jose Marzan Jr.   Ian Churchill
Norm Rapmund   Phil Jimenez   Andy Lanning
Lee Bermejo   Doug Mahnke   Tim Sale
Tom Derenick   Wayne Faucher   Karl Kerschl
Duncan Rouleau   Dale Eaglesham   Drew Geraci
Ed McGuinness   Dexter Vines   Ivan Reis
George Pérez   Dave Bullock
Kalman Andrasofszky**
ARTISTS

**Jeromy Cox   Guy Major   Renato Guedes
Dave Stewart   Tanya & Richard Horie
Rod Reis   Tom Smith   Michelle Madsen
Kalman Andrasofszky   Dave Bullock**
COLORISTS

**Travis Lanham   Pat Brosseau
Nick J. Napolitano   Comicraft**
LETTERERS

Special thanks to Joe Casey

**Superman created by
Jerry Siegel & Joe Shuster**

SUPERMAN: INFINITE CRISIS Published by DC Comics. Cover, introduction and compilation copyright © 2006 DC Comics. All Rights Reserved. Originally published in single magazine form in INFINITE CRISIS SECRET FILES & ORIGINS 2006, INFINITE CRISIS 5, SUPERMAN 226, ACTION COMICS 836 and ADVENTURES OF SUPERMAN 649. Copyright © 2006 DC Comics. All Rights Reserved. All characters, their distinctive likenesses and related elements featured in this publication are trademarks of DC Comics. The stories, characters and incidents featured in this publication are entirely fictional. DC Comics does not read or accept unsolicited submissions of ideas, stories or artwork. DC Comics, 1700 Broadway, New York, NY 10019. A Warner Bros. Entertainment Company.
Printed in Canada. First Printing. ISBN: 1-4012-0953-X. ISBN 13: 978-1-4012-0953-7.
Cover illustration by Phil Jimenez and Andy Lanning.
Publication design by Peter Hamboussi.

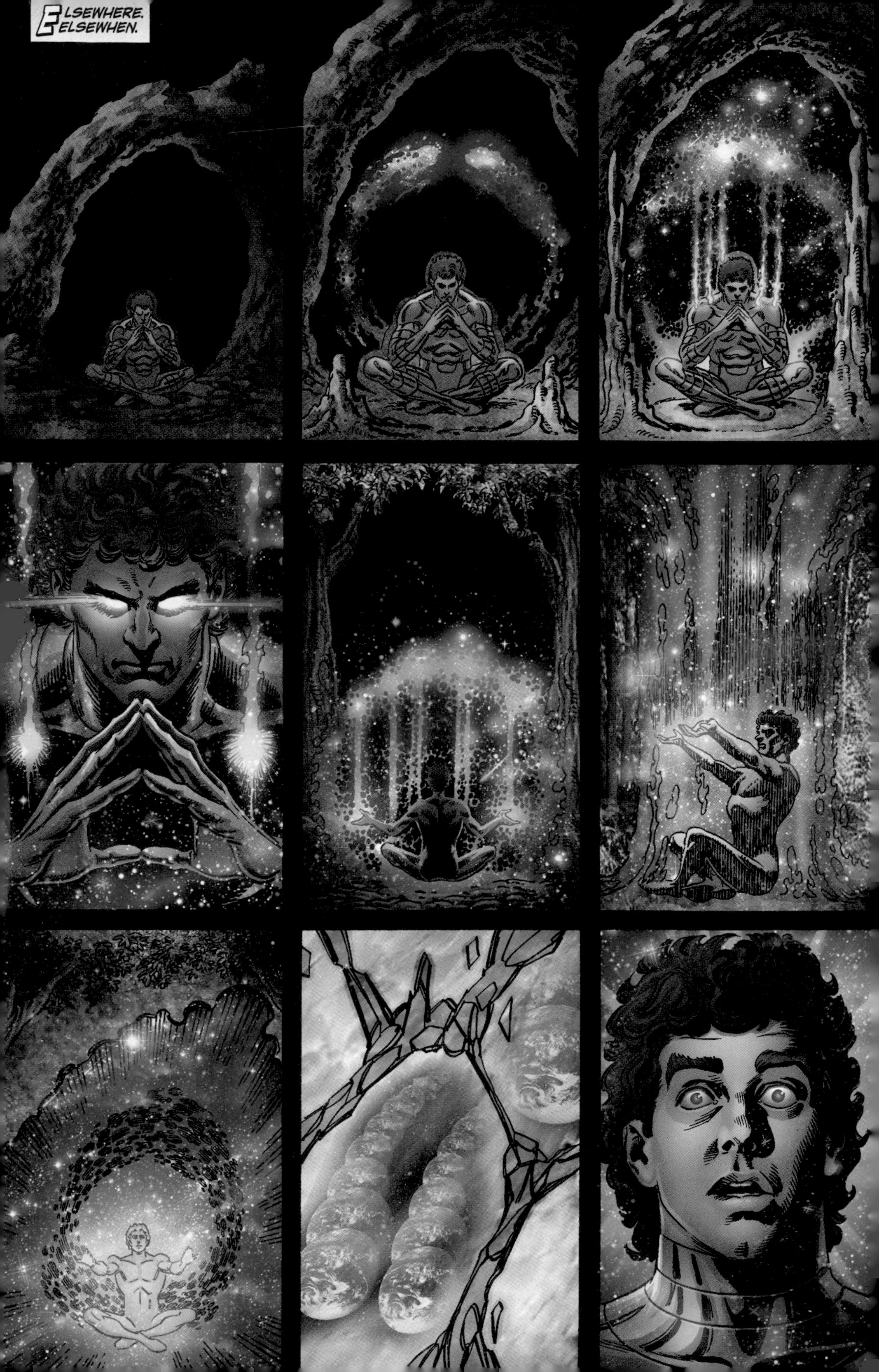
ELSEWHERE. ELSEWHEN.

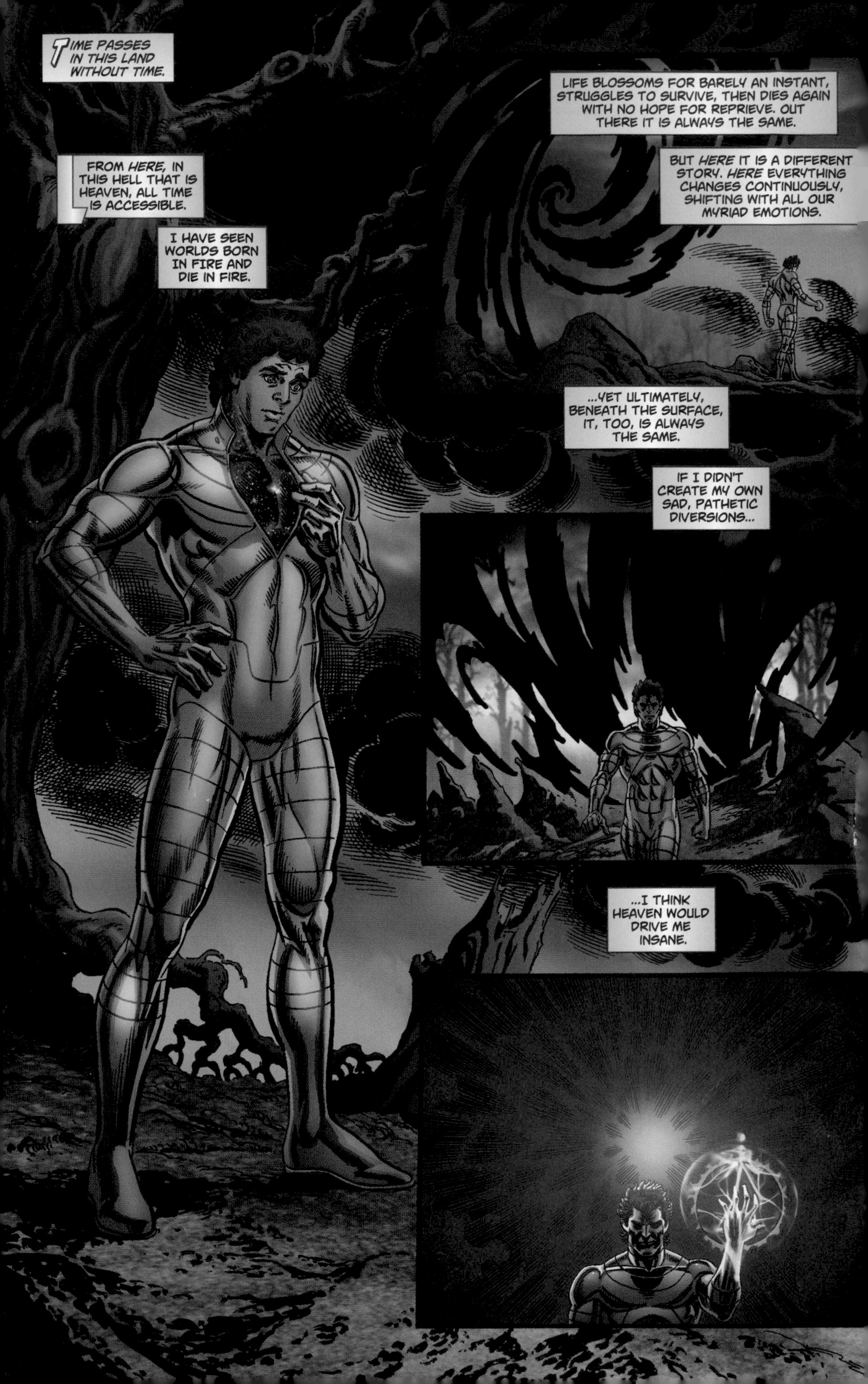
TIME PASSES IN THIS LAND WITHOUT TIME.
LIFE BLOSSOMS FOR BARELY AN INSTANT, STRUGGLES TO SURVIVE, THEN DIES AGAIN WITH NO HOPE FOR REPRIEVE. OUT THERE IT IS ALWAYS THE SAME.
FROM *HERE*, IN THIS HELL THAT IS HEAVEN, ALL TIME IS ACCESSIBLE.
BUT *HERE* IT IS A DIFFERENT STORY. *HERE* EVERYTHING CHANGES CONTINUOUSLY, SHIFTING WITH ALL OUR MYRIAD EMOTIONS.
I HAVE SEEN WORLDS BORN IN FIRE AND DIE IN FIRE.
...YET ULTIMATELY, BENEATH THE SURFACE, IT, TOO, IS ALWAYS THE SAME.
IF I DIDN'T CREATE MY OWN SAD, PATHETIC DIVERSIONS...
...I THINK HEAVEN WOULD DRIVE ME INSANE.

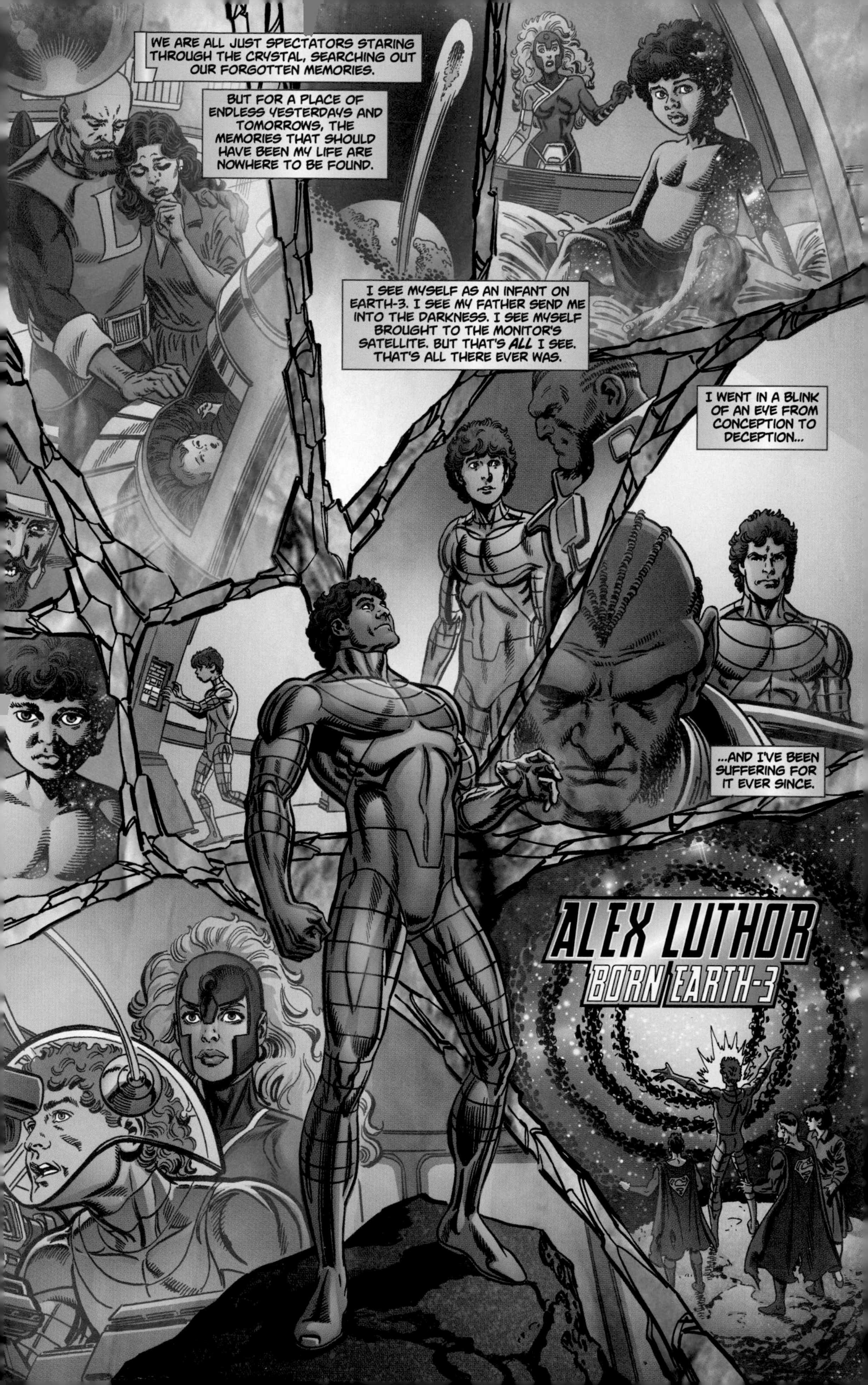
WE ARE ALL JUST SPECTATORS STARING THROUGH THE CRYSTAL, SEARCHING OUT OUR FORGOTTEN MEMORIES.
BUT FOR A PLACE OF ENDLESS YESTERDAYS AND TOMORROWS, THE MEMORIES THAT SHOULD HAVE BEEN MY LIFE ARE NOWHERE TO BE FOUND.
I SEE MYSELF AS AN INFANT ON EARTH-3. I SEE MY FATHER SEND ME INTO THE DARKNESS. I SEE MYSELF BROUGHT TO THE MONITOR'S SATELLITE. BUT THAT'S ALL I SEE. THAT'S ALL THERE EVER WAS.
I WENT IN A BLINK OF AN EYE FROM CONCEPTION TO DECEPTION...
...AND I'VE BEEN SUFFERING FOR IT EVER SINCE.
ALEX LUTHOR
BORN EARTH-3

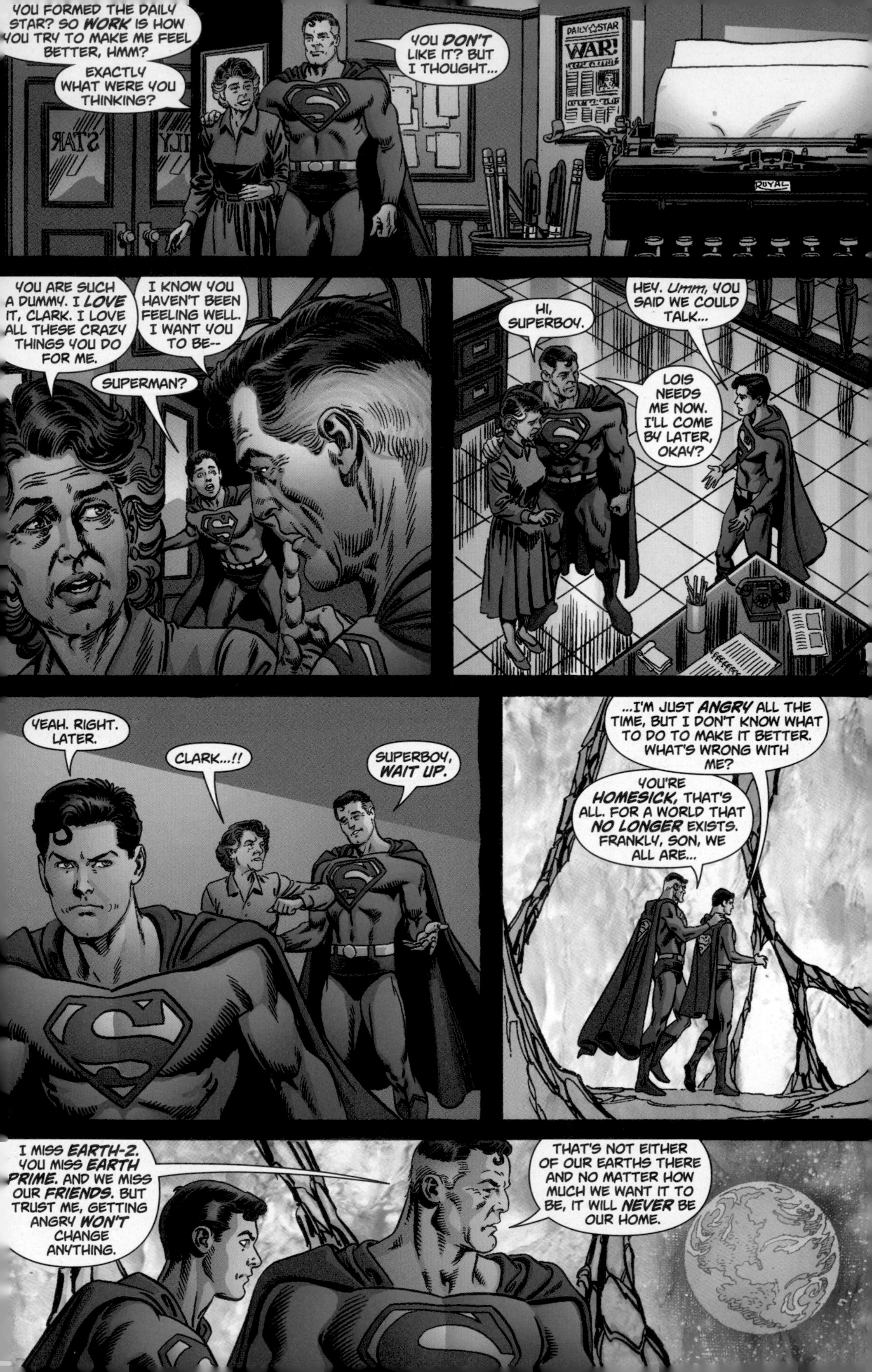

YOU FORMED THE DAILY STAR? SO WORK IS HOW YOU TRY TO MAKE ME FEEL BETTER, HMM?
EXACTLY WHAT WERE YOU THINKING?
YOU DON'T LIKE IT? BUT I THOUGHT...
DAILY STAR
WAR!
ROYAL
YOU ARE SUCH A DUMMY. I LOVE IT, CLARK. I LOVE ALL THESE CRAZY THINGS YOU DO FOR ME.
I KNOW YOU HAVEN'T BEEN FEELING WELL. I WANT YOU TO BE--
SUPERMAN?
HI, SUPERBOY.
HEY. Umm, YOU SAID WE COULD TALK...
LOIS NEEDS ME NOW. I'LL COME BY LATER, OKAY?
YEAH. RIGHT. LATER.
CLARK...!!
SUPERBOY, WAIT UP.
...I'M JUST ANGRY ALL THE TIME, BUT I DON'T KNOW WHAT TO DO TO MAKE IT BETTER. WHAT'S WRONG WITH ME?
YOU'RE HOMESICK, THAT'S ALL. FOR A WORLD THAT NO LONGER EXISTS. FRANKLY, SON, WE ALL ARE...
I MISS EARTH-2. YOU MISS EARTH PRIME. AND WE MISS OUR FRIENDS. BUT TRUST ME, GETTING ANGRY WON'T CHANGE ANYTHING.
THAT'S NOT EITHER OF OUR EARTHS THERE AND NO MATTER HOW MUCH WE WANT IT TO BE, IT WILL NEVER BE OUR HOME.

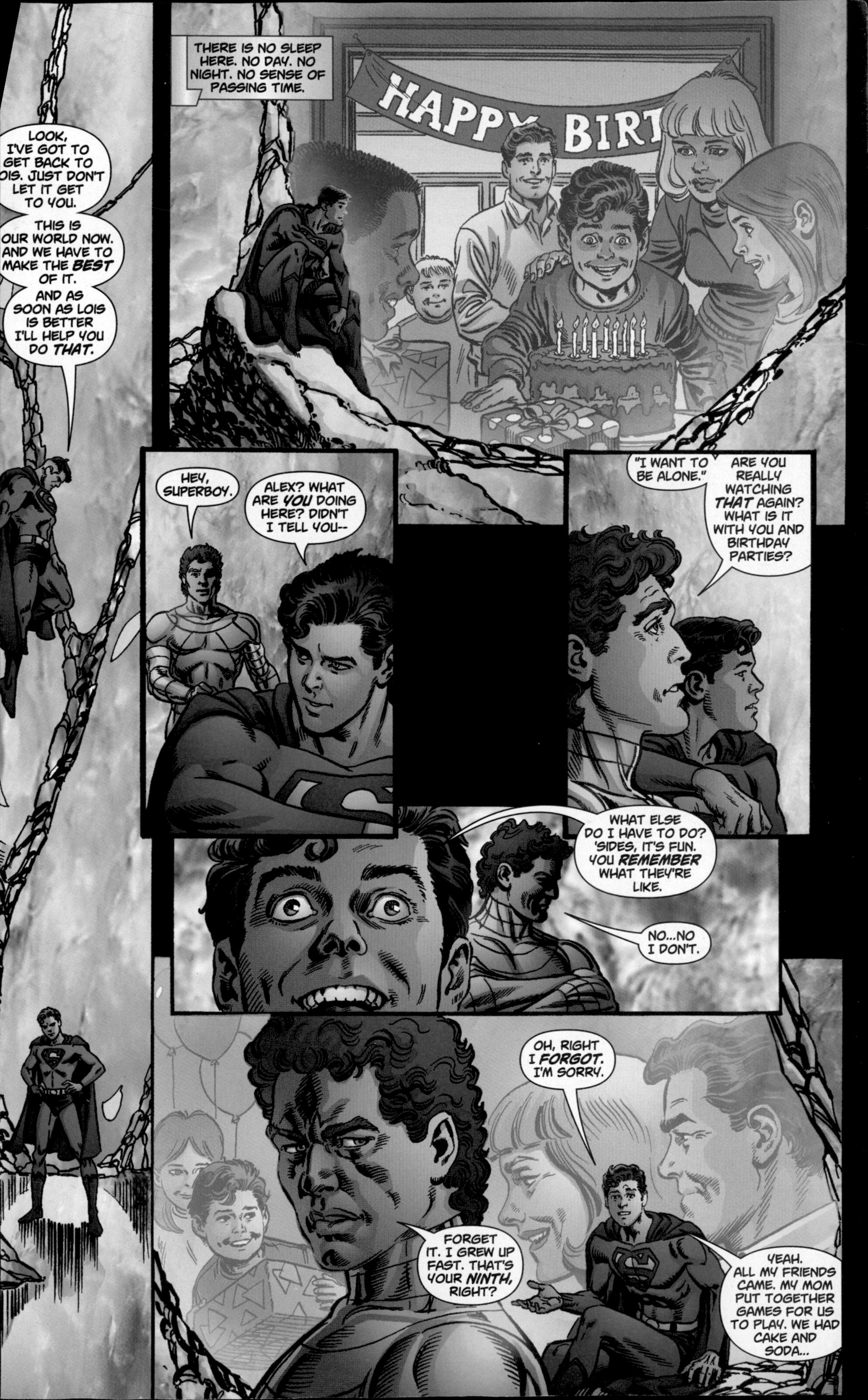
LOOK, I'VE GOT TO GET BACK TO LOIS. JUST DON'T LET IT GET TO YOU.
THIS IS OUR WORLD NOW. AND WE HAVE TO MAKE THE BEST OF IT.
AND AS SOON AS LOIS IS BETTER I'LL HELP YOU DO THAT.
THERE IS NO SLEEP HERE. NO DAY. NO NIGHT. NO SENSE OF PASSING TIME.
HAPPY BIRT
HEY, SUPERBOY.
ALEX? WHAT ARE YOU DOING HERE? DIDN'T I TELL YOU--
"I WANT TO BE ALONE."
ARE YOU REALLY WATCHING THAT AGAIN? WHAT IS IT WITH YOU AND BIRTHDAY PARTIES?
WHAT ELSE DO I HAVE TO DO? 'SIDES, IT'S FUN. YOU REMEMBER WHAT THEY'RE LIKE.
NO...NO I DON'T.
OH, RIGHT I FORGOT. I'M SORRY.
FORGET IT. I GREW UP FAST. THAT'S YOUR NINTH, RIGHT?
YEAH. ALL MY FRIENDS CAME. MY MOM PUT TOGETHER GAMES FOR US TO PLAY. WE HAD CAKE AND SODA...

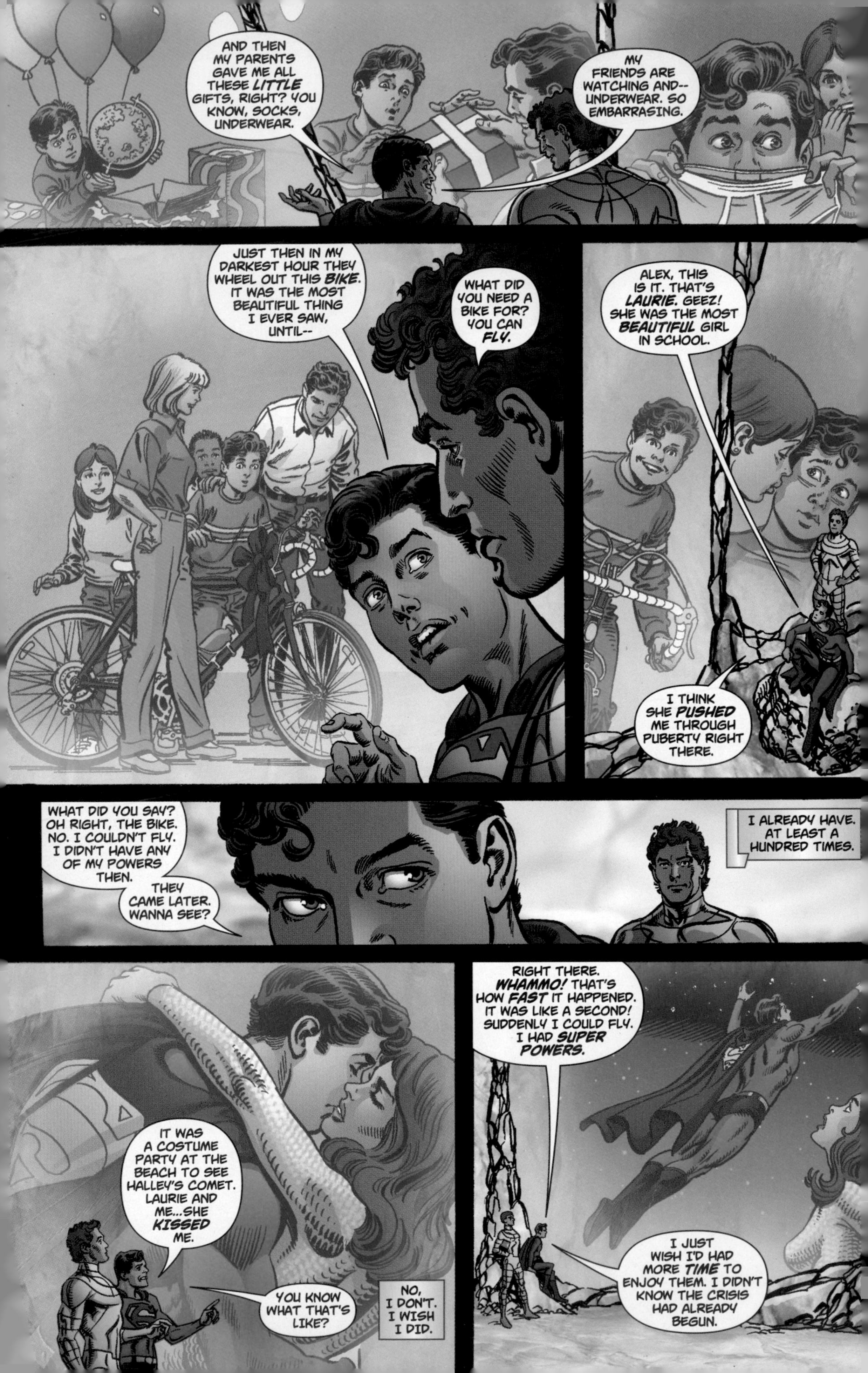
AND THEN MY PARENTS GAVE ME ALL THESE LITTLE GIFTS, RIGHT? YOU KNOW, SOCKS, UNDERWEAR.
MY FRIENDS ARE WATCHING AND-- UNDERWEAR. SO EMBARRASING.
JUST THEN IN MY DARKEST HOUR THEY WHEEL OUT THIS BIKE. IT WAS THE MOST BEAUTIFUL THING I EVER SAW, UNTIL--
WHAT DID YOU NEED A BIKE FOR? YOU CAN FLY.
ALEX, THIS IS IT. THAT'S LAURIE. GEEZ! SHE WAS THE MOST BEAUTIFUL GIRL IN SCHOOL.
I THINK SHE PUSHED ME THROUGH PUBERTY RIGHT THERE.
WHAT DID YOU SAY? OH RIGHT, THE BIKE. NO. I COULDN'T FLY. I DIDN'T HAVE ANY OF MY POWERS THEN.
THEY CAME LATER. WANNA SEE?
I ALREADY HAVE. AT LEAST A HUNDRED TIMES.
IT WAS A COSTUME PARTY AT THE BEACH TO SEE HALLEY'S COMET. LAURIE AND ME...SHE KISSED ME.
YOU KNOW WHAT THAT'S LIKE?
NO, I DON'T. I WISH I DID.
RIGHT THERE. WHAMMO! THAT'S HOW FAST IT HAPPENED. IT WAS LIKE A SECOND! SUDDENLY I COULD FLY. I HAD SUPER POWERS.
I JUST WISH I'D HAD MORE TIME TO ENJOY THEM. I DIDN'T KNOW THE CRISIS HAD ALREADY BEGUN.

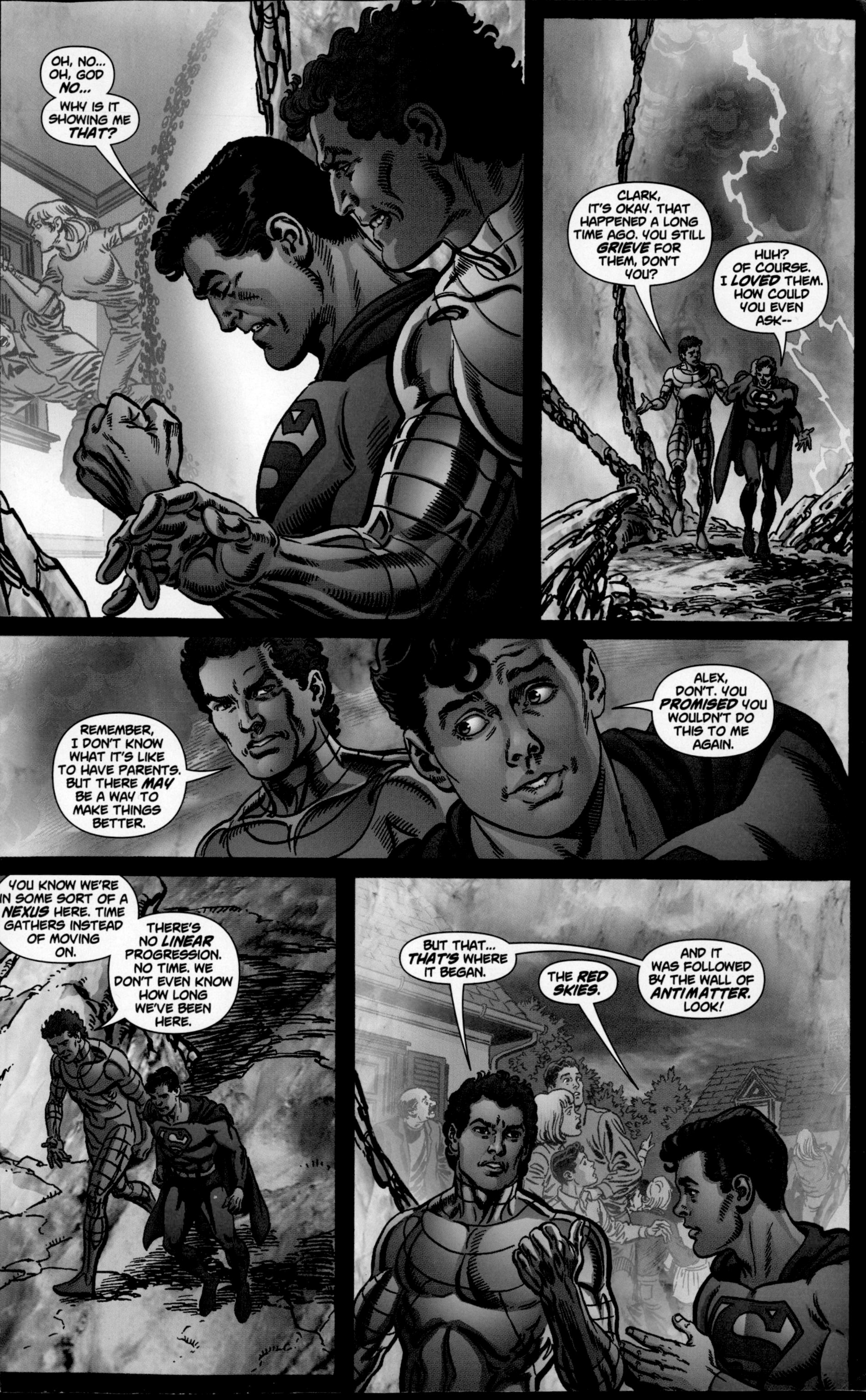
OH, NO... OH, GOD NO... WHY IS IT SHOWING ME THAT?
CLARK, IT'S OKAY. THAT HAPPENED A LONG TIME AGO. YOU STILL GRIEVE FOR THEM, DON'T YOU?
HUH? OF COURSE. I LOVED THEM. HOW COULD YOU EVEN ASK--
REMEMBER, I DON'T KNOW WHAT IT'S LIKE TO HAVE PARENTS. BUT THERE MAY BE A WAY TO MAKE THINGS BETTER.
ALEX, DON'T. YOU PROMISED YOU WOULDN'T DO THIS TO ME AGAIN.
YOU KNOW WE'RE IN SOME SORT OF A NEXUS HERE. TIME GATHERS INSTEAD OF MOVING ON.
THERE'S NO LINEAR PROGRESSION. NO TIME. WE DON'T EVEN KNOW HOW LONG WE'VE BEEN HERE.
BUT THAT... THAT'S WHERE IT BEGAN.
THE RED SKIES.
AND IT WAS FOLLOWED BY THE WALL OF ANTIMATTER. LOOK!

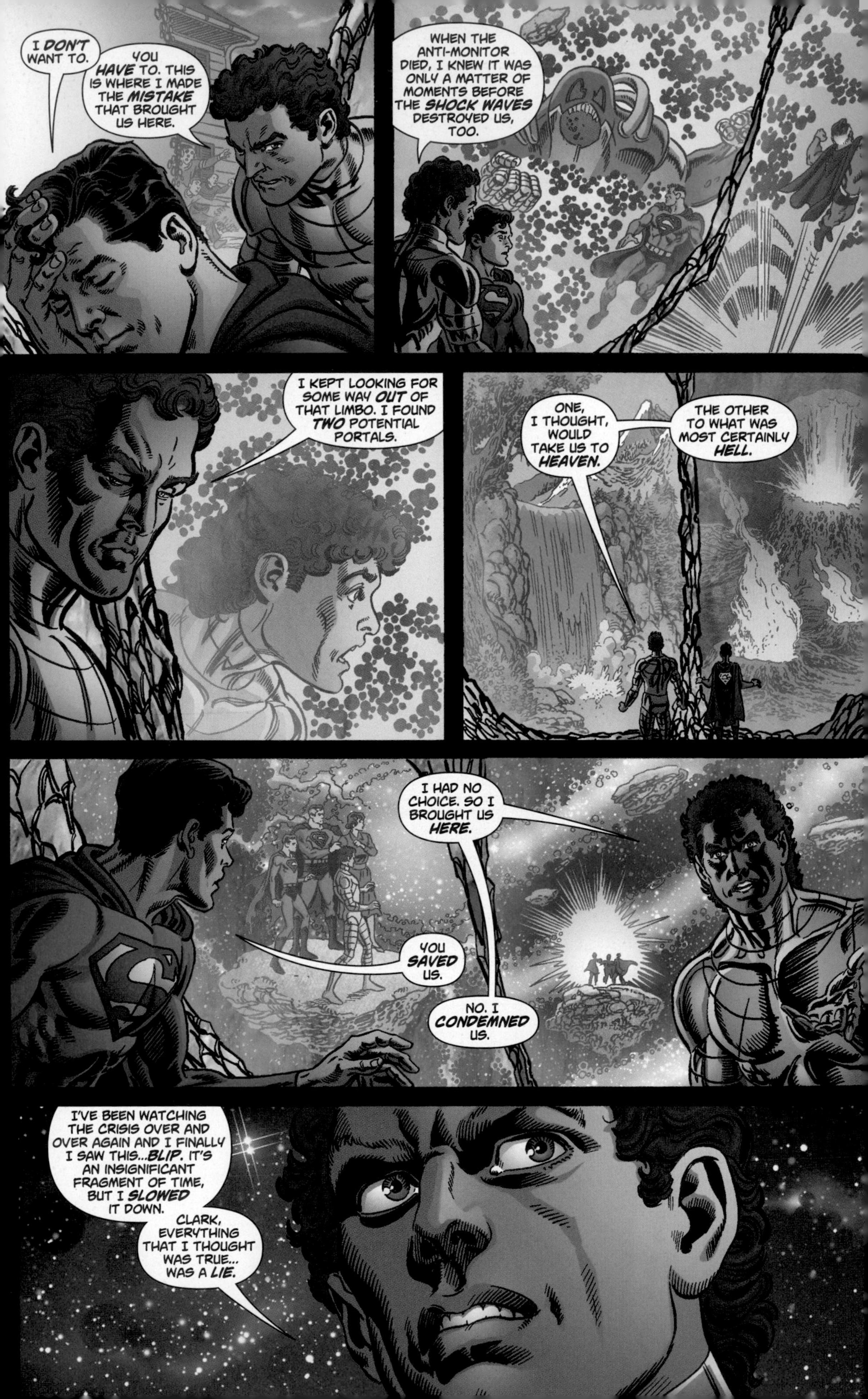
I DON'T WANT TO.
YOU HAVE TO. THIS IS WHERE I MADE THE MISTAKE THAT BROUGHT US HERE.
WHEN THE ANTI-MONITOR DIED, I KNEW IT WAS ONLY A MATTER OF MOMENTS BEFORE THE SHOCK WAVES DESTROYED US, TOO.
I KEPT LOOKING FOR SOME WAY OUT OF THAT LIMBO. I FOUND TWO POTENTIAL PORTALS.
ONE, I THOUGHT, WOULD TAKE US TO HEAVEN.
THE OTHER TO WHAT WAS MOST CERTAINLY HELL.
I HAD NO CHOICE. SO I BROUGHT US HERE.
YOU SAVED US.
NO. I CONDEMNED US.
I'VE BEEN WATCHING THE CRISIS OVER AND OVER AGAIN AND I FINALLY I SAW THIS...BLIP. IT'S AN INSIGNIFICANT FRAGMENT OF TIME, BUT I SLOWED IT DOWN.
CLARK, EVERYTHING THAT I THOUGHT WAS TRUE... WAS A LIE.

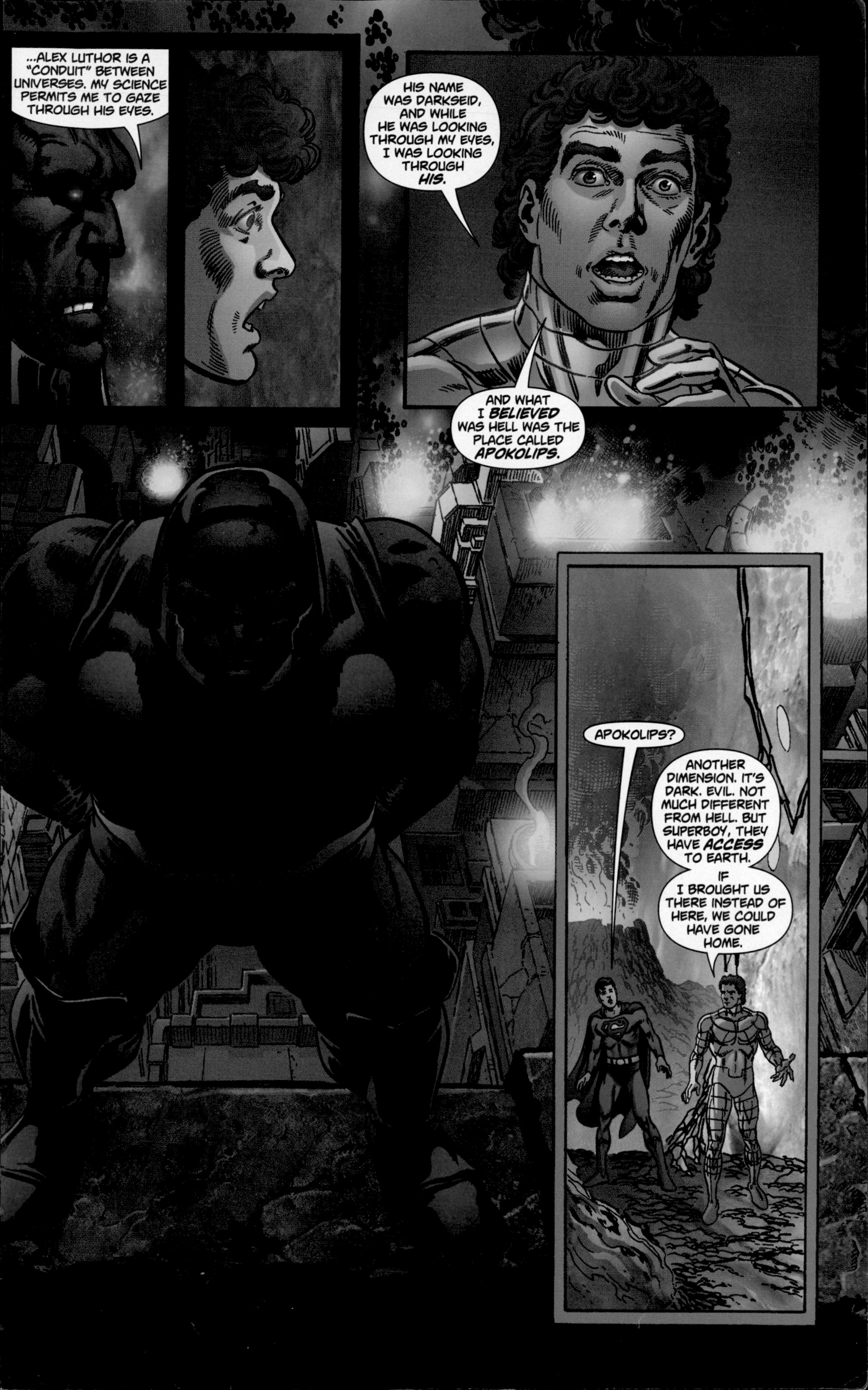
...ALEX LUTHOR IS A "CONDUIT" BETWEEN UNIVERSES. MY SCIENCE PERMITS ME TO GAZE THROUGH HIS EYES.
HIS NAME WAS DARKSEID, AND WHILE HE WAS LOOKING THROUGH MY EYES, I WAS LOOKING THROUGH HIS.
AND WHAT I BELIEVED WAS HELL WAS THE PLACE CALLED APOKOLIPS.
APOKOLIPS?
ANOTHER DIMENSION. IT'S DARK. EVIL. NOT MUCH DIFFERENT FROM HELL. BUT SUPERBOY, THEY HAVE ACCESS TO EARTH.
IF I BROUGHT US THERE INSTEAD OF HERE, WE COULD HAVE GONE HOME.

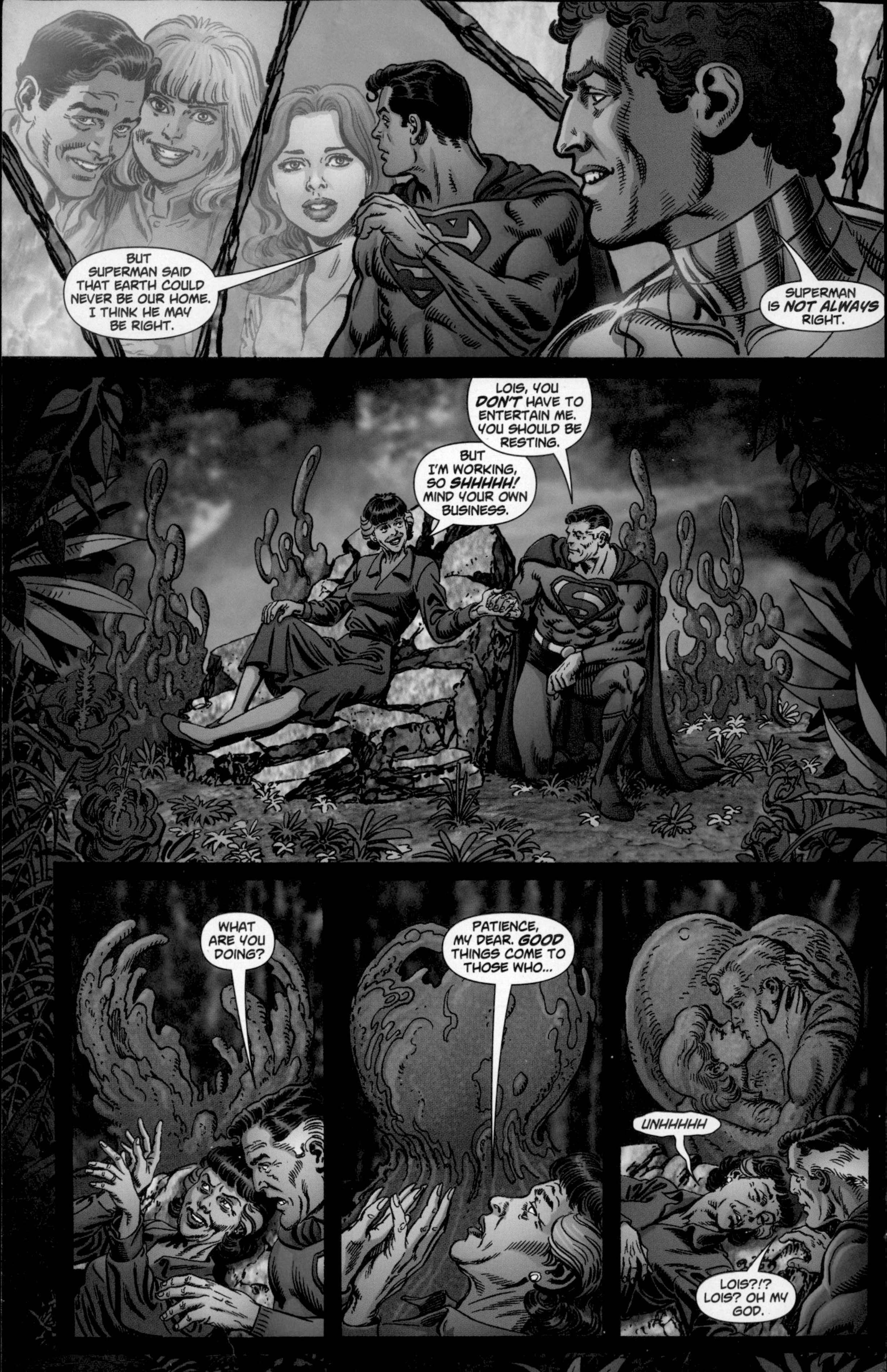
BUT SUPERMAN SAID THAT EARTH COULD NEVER BE OUR HOME. I THINK HE MAY BE RIGHT.
SUPERMAN IS NOT ALWAYS RIGHT.
LOIS, YOU DON'T HAVE TO ENTERTAIN ME. YOU SHOULD BE RESTING.
BUT I'M WORKING, SO SHHHHH! MIND YOUR OWN BUSINESS.
WHAT ARE YOU DOING?
PATIENCE, MY DEAR. GOOD THINGS COME TO THOSE WHO...
UNHHHHH
LOIS?!? LOIS? OH MY GOD.

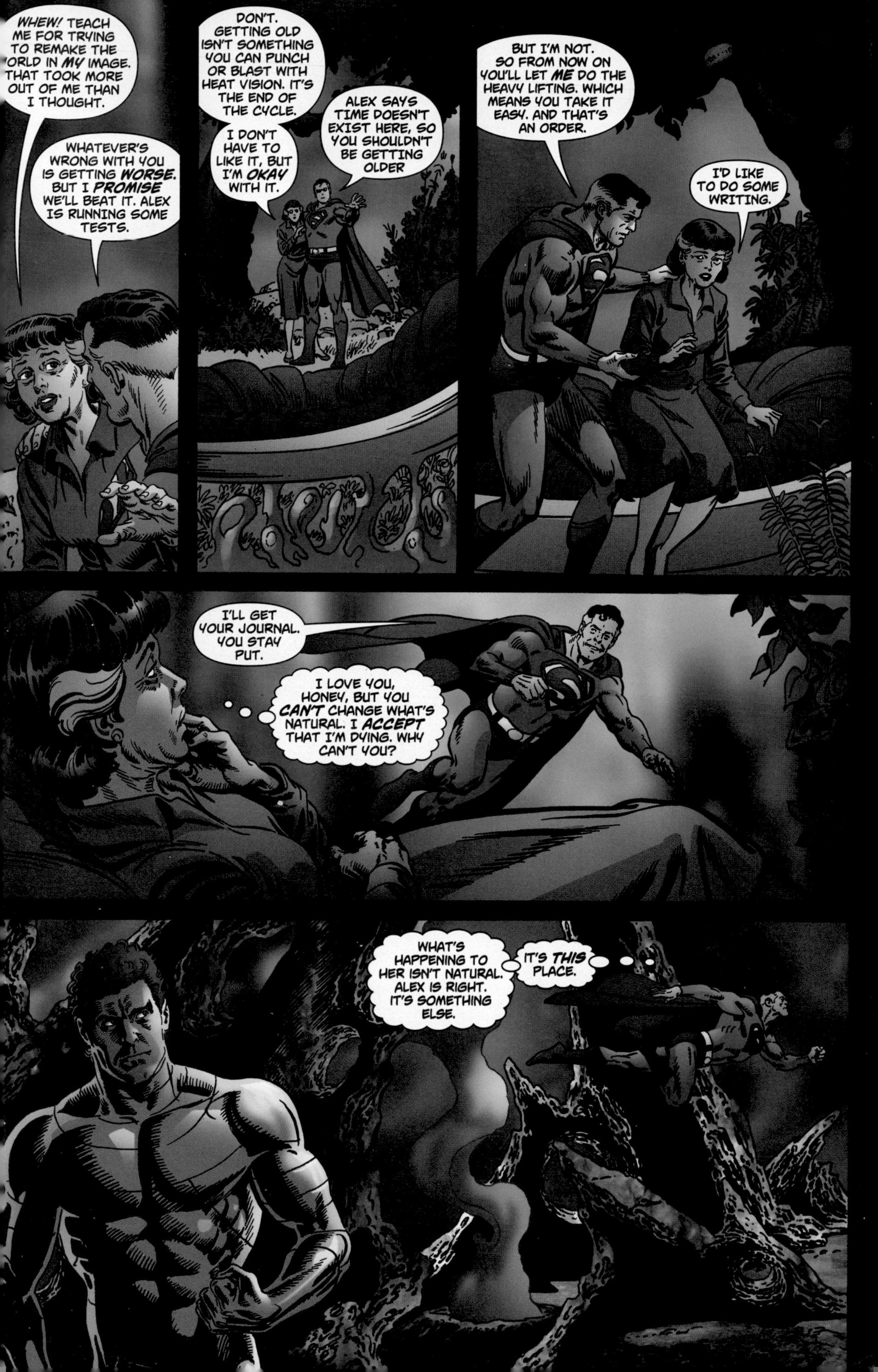
WHEW! TEACH ME FOR TRYING TO REMAKE THE ORLD IN MY IMAGE. THAT TOOK MORE OUT OF ME THAN I THOUGHT.
WHATEVER'S WRONG WITH YOU IS GETTING WORSE. BUT I PROMISE WE'LL BEAT IT. ALEX IS RUNNING SOME TESTS.
DON'T. GETTING OLD ISN'T SOMETHING YOU CAN PUNCH OR BLAST WITH HEAT VISION. IT'S THE END OF THE CYCLE.
I DON'T HAVE TO LIKE IT, BUT I'M OKAY WITH IT.
ALEX SAYS TIME DOESN'T EXIST HERE, SO YOU SHOULDN'T BE GETTING OLDER
BUT I'M NOT. SO FROM NOW ON YOU'LL LET ME DO THE HEAVY LIFTING. WHICH MEANS YOU TAKE IT EASY. AND THAT'S AN ORDER.
I'D LIKE TO DO SOME WRITING.
I'LL GET YOUR JOURNAL. YOU STAY PUT.
I LOVE YOU, HONEY, BUT YOU CAN'T CHANGE WHAT'S NATURAL. I ACCEPT THAT I'M DYING. WHY CAN'T YOU?
WHAT'S HAPPENING TO HER ISN'T NATURAL. ALEX IS RIGHT. IT'S SOMETHING ELSE.
IT'S THIS PLACE.

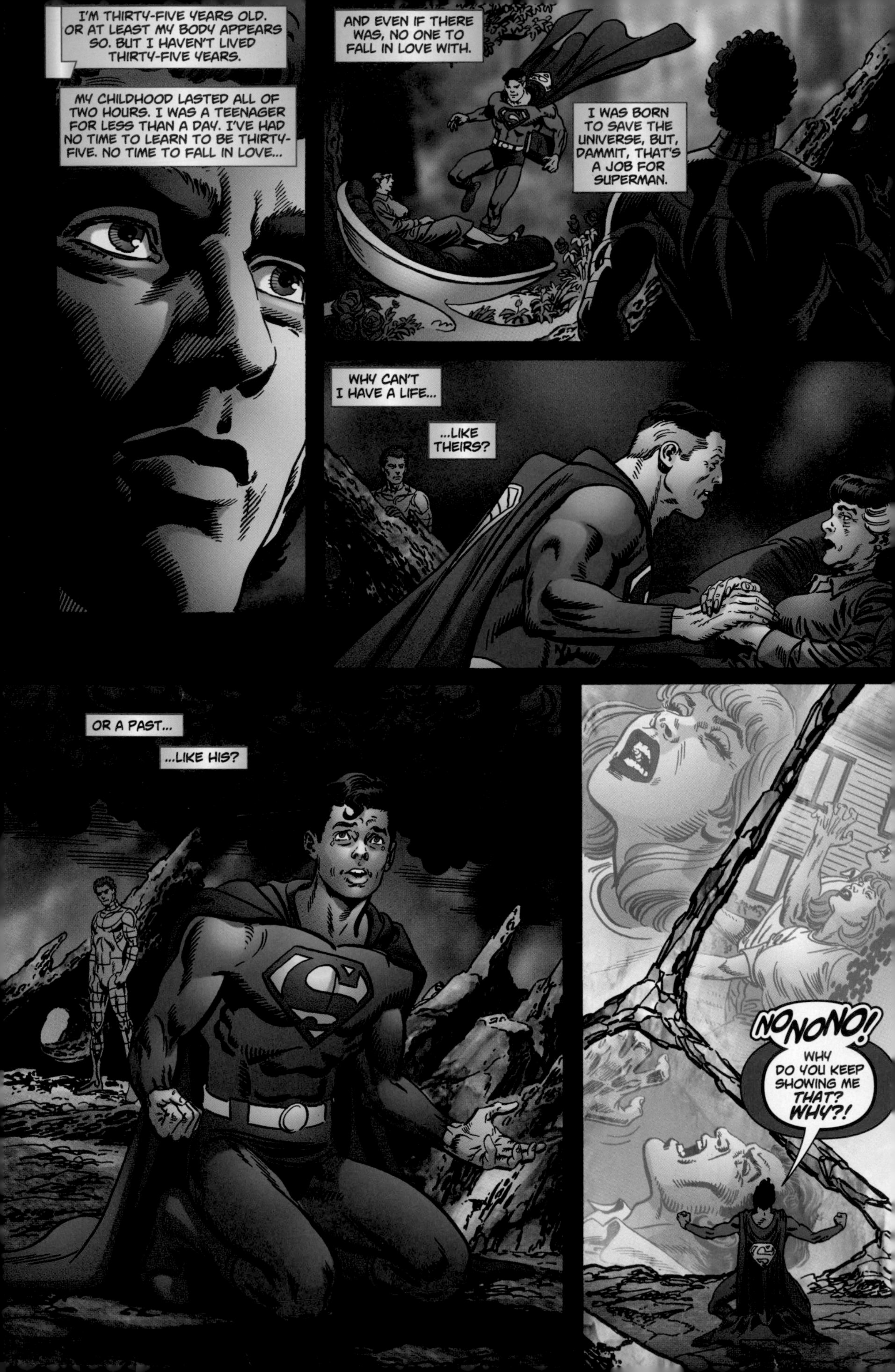

I'M THIRTY-FIVE YEARS OLD. OR AT LEAST MY BODY APPEARS SO. BUT I HAVEN'T LIVED THIRTY-FIVE YEARS.
MY CHILDHOOD LASTED ALL OF TWO HOURS. I WAS A TEENAGER FOR LESS THAN A DAY. I'VE HAD NO TIME TO LEARN TO BE THIRTY-FIVE. NO TIME TO FALL IN LOVE...
AND EVEN IF THERE WAS, NO ONE TO FALL IN LOVE WITH.
I WAS BORN TO SAVE THE UNIVERSE, BUT, DAMMIT, THAT'S A JOB FOR SUPERMAN.
WHY CAN'T I HAVE A LIFE...
...LIKE THEIRS?
OR A PAST...
...LIKE HIS?
NONONO!
WHY DO YOU KEEP SHOWING ME THAT? WHY?!

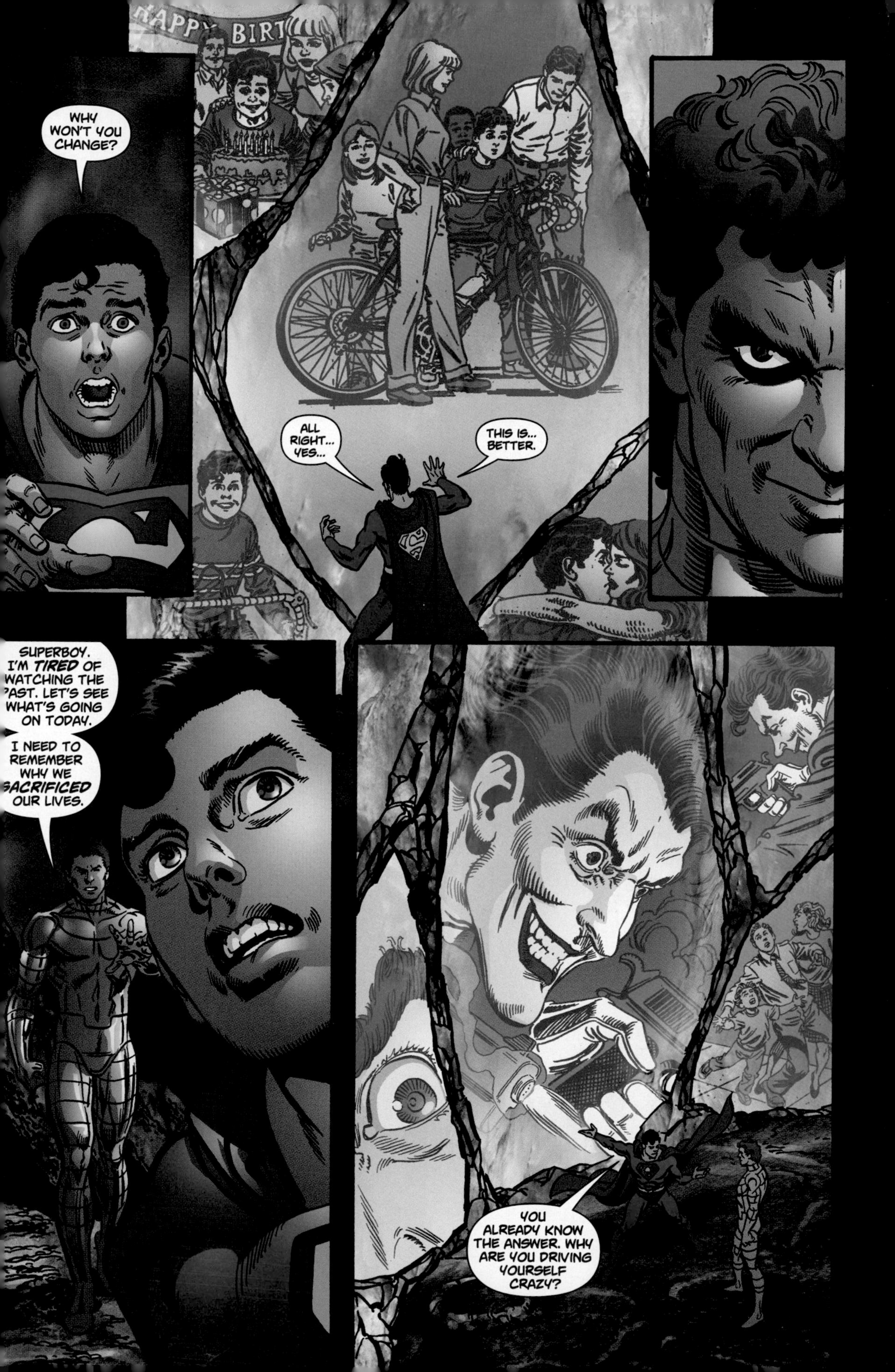

HAPPY BIRT
WHY WON'T YOU CHANGE?
ALL RIGHT... YES...
THIS IS... BETTER.
SUPERBOY. I'M *TIRED* OF WATCHING THE PAST. LET'S SEE WHAT'S GOING ON TODAY.
I NEED TO REMEMBER WHY WE *SACRIFICED* OUR LIVES.
YOU ALREADY KNOW THE ANSWER. WHY ARE YOU DRIVING YOURSELF CRAZY?

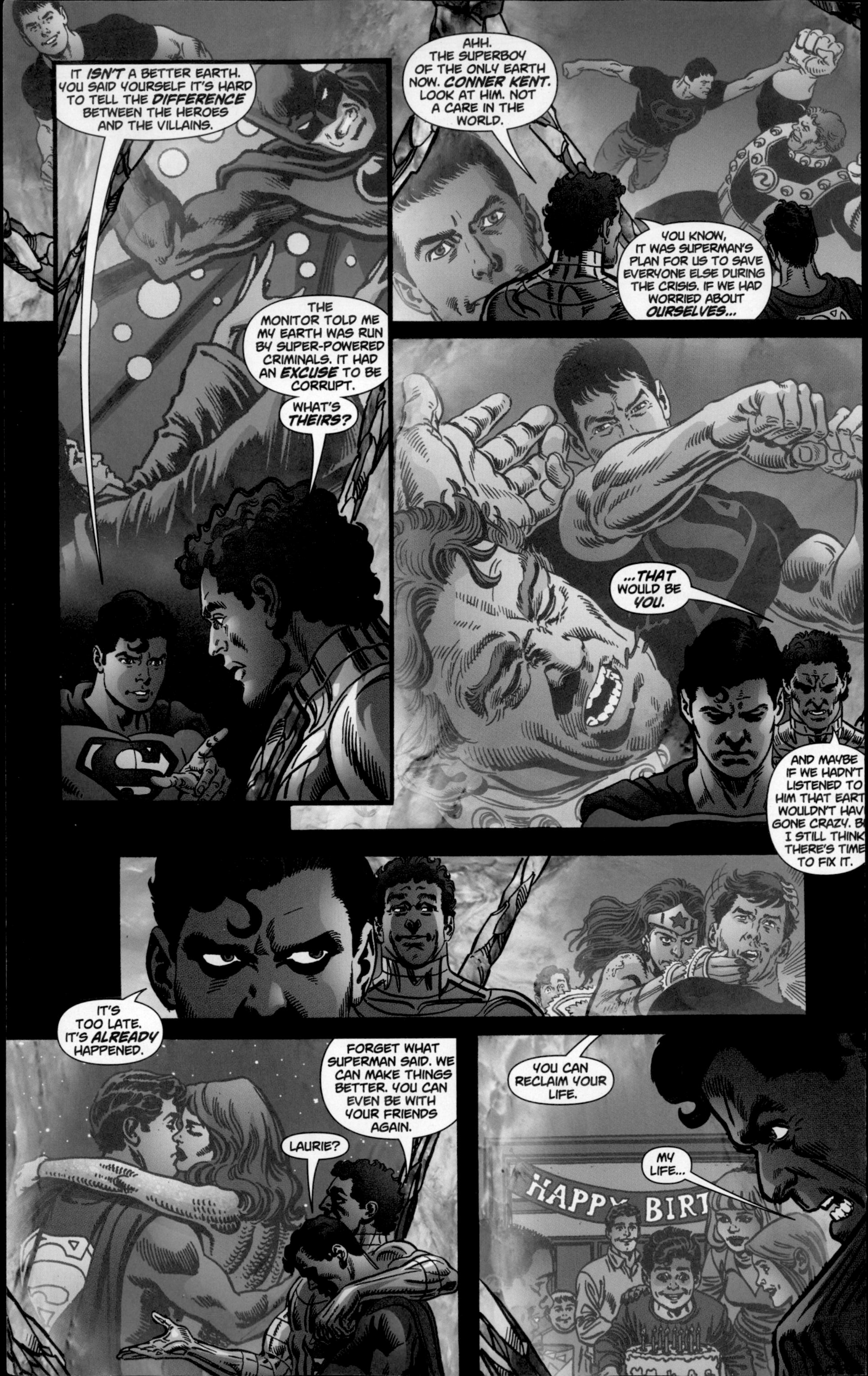
IT ISN'T A BETTER EARTH. YOU SAID YOURSELF IT'S HARD TO TELL THE DIFFERENCE BETWEEN THE HEROES AND THE VILLAINS.
AHH. THE SUPERBOY OF THE ONLY EARTH NOW. CONNER KENT. LOOK AT HIM. NOT A CARE IN THE WORLD.
YOU KNOW, IT WAS SUPERMAN'S PLAN FOR US TO SAVE EVERYONE ELSE DURING THE CRISIS. IF WE HAD WORRIED ABOUT OURSELVES...
THE MONITOR TOLD ME MY EARTH WAS RUN BY SUPER-POWERED CRIMINALS. IT HAD AN EXCUSE TO BE CORRUPT.
WHAT'S THEIRS?
...THAT WOULD BE YOU.
AND MAYBE IF WE HADN'T LISTENED TO HIM THAT EART WOULDN'T HAV GONE CRAZY. B I STILL THINK THERE'S TIME TO FIX IT.
IT'S TOO LATE. IT'S ALREADY HAPPENED.
FORGET WHAT SUPERMAN SAID. WE CAN MAKE THINGS BETTER. YOU CAN EVEN BE WITH YOUR FRIENDS AGAIN.
LAURIE?
YOU CAN RECLAIM YOUR LIFE.
MY LIFE...
HAPPY BIRT

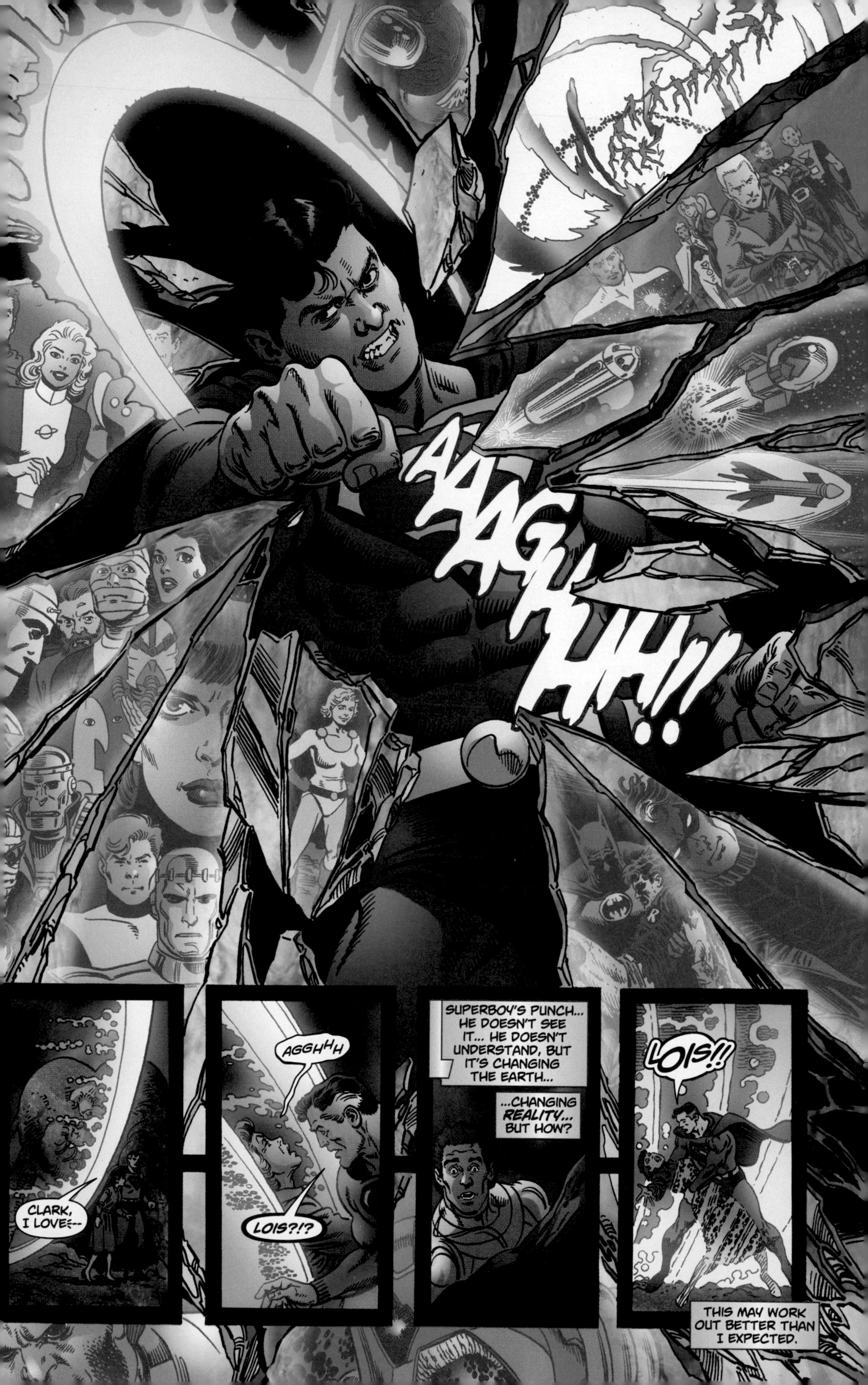
AAAGGHHH!!
CLARK, I LOVE--
AGGHHH
LOIS?!?
SUPERBOY'S PUNCH... HE DOESN'T SEE IT... HE DOESN'T UNDERSTAND, BUT IT'S CHANGING THE EARTH...
...CHANGING REALITY... BUT HOW?
LOIS!!
THIS MAY WORK OUT BETTER THAN I EXPECTED.

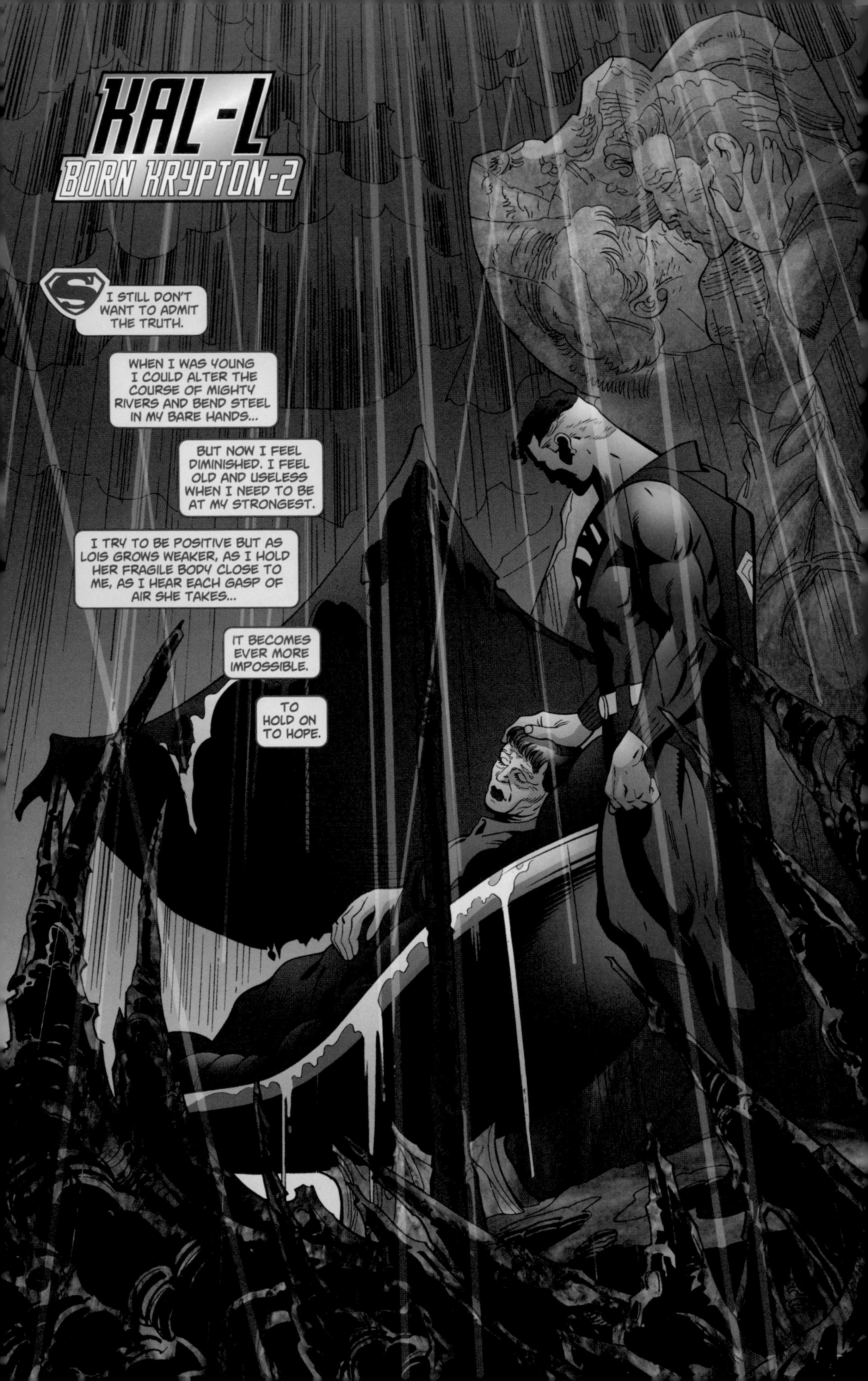
KAL-L
BORN KRYPTON-2
I STILL DON'T WANT TO ADMIT THE TRUTH.
WHEN I WAS YOUNG I COULD ALTER THE COURSE OF MIGHTY RIVERS AND BEND STEEL IN MY BARE HANDS...
BUT NOW I FEEL DIMINISHED. I FEEL OLD AND USELESS WHEN I NEED TO BE AT MY STRONGEST.
I TRY TO BE POSITIVE BUT AS LOIS GROWS WEAKER, AS I HOLD HER FRAGILE BODY CLOSE TO ME, AS I HEAR EACH GASP OF AIR SHE TAKES...
IT BECOMES EVER MORE IMPOSSIBLE.
TO HOLD ON TO HOPE.

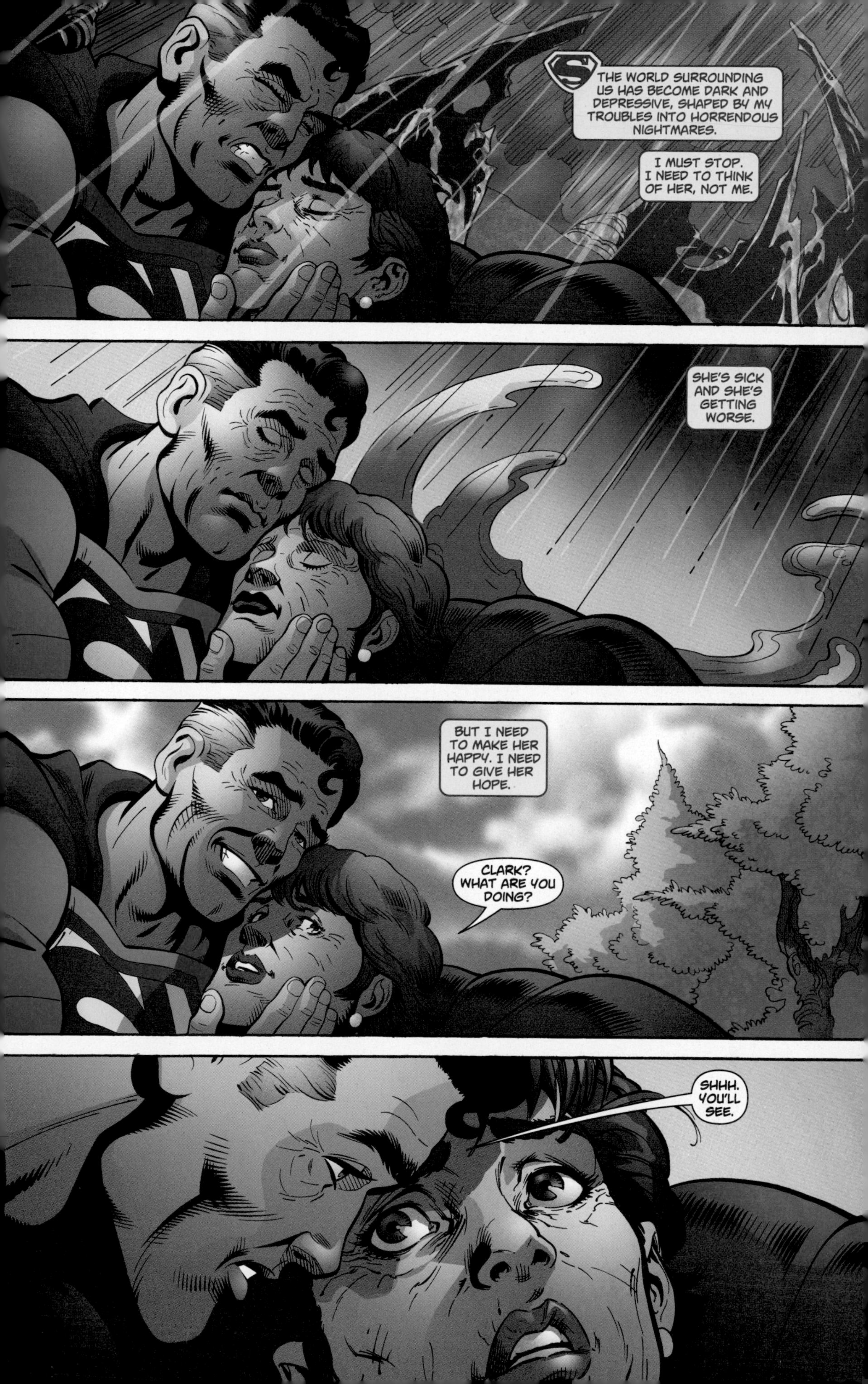
THE WORLD SURROUNDING US HAS BECOME DARK AND DEPRESSIVE, SHAPED BY MY TROUBLES INTO HORRENDOUS NIGHTMARES.
I MUST STOP. I NEED TO THINK OF HER, NOT ME.
SHE'S SICK AND SHE'S GETTING WORSE.
BUT I NEED TO MAKE HER HAPPY. I NEED TO GIVE HER HOPE.
CLARK? WHAT ARE YOU DOING?
SHHH. YOU'LL SEE.

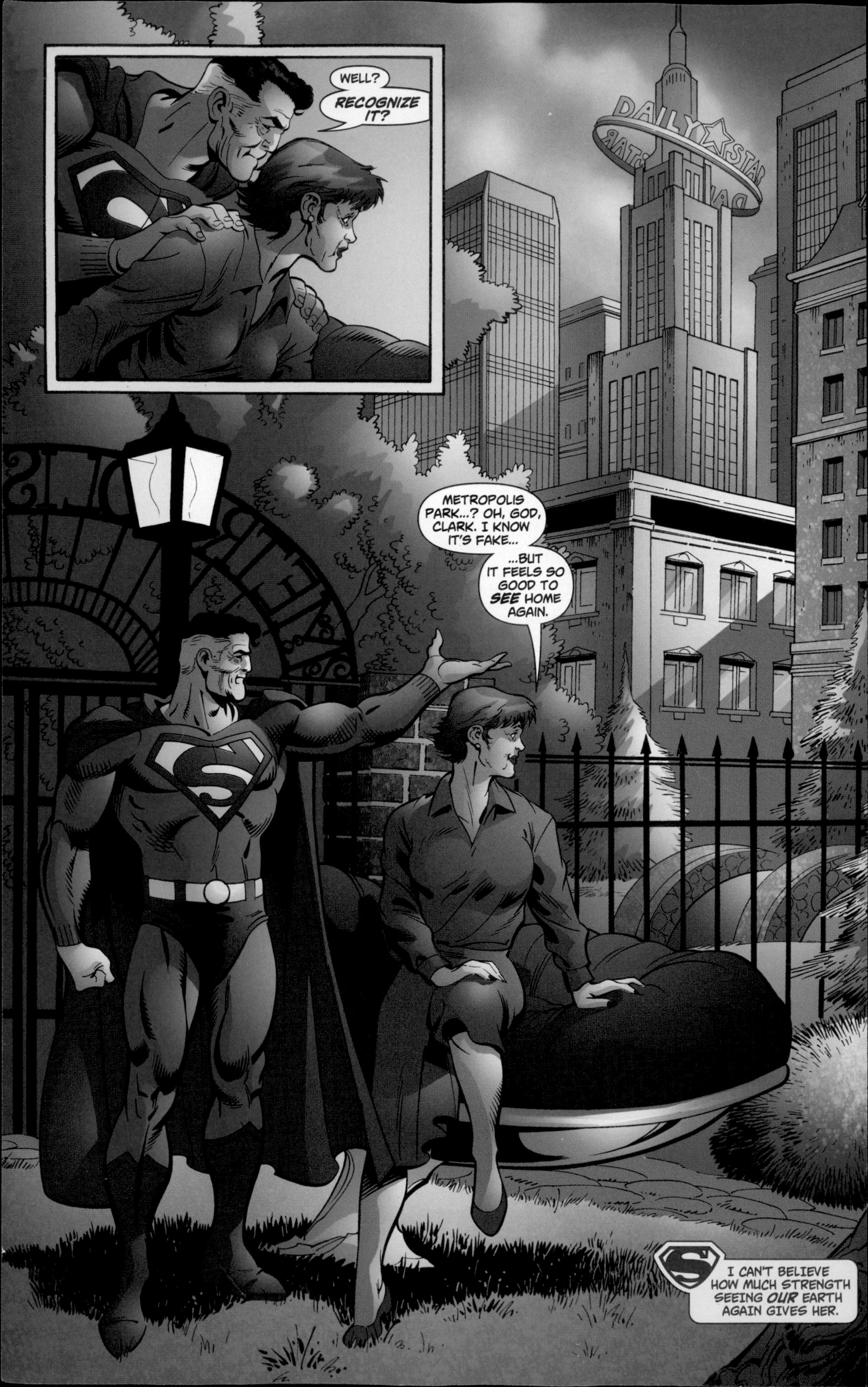
WELL? RECOGNIZE IT?
METROPOLIS PARK...? OH, GOD, CLARK. I KNOW IT'S FAKE...
...BUT IT FEELS SO GOOD TO SEE HOME AGAIN.
I CAN'T BELIEVE HOW MUCH STRENGTH SEEING OUR EARTH AGAIN GIVES HER.
DAILY STAR

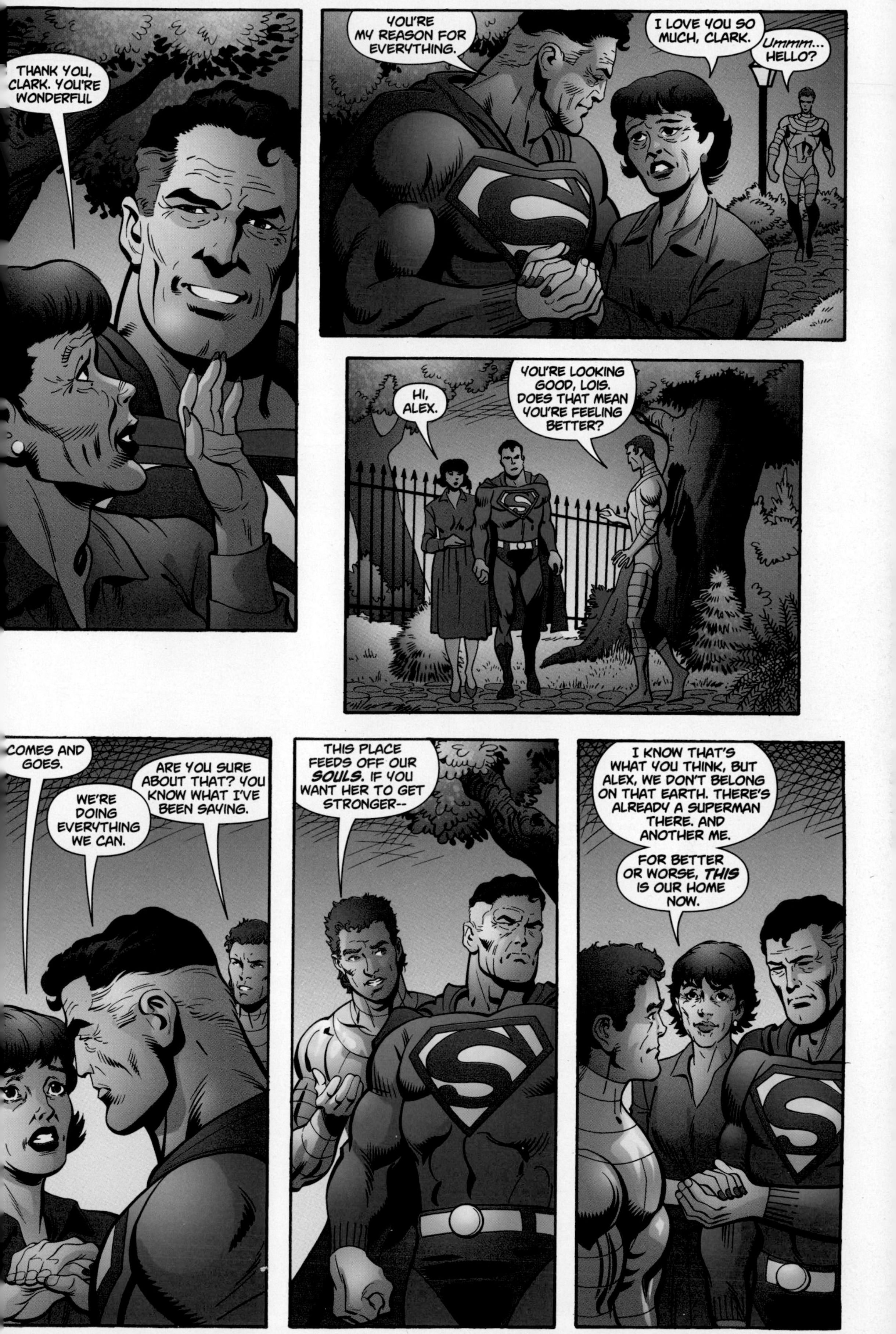
THANK YOU, CLARK. YOU'RE WONDERFUL
YOU'RE MY REASON FOR EVERYTHING.
I LOVE YOU SO MUCH, CLARK.
Ummmm... HELLO?
HI, ALEX.
YOU'RE LOOKING GOOD, LOIS. DOES THAT MEAN YOU'RE FEELING BETTER?
COMES AND GOES.
ARE YOU SURE ABOUT THAT? YOU KNOW WHAT I'VE BEEN SAYING.
WE'RE DOING EVERYTHING WE CAN.
THIS PLACE FEEDS OFF OUR SOULS. IF YOU WANT HER TO GET STRONGER--
I KNOW THAT'S WHAT YOU THINK, BUT ALEX, WE DON'T BELONG ON THAT EARTH. THERE'S ALREADY A SUPERMAN THERE. AND ANOTHER ME.
FOR BETTER OR WORSE, THIS IS OUR HOME NOW.

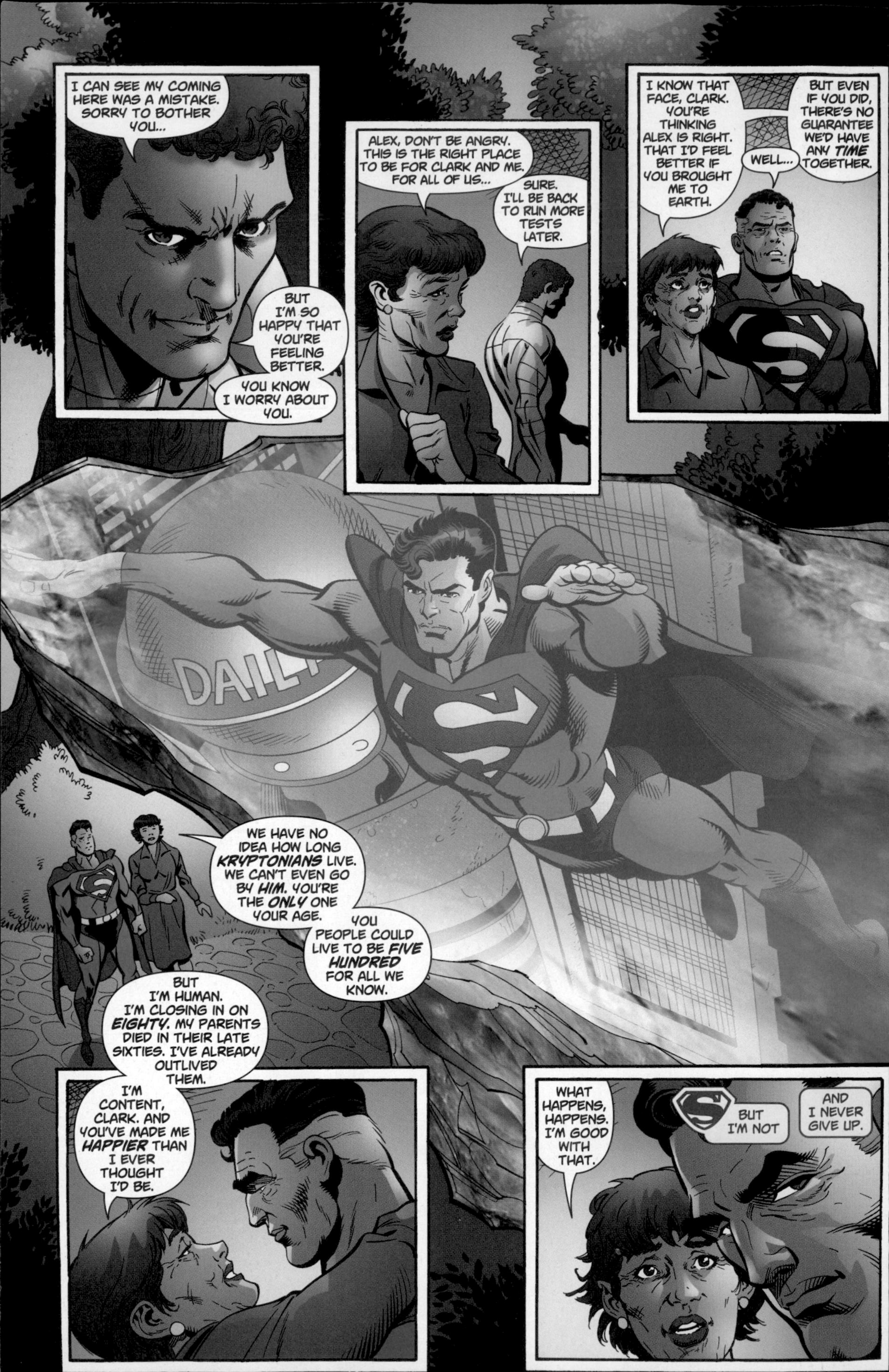
I CAN SEE MY COMING HERE WAS A MISTAKE. SORRY TO BOTHER YOU...
BUT I'M SO HAPPY THAT YOU'RE FEELING BETTER.
YOU KNOW I WORRY ABOUT YOU.
ALEX, DON'T BE ANGRY. THIS IS THE RIGHT PLACE TO BE FOR CLARK AND ME. FOR ALL OF US...
SURE. I'LL BE BACK TO RUN MORE TESTS LATER.
I KNOW THAT FACE, CLARK. YOU'RE THINKING ALEX IS RIGHT. THAT I'D FEEL BETTER IF YOU BROUGHT ME TO EARTH.
WELL...
BUT EVEN IF YOU DID, THERE'S NO GUARANTEE WE'D HAVE ANY TIME TOGETHER.
DAILY
WE HAVE NO IDEA HOW LONG KRYPTONIANS LIVE. WE CAN'T EVEN GO BY HIM. YOU'RE THE ONLY ONE YOUR AGE.
YOU PEOPLE COULD LIVE TO BE FIVE HUNDRED FOR ALL WE KNOW.
BUT I'M HUMAN. I'M CLOSING IN ON EIGHTY. MY PARENTS DIED IN THEIR LATE SIXTIES. I'VE ALREADY OUTLIVED THEM.
I'M CONTENT, CLARK. AND YOU'VE MADE ME HAPPIER THAN I EVER THOUGHT I'D BE.
WHAT HAPPENS, HAPPENS. I'M GOOD WITH THAT.
BUT I'M NOT.
AND I NEVER GIVE UP.

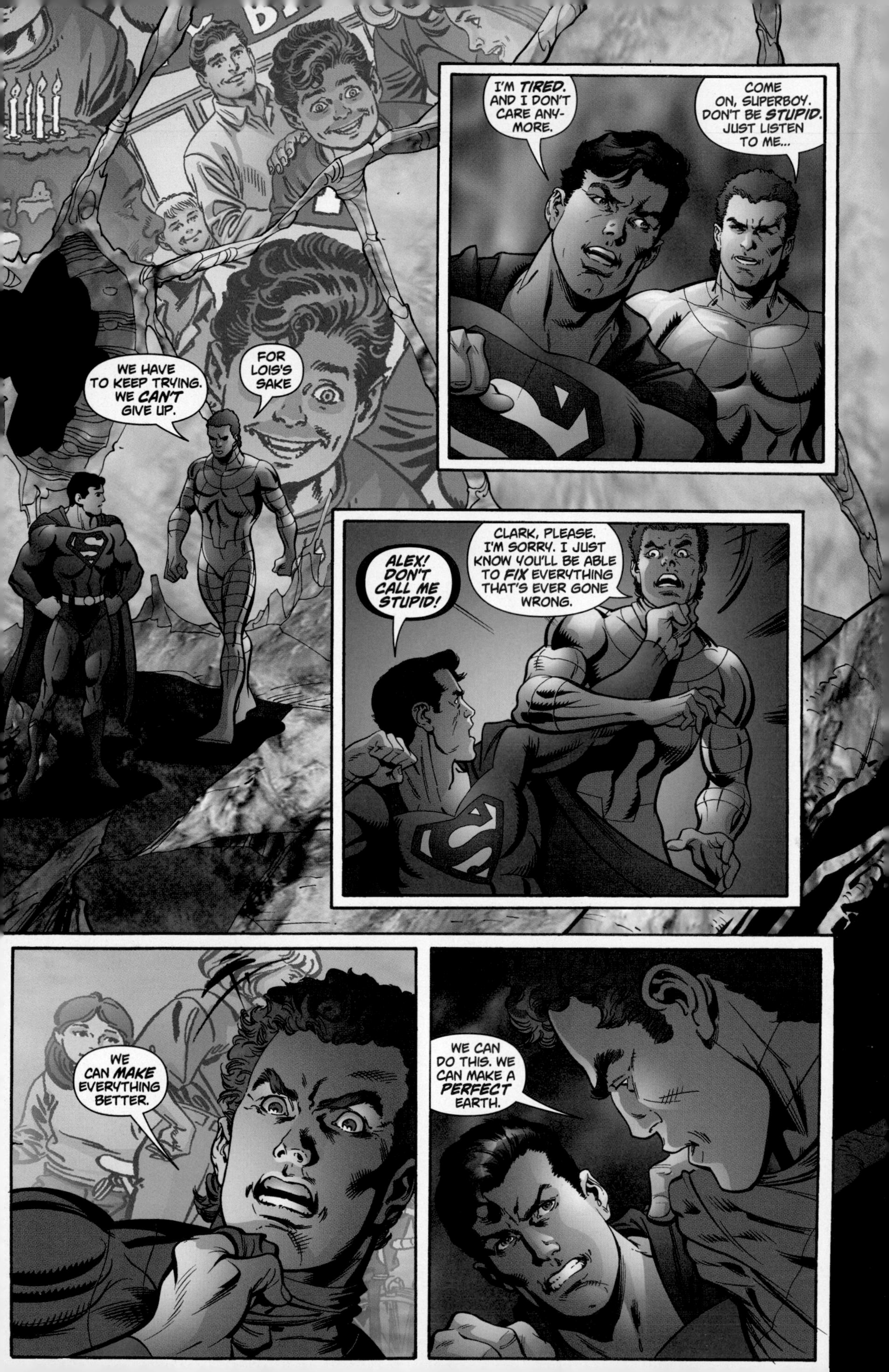
I'M TIRED. AND I DON'T CARE ANYMORE.
COME ON, SUPERBOY. DON'T BE STUPID. JUST LISTEN TO ME...
WE HAVE TO KEEP TRYING. WE CAN'T GIVE UP.
FOR LOIS'S SAKE
ALEX! DON'T CALL ME STUPID!
CLARK, PLEASE. I'M SORRY. I JUST KNOW YOU'LL BE ABLE TO FIX EVERYTHING THAT'S EVER GONE WRONG.
WE CAN MAKE EVERYTHING BETTER.
WE CAN DO THIS. WE CAN MAKE A PERFECT EARTH.

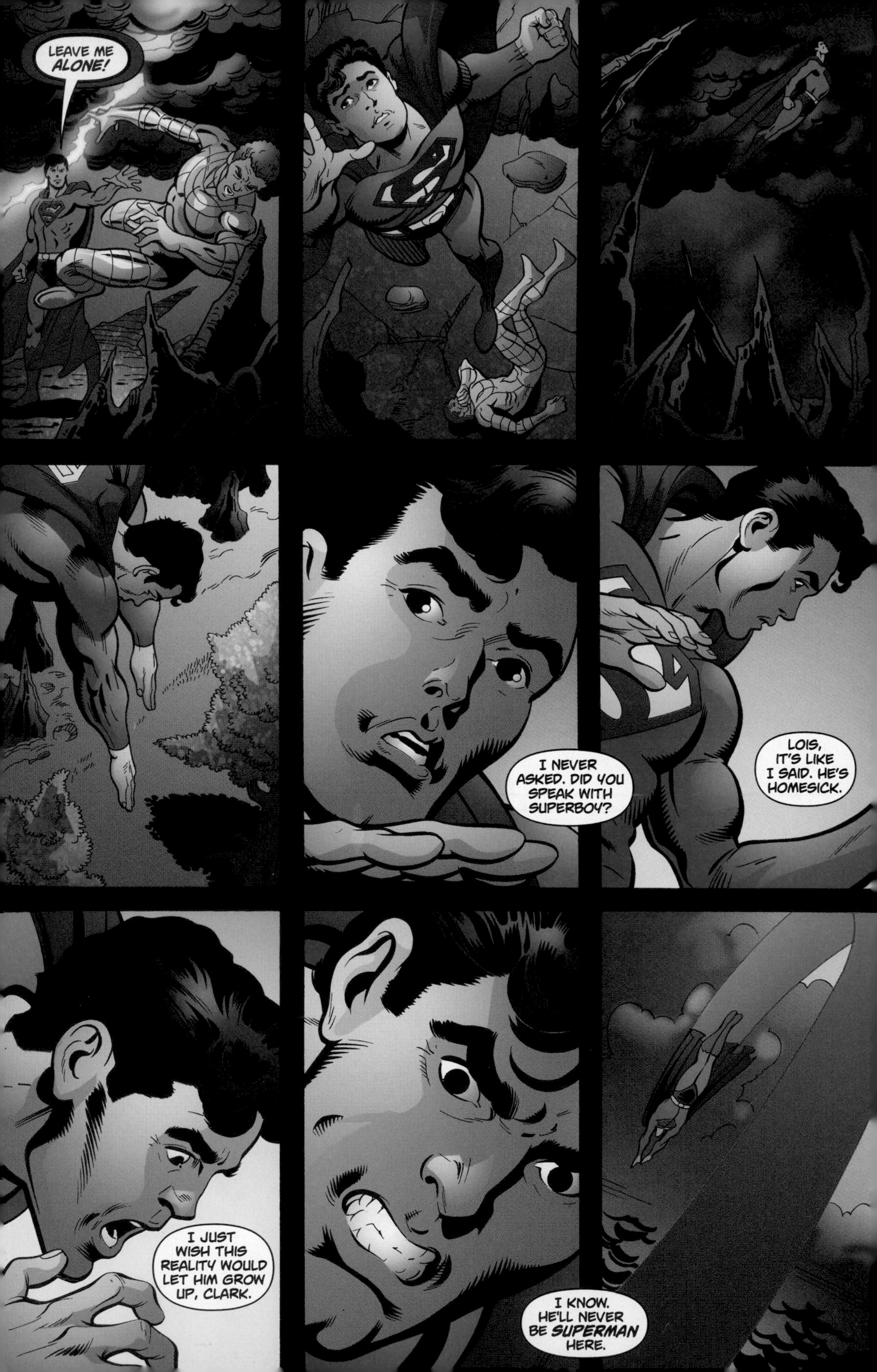
LEAVE ME ALONE!
I NEVER ASKED. DID YOU SPEAK WITH SUPERBOY?
LOIS, IT'S LIKE I SAID. HE'S HOMESICK.
I JUST WISH THIS REALITY WOULD LET HIM GROW UP, CLARK.
I KNOW. HE'LL NEVER BE SUPERMAN HERE.

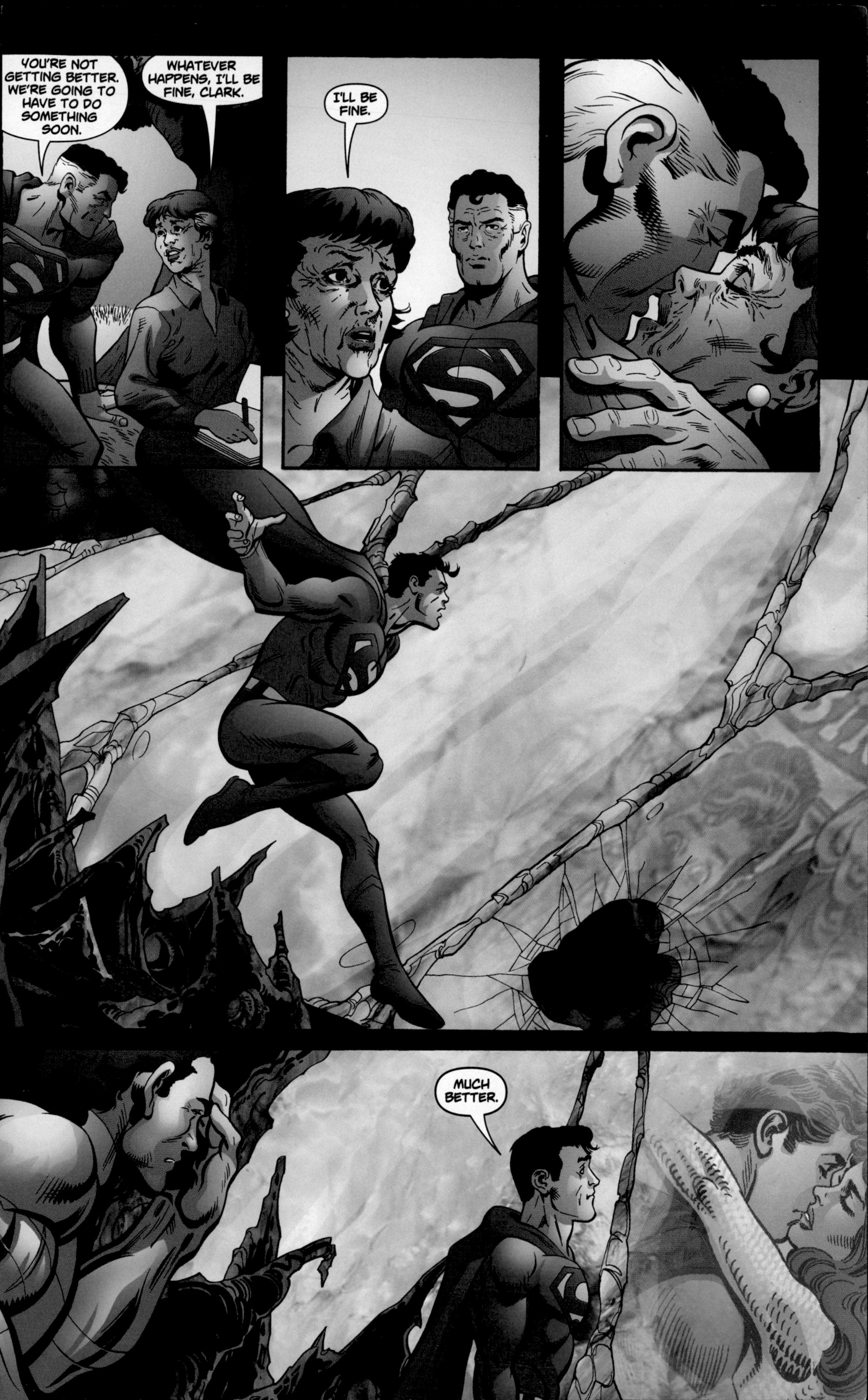
YOU'RE NOT GETTING BETTER. WE'RE GOING TO HAVE TO DO SOMETHING SOON.
WHATEVER HAPPENS, I'LL BE FINE, CLARK.
I'LL BE FINE.
MUCH BETTER.

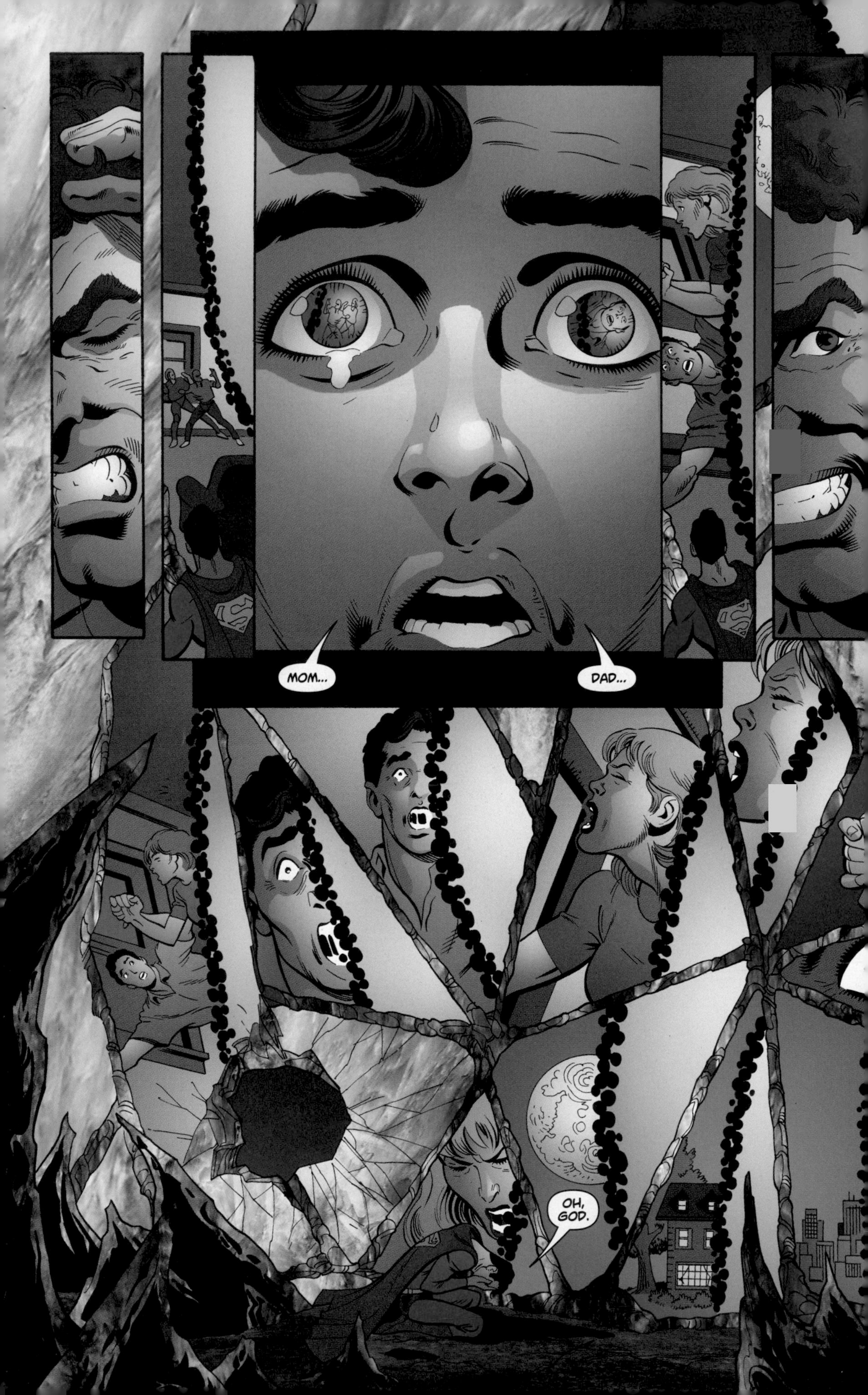
MOM...
DAD...
OH, GOD.

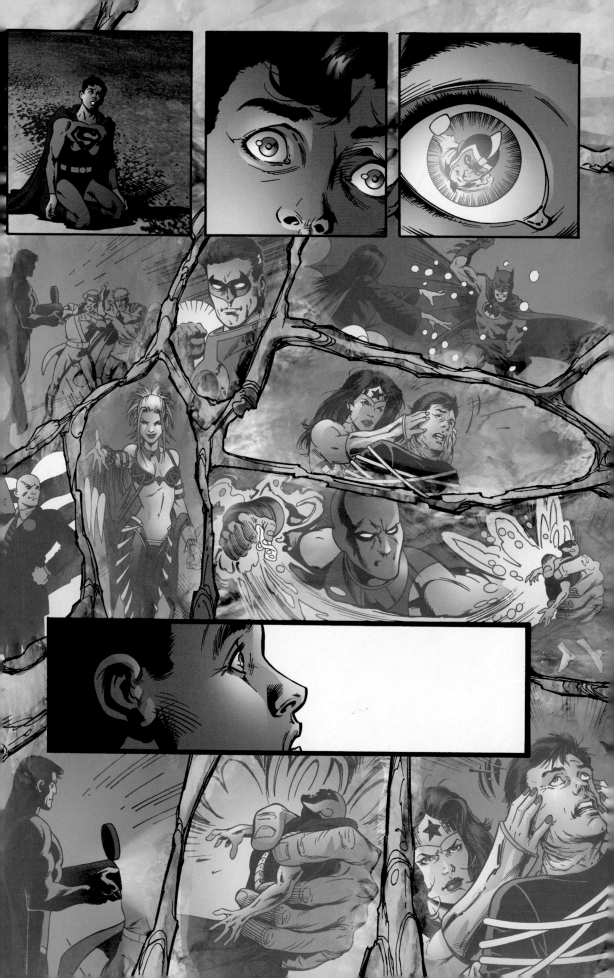

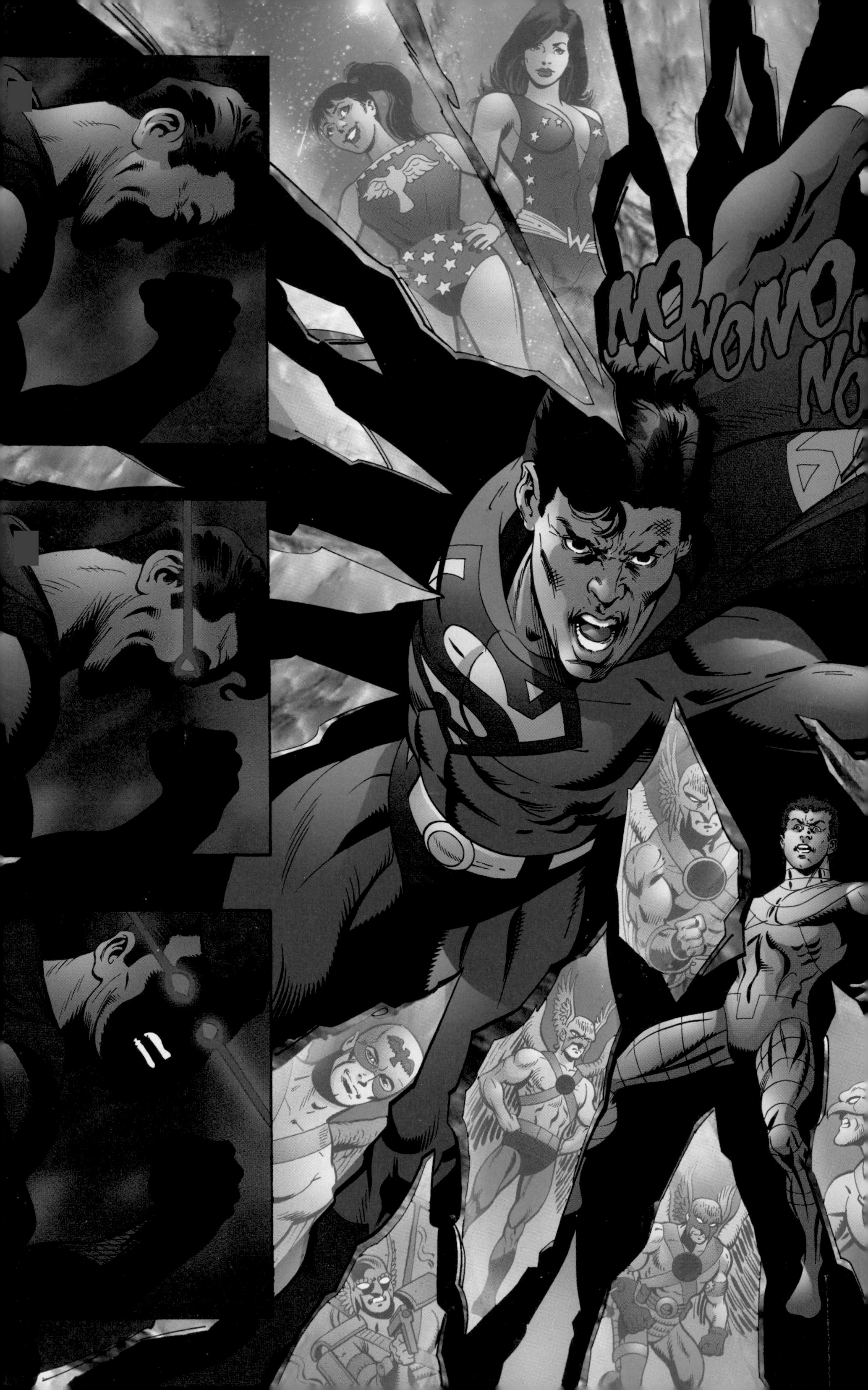
NONONO
NO

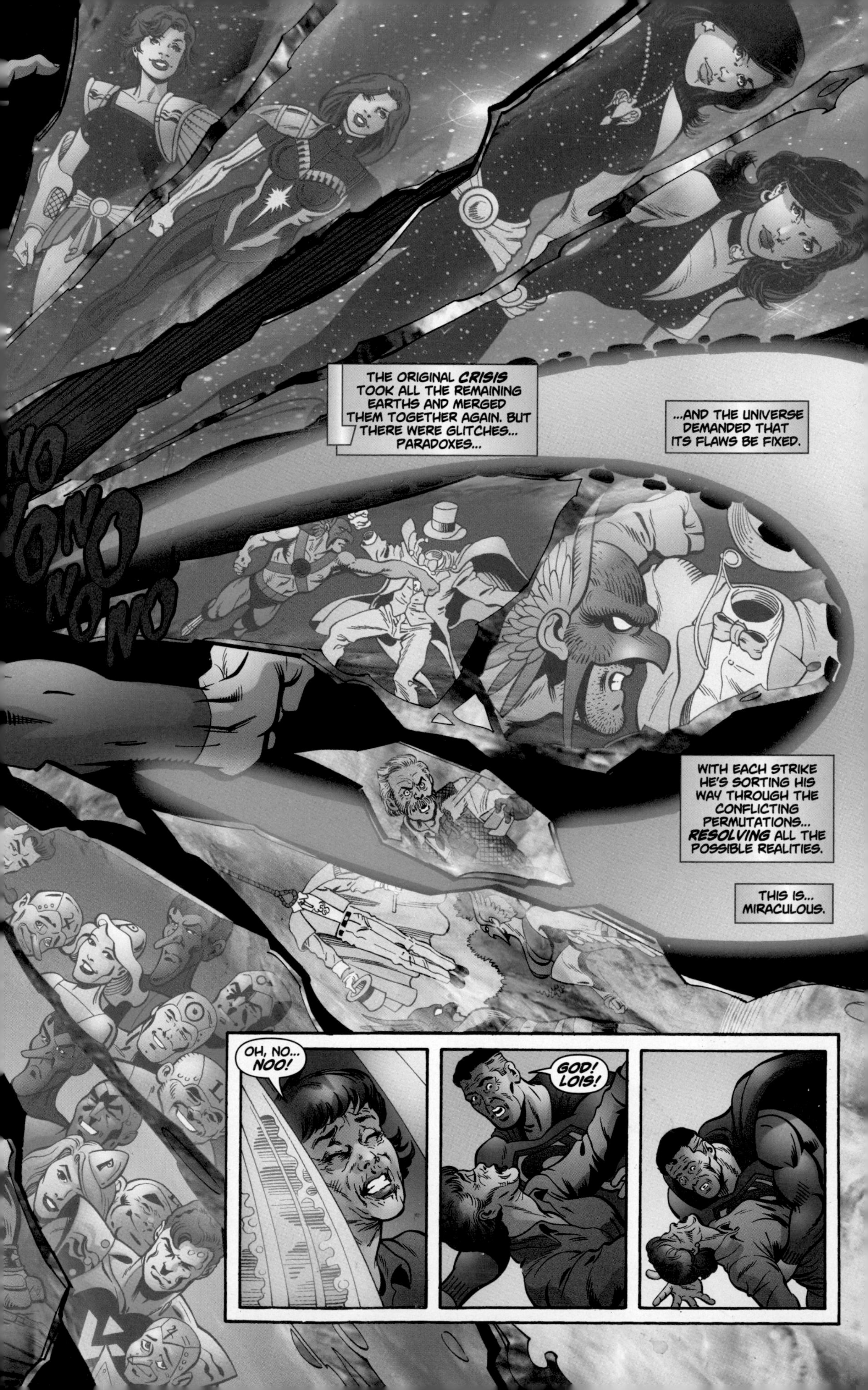
THE ORIGINAL CRISIS TOOK ALL THE REMAINING EARTHS AND MERGED THEM TOGETHER AGAIN. BUT THERE WERE GLITCHES... PARADOXES...
...AND THE UNIVERSE DEMANDED THAT ITS FLAWS BE FIXED.
NO NO NO NO NO NO NO
WITH EACH STRIKE HE'S SORTING HIS WAY THROUGH THE CONFLICTING PERMUTATIONS... RESOLVING ALL THE POSSIBLE REALITIES.
THIS IS... MIRACULOUS.
OH, NO... NOO!
GOD! LOIS!

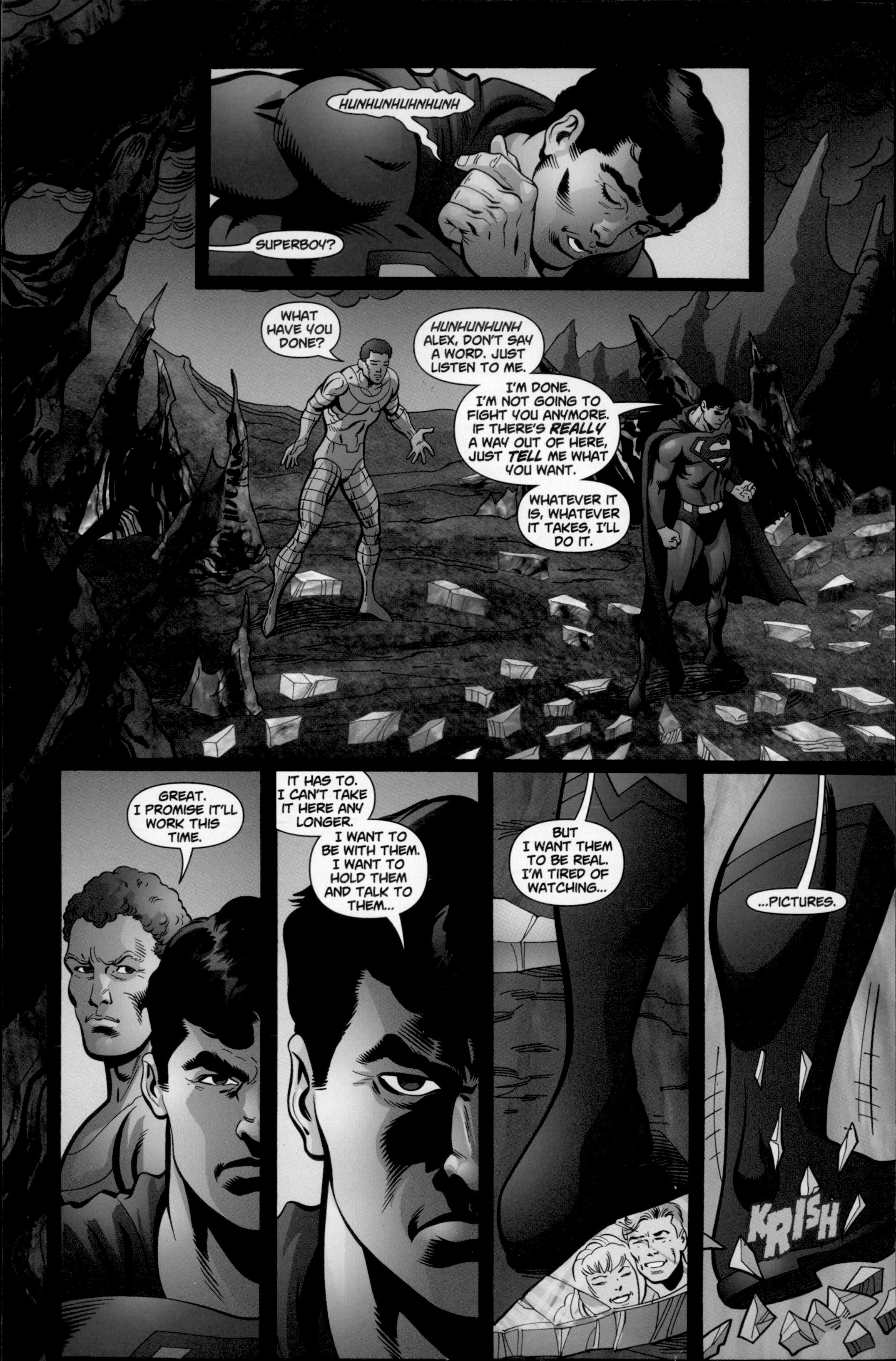
HUNHUNHUHNHUNH
SUPERBOY?
WHAT HAVE YOU DONE?
HUNHUNHUNH ALEX, DON'T SAY A WORD. JUST LISTEN TO ME.
I'M DONE. I'M NOT GOING TO FIGHT YOU ANYMORE. IF THERE'S REALLY A WAY OUT OF HERE, JUST TELL ME WHAT YOU WANT.
WHATEVER IT IS, WHATEVER IT TAKES, I'LL DO IT.
GREAT. I PROMISE IT'LL WORK THIS TIME.
IT HAS TO. I CAN'T TAKE IT HERE ANY LONGER.
I WANT TO BE WITH THEM. I WANT TO HOLD THEM AND TALK TO THEM...
BUT I WANT THEM TO BE REAL. I'M TIRED OF WATCHING...
...PICTURES.
KRISH

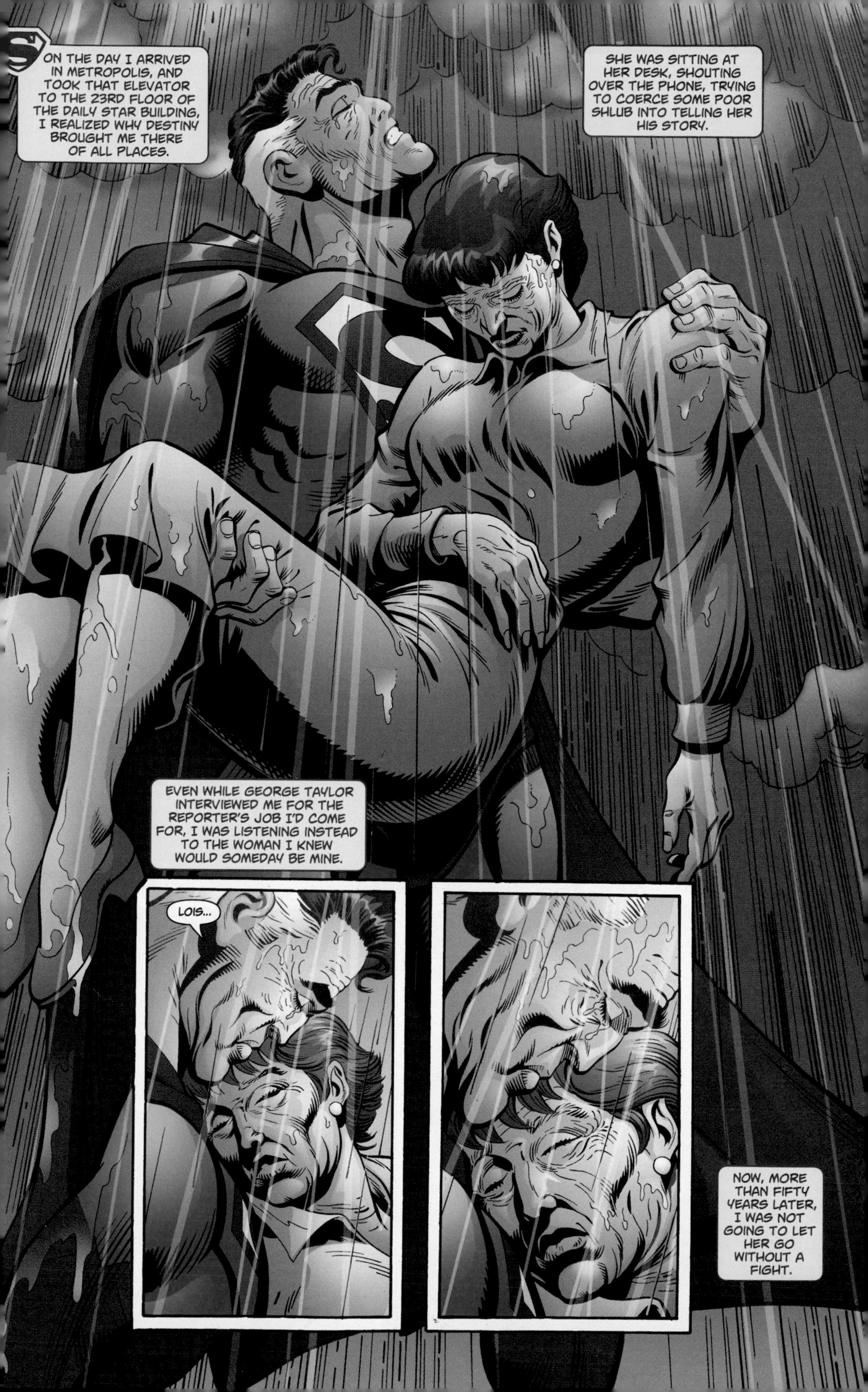
ON THE DAY I ARRIVED IN METROPOLIS, AND TOOK THAT ELEVATOR TO THE 23RD FLOOR OF THE DAILY STAR BUILDING, I REALIZED WHY DESTINY BROUGHT ME THERE OF ALL PLACES.
SHE WAS SITTING AT HER DESK, SHOUTING OVER THE PHONE, TRYING TO COERCE SOME POOR SHLUB INTO TELLING HER HIS STORY.
EVEN WHILE GEORGE TAYLOR INTERVIEWED ME FOR THE REPORTER'S JOB I'D COME FOR, I WAS LISTENING INSTEAD TO THE WOMAN I KNEW WOULD SOMEDAY BE MINE.
LOIS...
NOW, MORE THAN FIFTY YEARS LATER, I WAS NOT GOING TO LET HER GO WITHOUT A FIGHT.

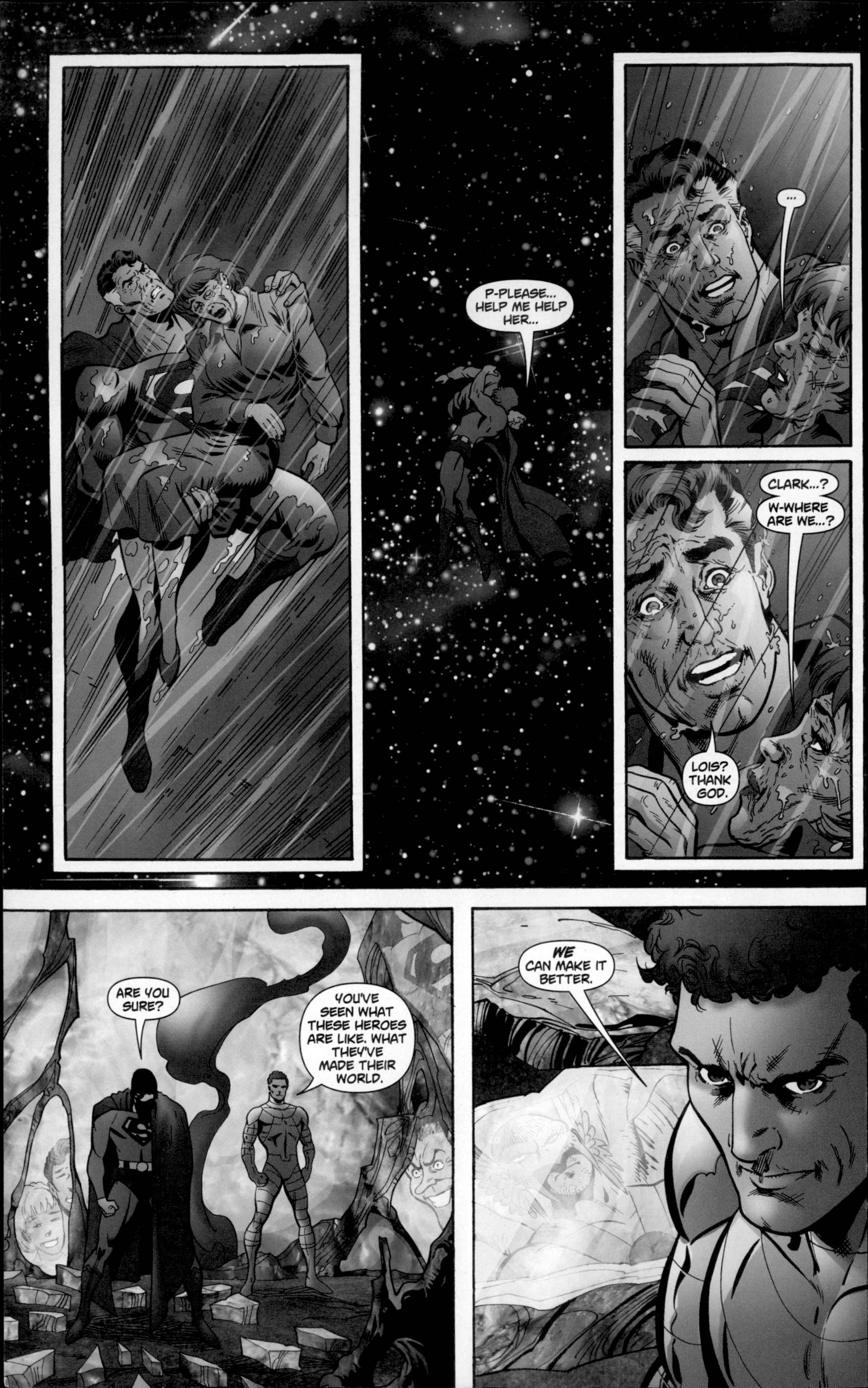
P-PLEASE... HELP ME HELP HER...
...
CLARK...?
W-WHERE ARE WE...?
LOIS? THANK GOD.
ARE YOU SURE?
YOU'VE SEEN WHAT THESE HEROES ARE LIKE. WHAT THEY'VE MADE THEIR WORLD.
WE CAN MAKE IT BETTER.

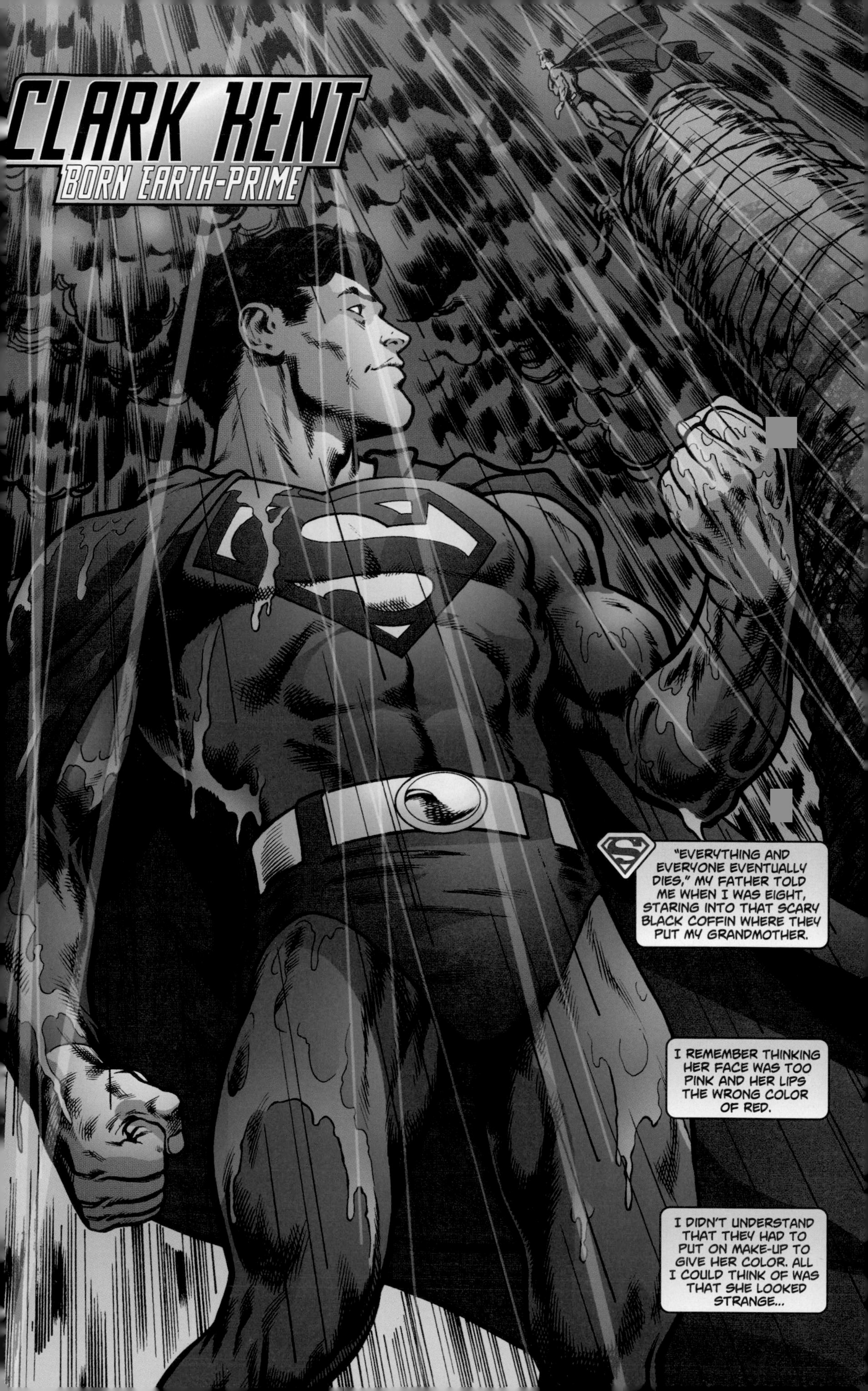
CLARK KENT
BORN EARTH-PRIME
"EVERYTHING AND EVERYONE EVENTUALLY DIES," MY FATHER TOLD ME WHEN I WAS EIGHT, STARING INTO THAT SCARY BLACK COFFIN WHERE THEY PUT MY GRANDMOTHER.
I REMEMBER THINKING HER FACE WAS TOO PINK AND HER LIPS THE WRONG COLOR OF RED.
I DIDN'T UNDERSTAND THAT THEY HAD TO PUT ON MAKE-UP TO GIVE HER COLOR. ALL I COULD THINK OF WAS THAT SHE LOOKED STRANGE...

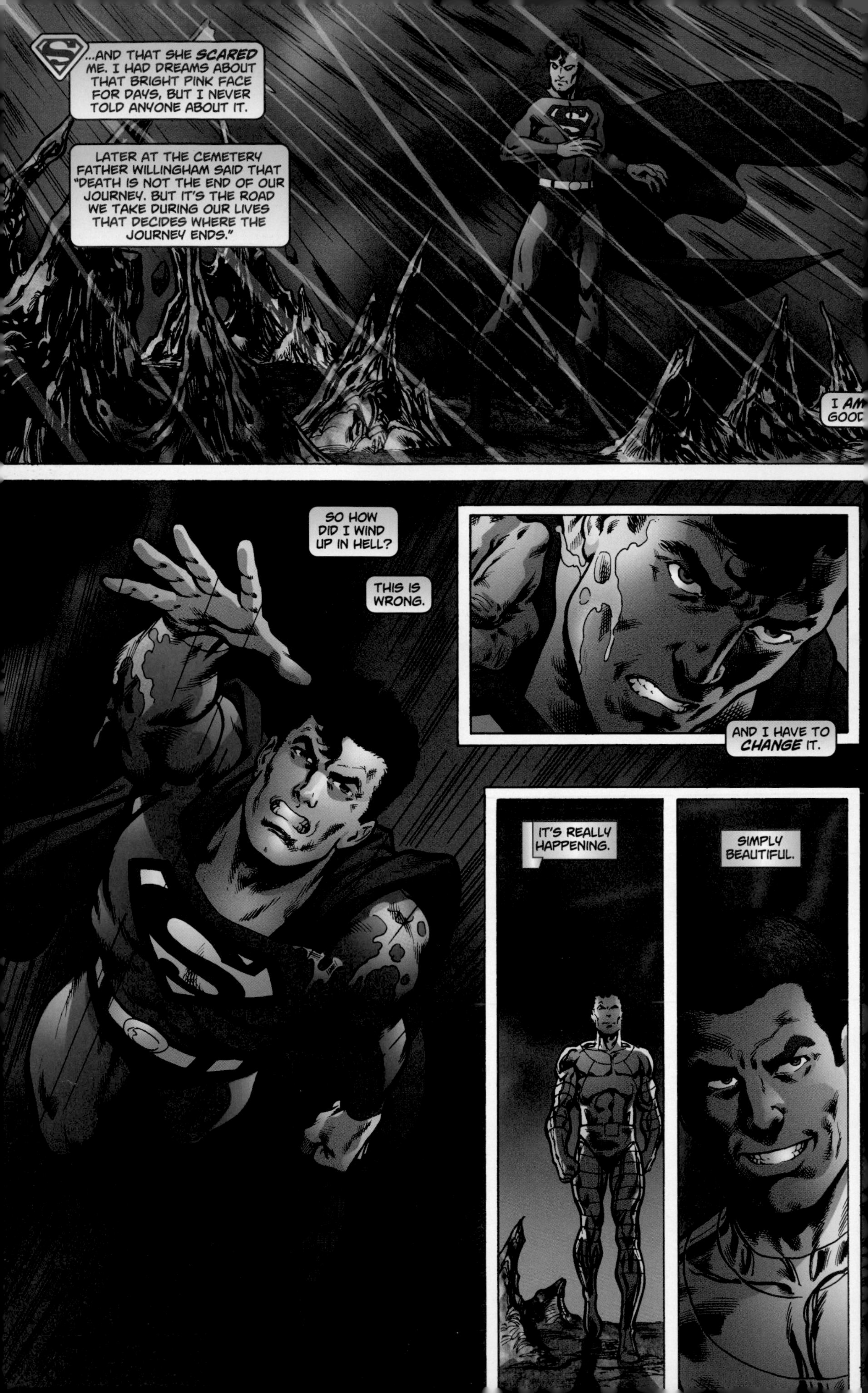
...AND THAT SHE SCARED ME. I HAD DREAMS ABOUT THAT BRIGHT PINK FACE FOR DAYS, BUT I NEVER TOLD ANYONE ABOUT IT.
LATER AT THE CEMETERY FATHER WILLINGHAM SAID THAT "DEATH IS NOT THE END OF OUR JOURNEY. BUT IT'S THE ROAD WE TAKE DURING OUR LIVES THAT DECIDES WHERE THE JOURNEY ENDS."
SO HOW DID I WIND UP IN HELL?
THIS IS WRONG.
AND I HAVE TO CHANGE IT.
IT'S REALLY HAPPENING.
SIMPLY BEAUTIFUL.

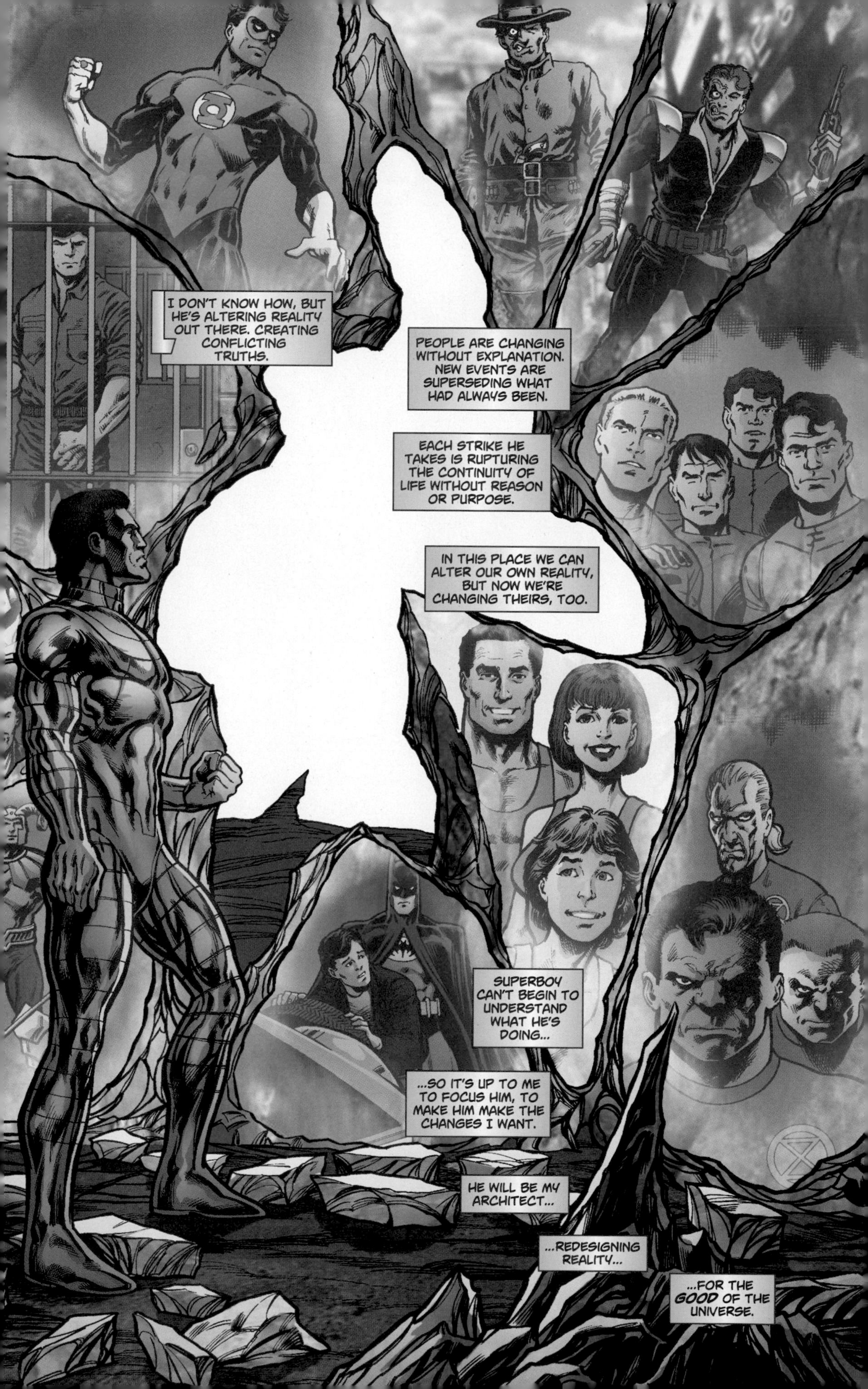
I DON'T KNOW HOW, BUT HE'S ALTERING REALITY OUT THERE. CREATING CONFLICTING TRUTHS.
PEOPLE ARE CHANGING WITHOUT EXPLANATION. NEW EVENTS ARE SUPERSEDING WHAT HAD ALWAYS BEEN.
EACH STRIKE HE TAKES IS RUPTURING THE CONTINUITY OF LIFE WITHOUT REASON OR PURPOSE.
IN THIS PLACE WE CAN ALTER OUR OWN REALITY, BUT NOW WE'RE CHANGING THEIRS, TOO.
SUPERBOY CAN'T BEGIN TO UNDERSTAND WHAT HE'S DOING...
...SO IT'S UP TO ME TO FOCUS HIM, TO MAKE HIM MAKE THE CHANGES I WANT.
HE WILL BE MY ARCHITECT...
...REDESIGNING REALITY...
...FOR THE *GOOD* OF THE UNIVERSE.

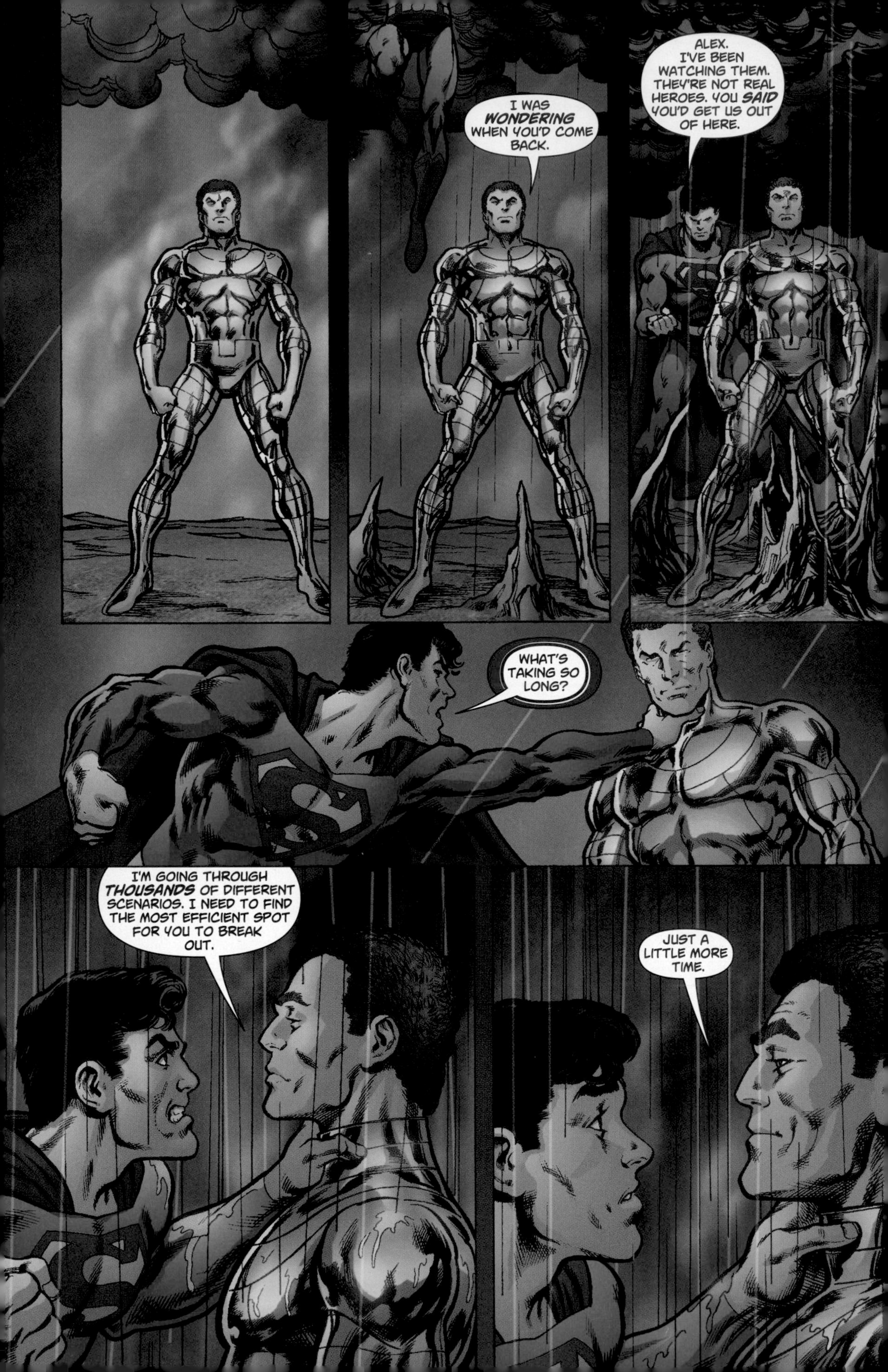
I WAS WONDERING WHEN YOU'D COME BACK.
ALEX. I'VE BEEN WATCHING THEM. THEY'RE NOT REAL HEROES. YOU SAID YOU'D GET US OUT OF HERE.
WHAT'S TAKING SO LONG?
I'M GOING THROUGH THOUSANDS OF DIFFERENT SCENARIOS. I NEED TO FIND THE MOST EFFICIENT SPOT FOR YOU TO BREAK OUT.
JUST A LITTLE MORE TIME.

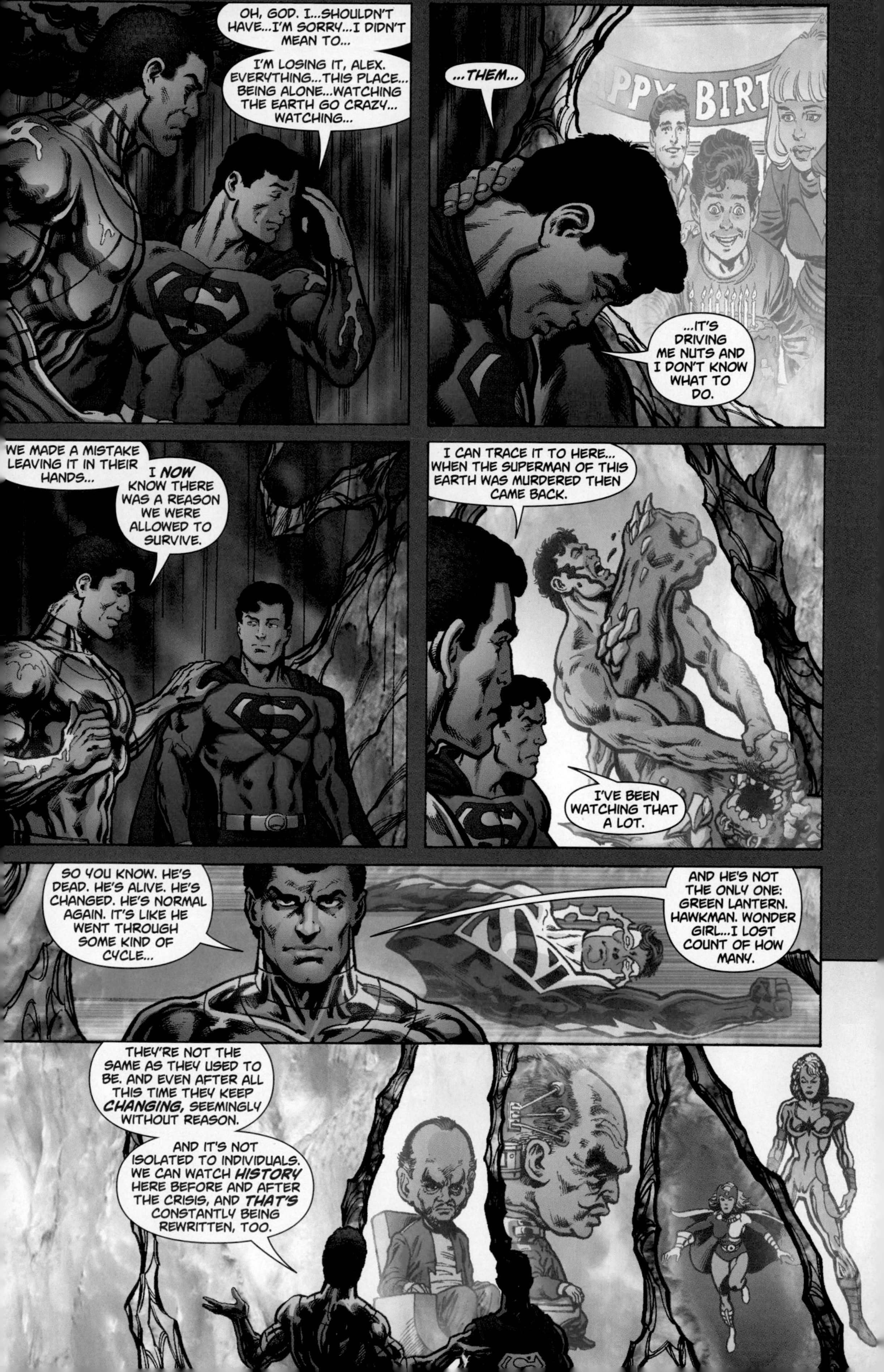
OH, GOD. I...SHOULDN'T HAVE...I'M SORRY...I DIDN'T MEAN TO...
I'M LOSING IT, ALEX. EVERYTHING...THIS PLACE... BEING ALONE...WATCHING THE EARTH GO CRAZY... WATCHING...
...THEM...
PPY BIRT
...IT'S DRIVING ME NUTS AND I DON'T KNOW WHAT TO DO.
WE MADE A MISTAKE LEAVING IT IN THEIR HANDS...
I NOW KNOW THERE WAS A REASON WE WERE ALLOWED TO SURVIVE.
I CAN TRACE IT TO HERE... WHEN THE SUPERMAN OF THIS EARTH WAS MURDERED THEN CAME BACK.
I'VE BEEN WATCHING THAT A LOT.
SO YOU KNOW. HE'S DEAD. HE'S ALIVE. HE'S CHANGED. HE'S NORMAL AGAIN. IT'S LIKE HE WENT THROUGH SOME KIND OF CYCLE...
AND HE'S NOT THE ONLY ONE: GREEN LANTERN. HAWKMAN. WONDER GIRL...I LOST COUNT OF HOW MANY.
THEY'RE NOT THE SAME AS THEY USED TO BE. AND EVEN AFTER ALL THIS TIME THEY KEEP CHANGING, SEEMINGLY WITHOUT REASON.
AND IT'S NOT ISOLATED TO INDIVIDUALS. WE CAN WATCH HISTORY HERE BEFORE AND AFTER THE CRISIS, AND THAT'S CONSTANTLY BEING REWRITTEN, TOO.

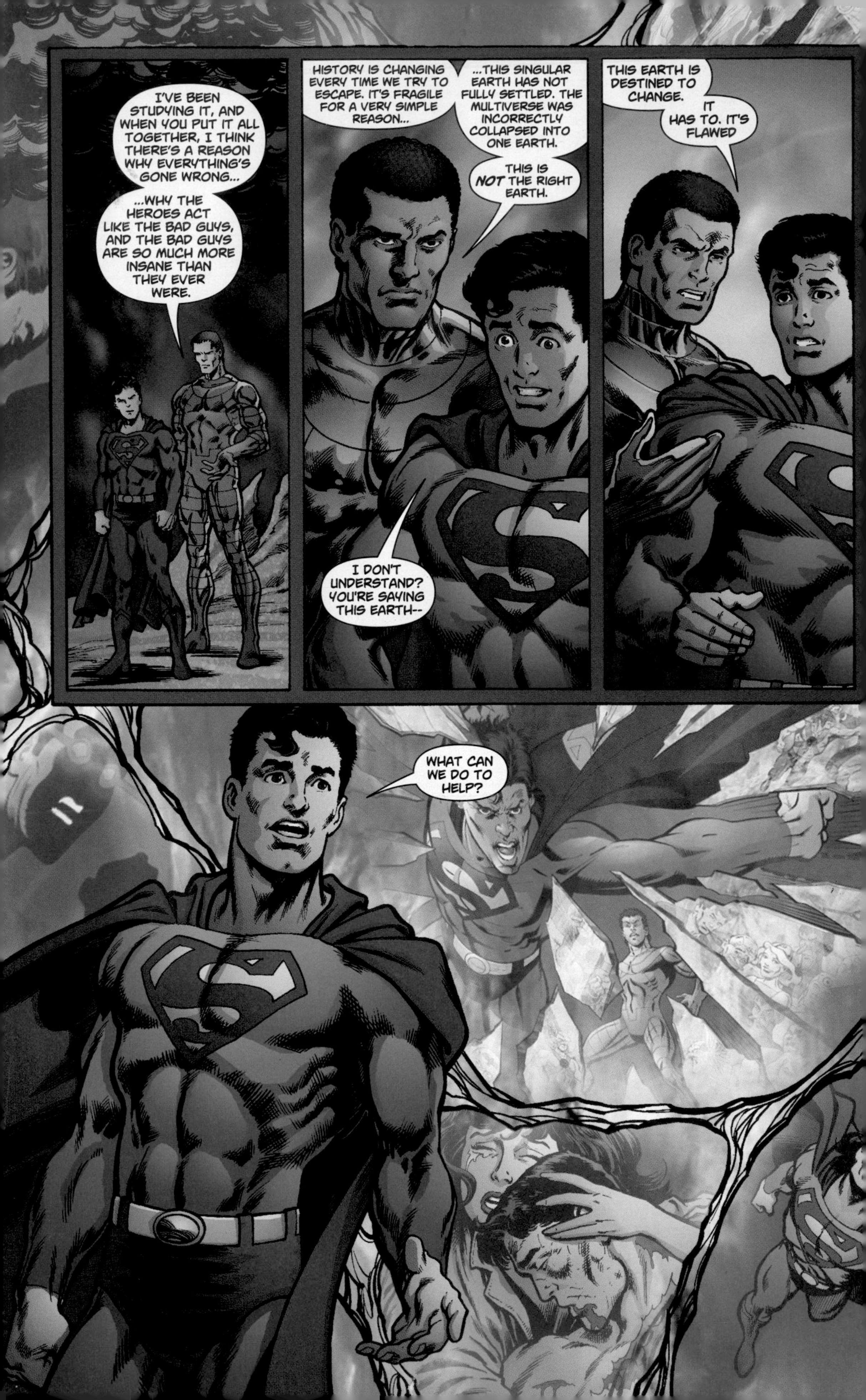
I'VE BEEN STUDYING IT, AND WHEN YOU PUT IT ALL TOGETHER, I THINK THERE'S A REASON WHY EVERYTHING'S GONE WRONG...
...WHY THE HEROES ACT LIKE THE BAD GUYS, AND THE BAD GUYS ARE SO MUCH MORE INSANE THAN THEY EVER WERE.
HISTORY IS CHANGING EVERY TIME WE TRY TO ESCAPE. IT'S FRAGILE FOR A VERY SIMPLE REASON...
...THIS SINGULAR EARTH HAS NOT FULLY SETTLED. THE MULTIVERSE WAS INCORRECTLY COLLAPSED INTO ONE EARTH.
THIS IS NOT THE RIGHT EARTH.
I DON'T UNDERSTAND? YOU'RE SAYING THIS EARTH--
THIS EARTH IS DESTINED TO CHANGE.
IT HAS TO. IT'S FLAWED
WHAT CAN WE DO TO HELP?

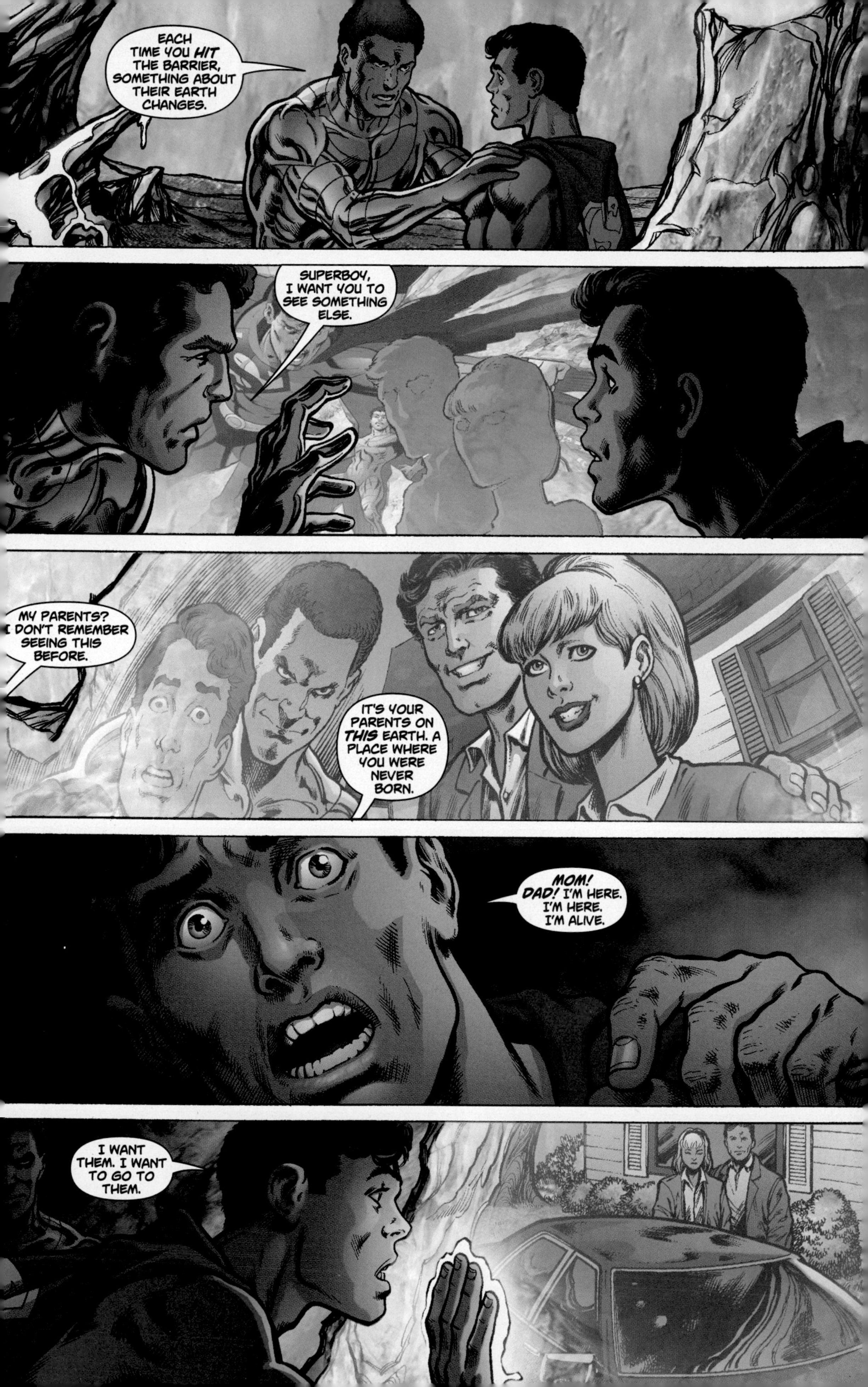
EACH TIME YOU HIT THE BARRIER, SOMETHING ABOUT THEIR EARTH CHANGES.
SUPERBOY, I WANT YOU TO SEE SOMETHING ELSE.
MY PARENTS? I DON'T REMEMBER SEEING THIS BEFORE.
IT'S YOUR PARENTS ON THIS EARTH. A PLACE WHERE YOU WERE NEVER BORN.
MOM! DAD! I'M HERE. I'M HERE. I'M ALIVE.
I WANT THEM. I WANT TO GO TO THEM.

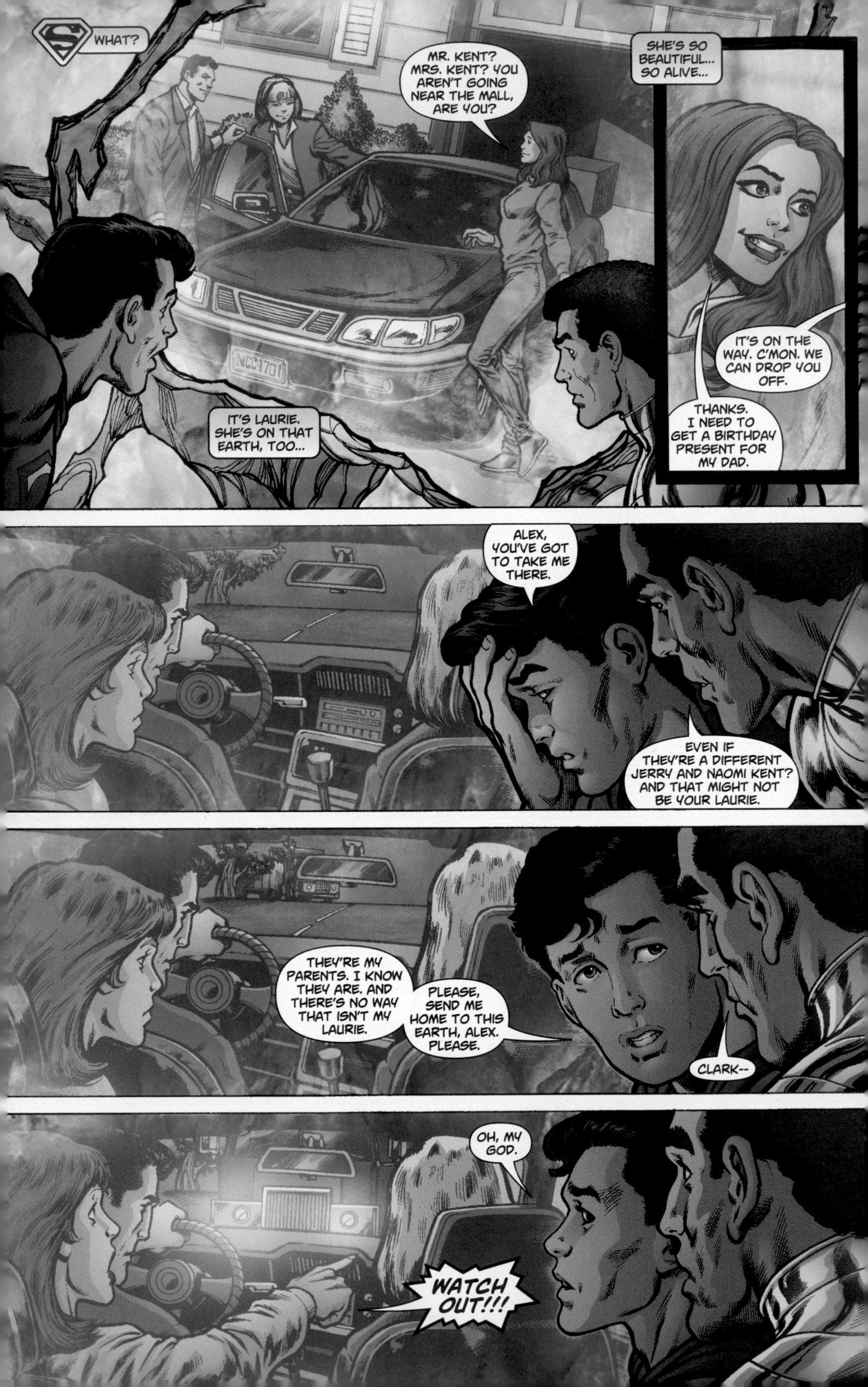
WHAT?
SHE'S SO BEAUTIFUL... SO ALIVE...
MR. KENT? MRS. KENT? YOU AREN'T GOING NEAR THE MALL, ARE YOU?
IT'S LAURIE. SHE'S ON THAT EARTH, TOO...
IT'S ON THE WAY. C'MON. WE CAN DROP YOU OFF.
THANKS. I NEED TO GET A BIRTHDAY PRESENT FOR MY DAD.
NCC1701
ALEX, YOU'VE GOT TO TAKE ME THERE.
EVEN IF THEY'RE A DIFFERENT JERRY AND NAOMI KENT? AND THAT MIGHT NOT BE YOUR LAURIE.
THEY'RE MY PARENTS. I KNOW THEY ARE. AND THERE'S NO WAY THAT ISN'T MY LAURIE.
PLEASE, SEND ME HOME TO THIS EARTH, ALEX. PLEASE.
CLARK--
OH, MY GOD.
WATCH OUT!!!

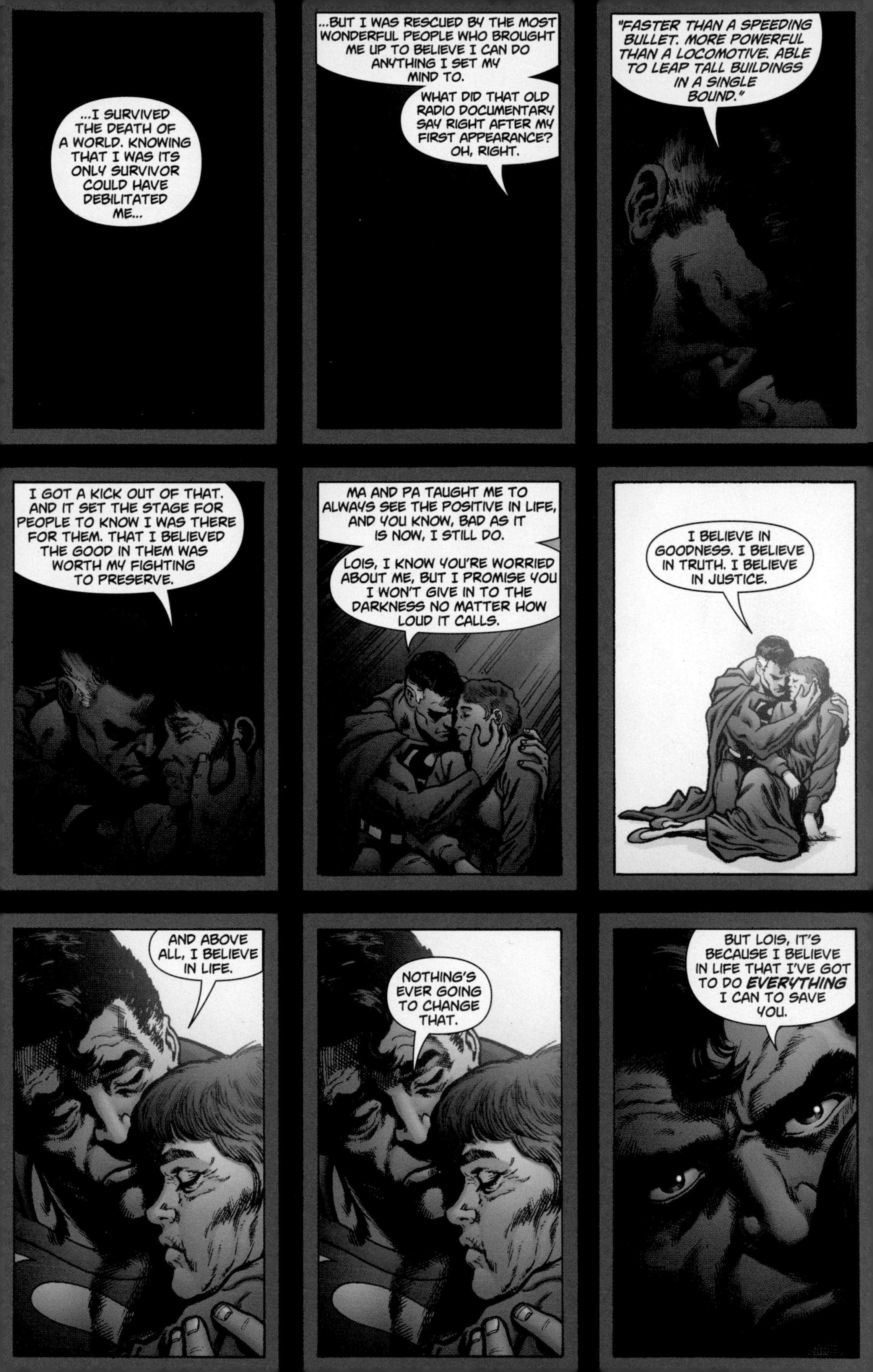
...I SURVIVED THE DEATH OF A WORLD. KNOWING THAT I WAS ITS ONLY SURVIVOR COULD HAVE DEBILITATED ME...
...BUT I WAS RESCUED BY THE MOST WONDERFUL PEOPLE WHO BROUGHT ME UP TO BELIEVE I CAN DO ANYTHING I SET MY MIND TO.
WHAT DID THAT OLD RADIO DOCUMENTARY SAY RIGHT AFTER MY FIRST APPEARANCE? OH, RIGHT.
"FASTER THAN A SPEEDING BULLET. MORE POWERFUL THAN A LOCOMOTIVE. ABLE TO LEAP TALL BUILDINGS IN A SINGLE BOUND."
I GOT A KICK OUT OF THAT. AND IT SET THE STAGE FOR PEOPLE TO KNOW I WAS THERE FOR THEM. THAT I BELIEVED THE GOOD IN THEM WAS WORTH MY FIGHTING TO PRESERVE.
MA AND PA TAUGHT ME TO ALWAYS SEE THE POSITIVE IN LIFE, AND YOU KNOW, BAD AS IT IS NOW, I STILL DO.
LOIS, I KNOW YOU'RE WORRIED ABOUT ME, BUT I PROMISE YOU I WON'T GIVE IN TO THE DARKNESS NO MATTER HOW LOUD IT CALLS.
I BELIEVE IN GOODNESS. I BELIEVE IN TRUTH. I BELIEVE IN JUSTICE.
AND ABOVE ALL, I BELIEVE IN LIFE.
NOTHING'S EVER GOING TO CHANGE THAT.
BUT LOIS, IT'S BECAUSE I BELIEVE IN LIFE THAT I'VE GOT TO DO *EVERYTHING* I CAN TO SAVE YOU.

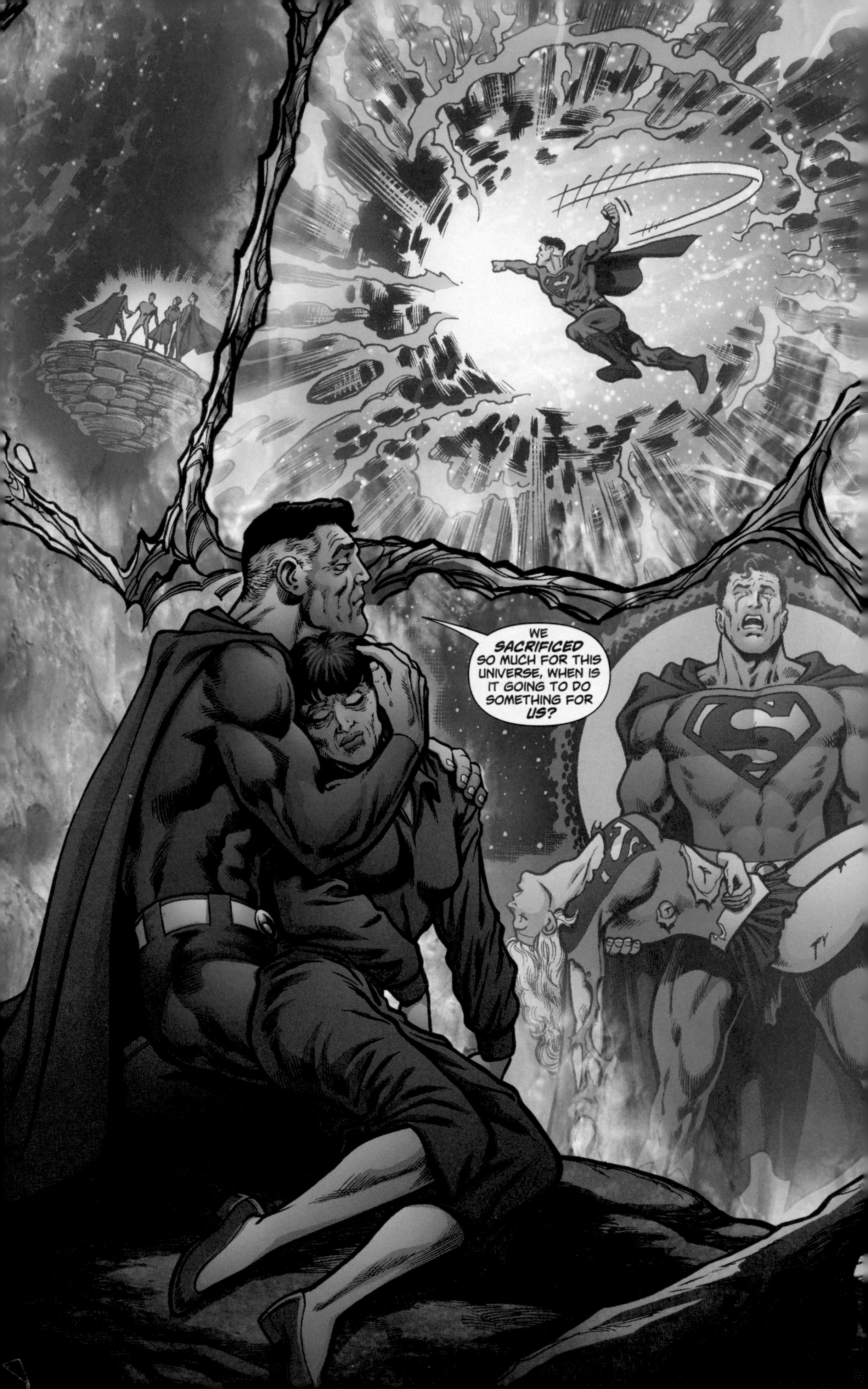
WE SACRIFICED SO MUCH FOR THIS UNIVERSE, WHEN IS IT GOING TO DO SOMETHING FOR US?

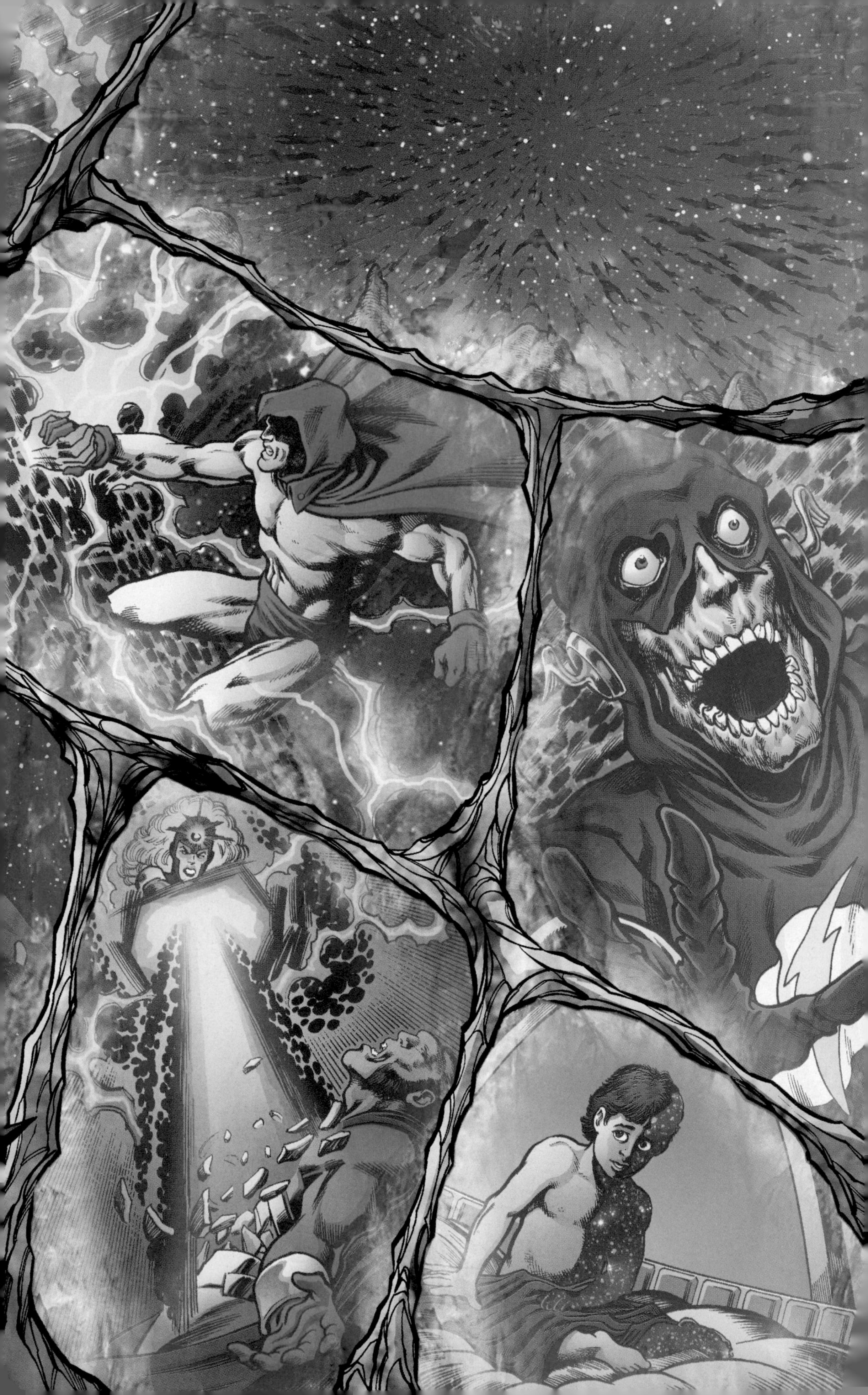

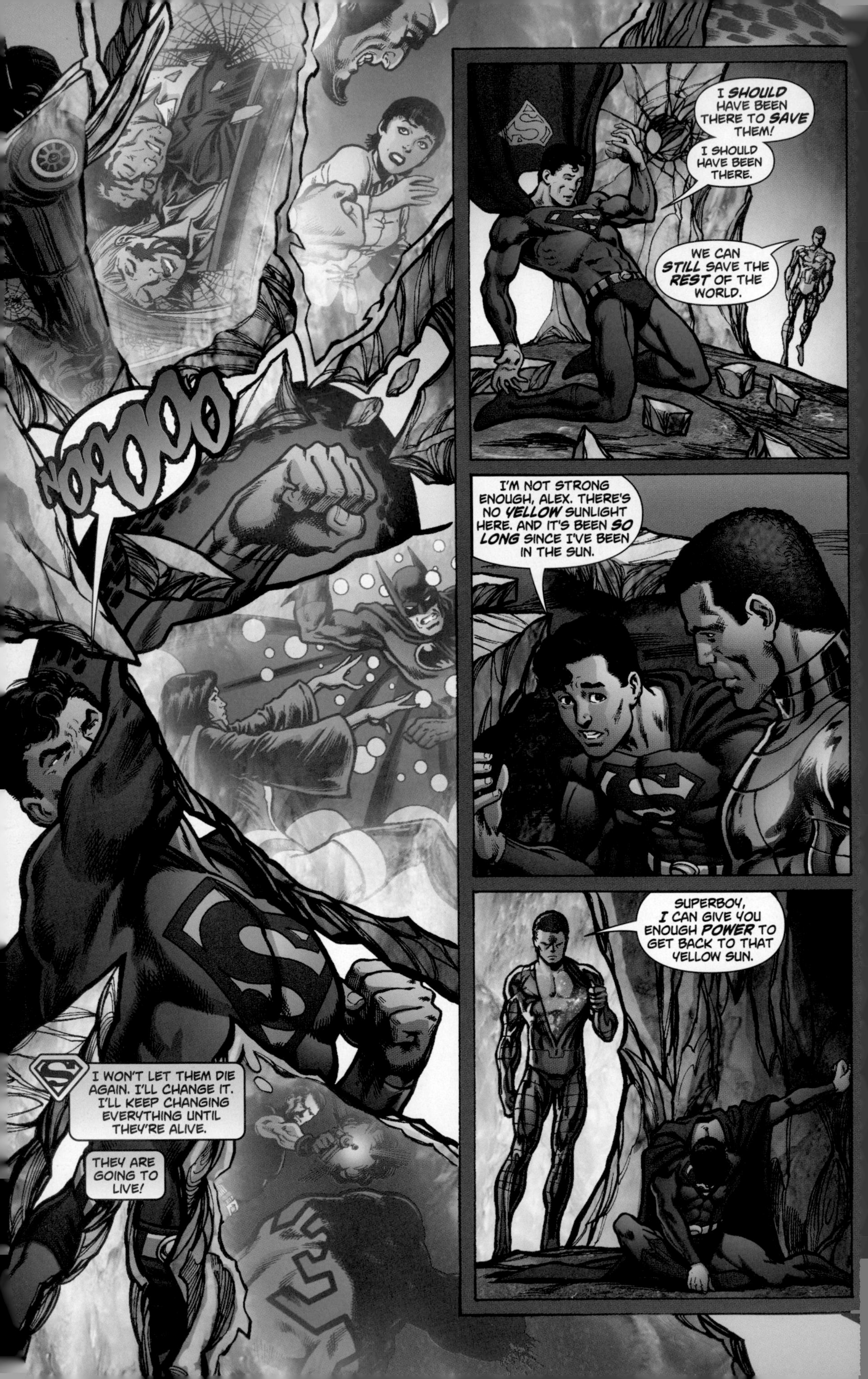
NOOOOO
I WON'T LET THEM DIE AGAIN. I'LL CHANGE IT. I'LL KEEP CHANGING EVERYTHING UNTIL THEY'RE ALIVE.
THEY ARE GOING TO LIVE!
I SHOULD HAVE BEEN THERE TO SAVE THEM!
I SHOULD HAVE BEEN THERE.
WE CAN STILL SAVE THE REST OF THE WORLD.
I'M NOT STRONG ENOUGH, ALEX. THERE'S NO YELLOW SUNLIGHT HERE. AND IT'S BEEN SO LONG SINCE I'VE BEEN IN THE SUN.
SUPERBOY, I CAN GIVE YOU ENOUGH POWER TO GET BACK TO THAT YELLOW SUN.

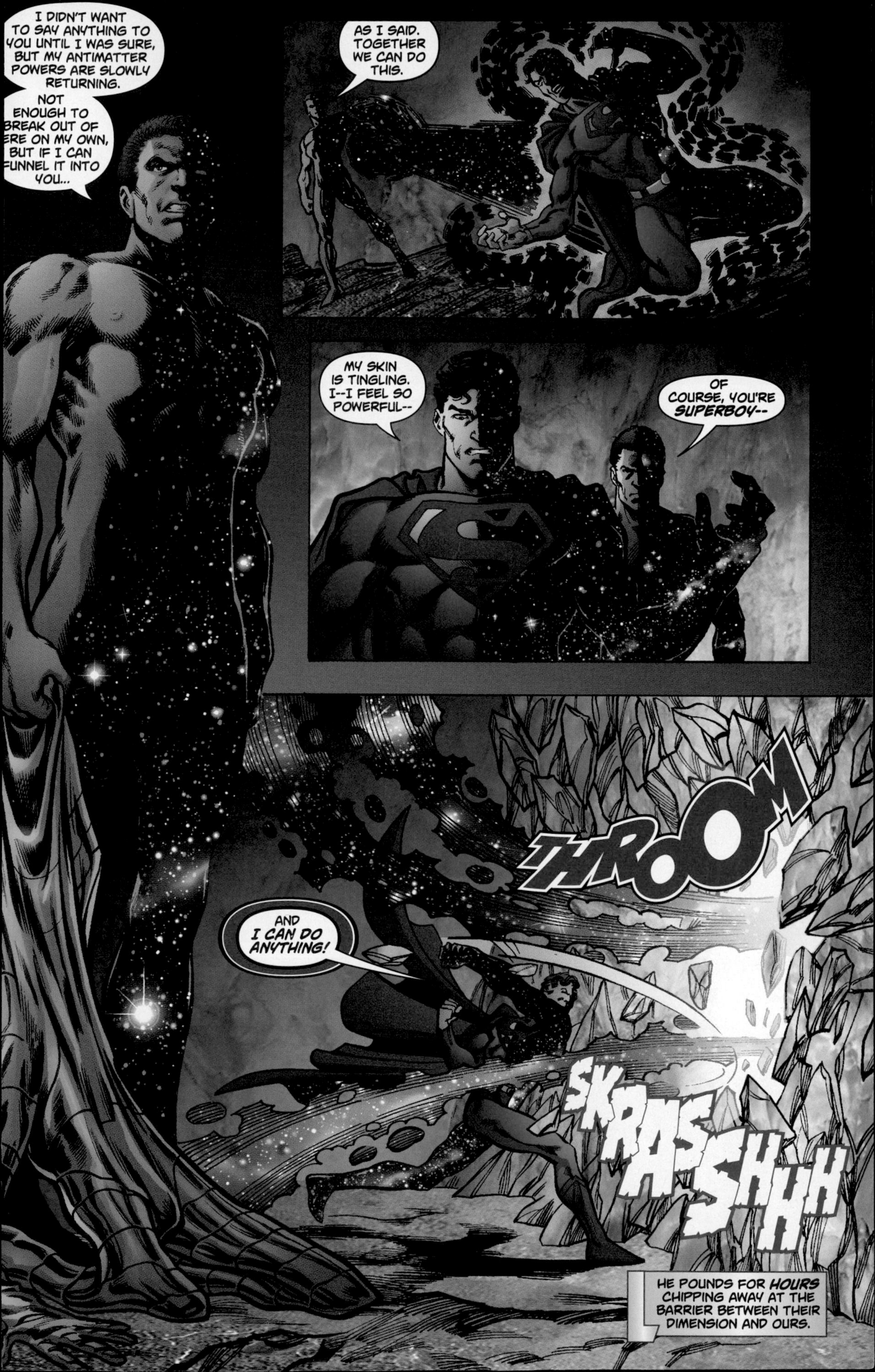
I DIDN'T WANT TO SAY ANYTHING TO YOU UNTIL I WAS SURE, BUT MY ANTIMATTER POWERS ARE SLOWLY RETURNING.
NOT ENOUGH TO BREAK OUT OF ERE ON MY OWN, BUT IF I CAN FUNNEL IT INTO YOU...
AS I SAID. TOGETHER WE CAN DO THIS.
MY SKIN IS TINGLING. I--I FEEL SO POWERFUL--
OF COURSE, YOU'RE SUPERBOY--
THROOOM
AND I CAN DO ANYTHING!
SKRASSHH
HE POUNDS FOR HOURS CHIPPING AWAY AT THE BARRIER BETWEEN THEIR DIMENSION AND OURS.

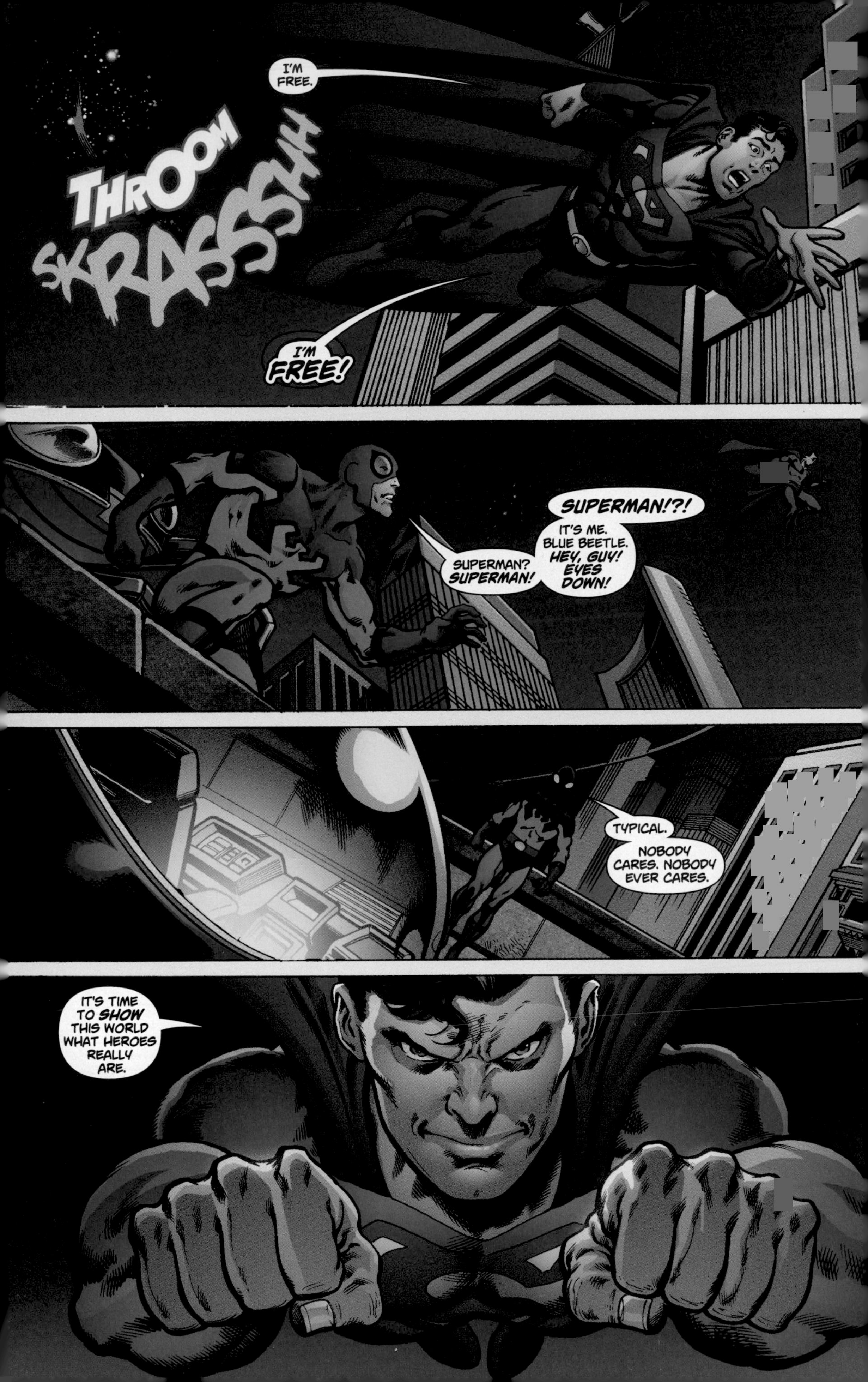
I'M FREE.
THROOM
SKRASSSH
I'M FREE!
SUPERMAN? SUPERMAN!
SUPERMAN!?!
IT'S ME. BLUE BEETLE. HEY, GUY! EYES DOWN!
TYPICAL.
NOBODY CARES. NOBODY EVER CARES.
IT'S TIME TO SHOW THIS WORLD WHAT HEROES REALLY ARE.

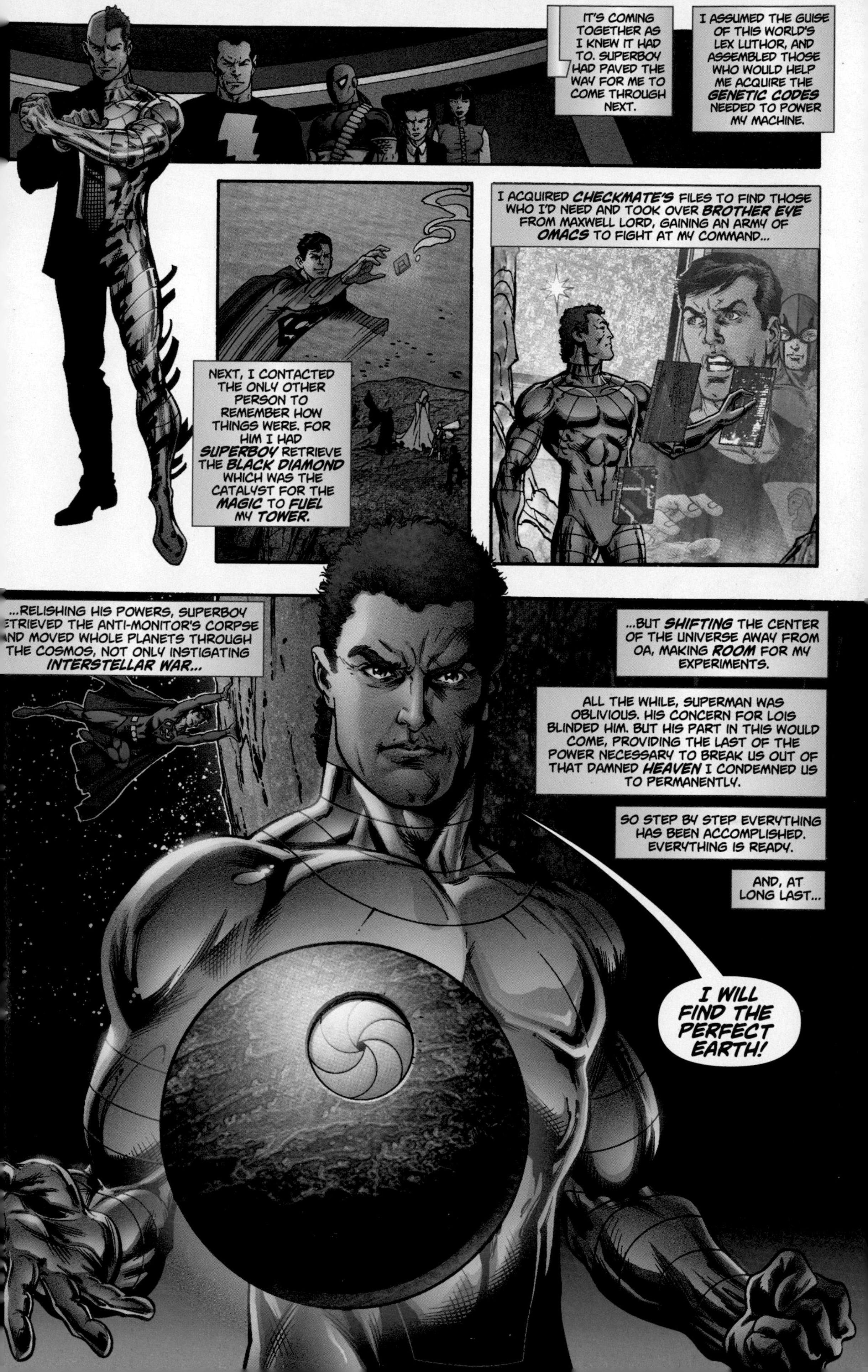
IT'S COMING TOGETHER AS I KNEW IT HAD TO. SUPERBOY HAD PAVED THE WAY FOR ME TO COME THROUGH NEXT.
I ASSUMED THE GUISE OF THIS WORLD'S LEX LUTHOR, AND ASSEMBLED THOSE WHO WOULD HELP ME ACQUIRE THE GENETIC CODES NEEDED TO POWER MY MACHINE.
NEXT, I CONTACTED THE ONLY OTHER PERSON TO REMEMBER HOW THINGS WERE. FOR HIM I HAD SUPERBOY RETRIEVE THE BLACK DIAMOND WHICH WAS THE CATALYST FOR THE MAGIC TO FUEL MY TOWER.
I ACQUIRED CHECKMATE'S FILES TO FIND THOSE WHO I'D NEED AND TOOK OVER BROTHER EYE FROM MAXWELL LORD, GAINING AN ARMY OF OMACS TO FIGHT AT MY COMMAND...
...RELISHING HIS POWERS, SUPERBOY RETRIEVED THE ANTI-MONITOR'S CORPSE AND MOVED WHOLE PLANETS THROUGH THE COSMOS, NOT ONLY INSTIGATING INTERSTELLAR WAR...
...BUT SHIFTING THE CENTER OF THE UNIVERSE AWAY FROM OA, MAKING ROOM FOR MY EXPERIMENTS.
ALL THE WHILE, SUPERMAN WAS OBLIVIOUS. HIS CONCERN FOR LOIS BLINDED HIM. BUT HIS PART IN THIS WOULD COME, PROVIDING THE LAST OF THE POWER NECESSARY TO BREAK US OUT OF THAT DAMNED HEAVEN I CONDEMNED US TO PERMANENTLY.
SO STEP BY STEP EVERYTHING HAS BEEN ACCOMPLISHED. EVERYTHING IS READY.
AND, AT LONG LAST...
I WILL FIND THE PERFECT EARTH!

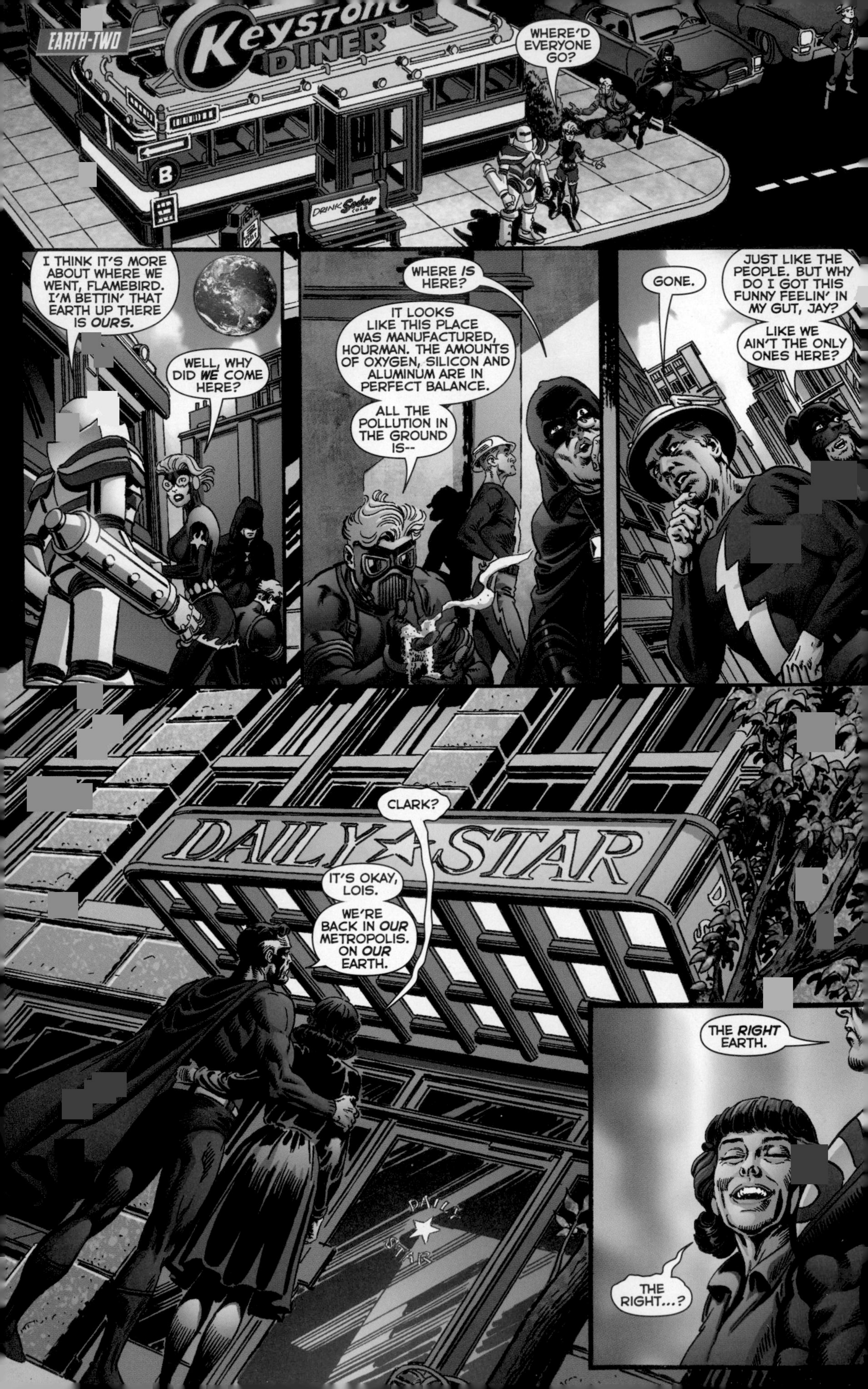
EARTH-TWO
Keystone DINER
WHERE'D EVERYONE GO?
I THINK IT'S MORE ABOUT WHERE WE WENT, FLAMEBIRD. I'M BETTIN' THAT EARTH UP THERE IS *OURS.*
WELL, WHY DID *WE* COME HERE?
WHERE *IS* HERE?
IT LOOKS LIKE THIS PLACE WAS MANUFACTURED, HOURMAN. THE AMOUNTS OF OXYGEN, SILICON AND ALUMINUM ARE IN PERFECT BALANCE.
ALL THE POLLUTION IN THE GROUND IS--
GONE.
JUST LIKE THE PEOPLE. BUT WHY DO I GOT THIS FUNNY FEELIN' IN MY GUT, JAY?
LIKE WE AIN'T THE ONLY ONES HERE?
DAILY STAR
CLARK?
IT'S OKAY, LOIS.
WE'RE BACK IN *OUR* METROPOLIS. ON *OUR* EARTH.
THE *RIGHT* EARTH.
THE RIGHT...?

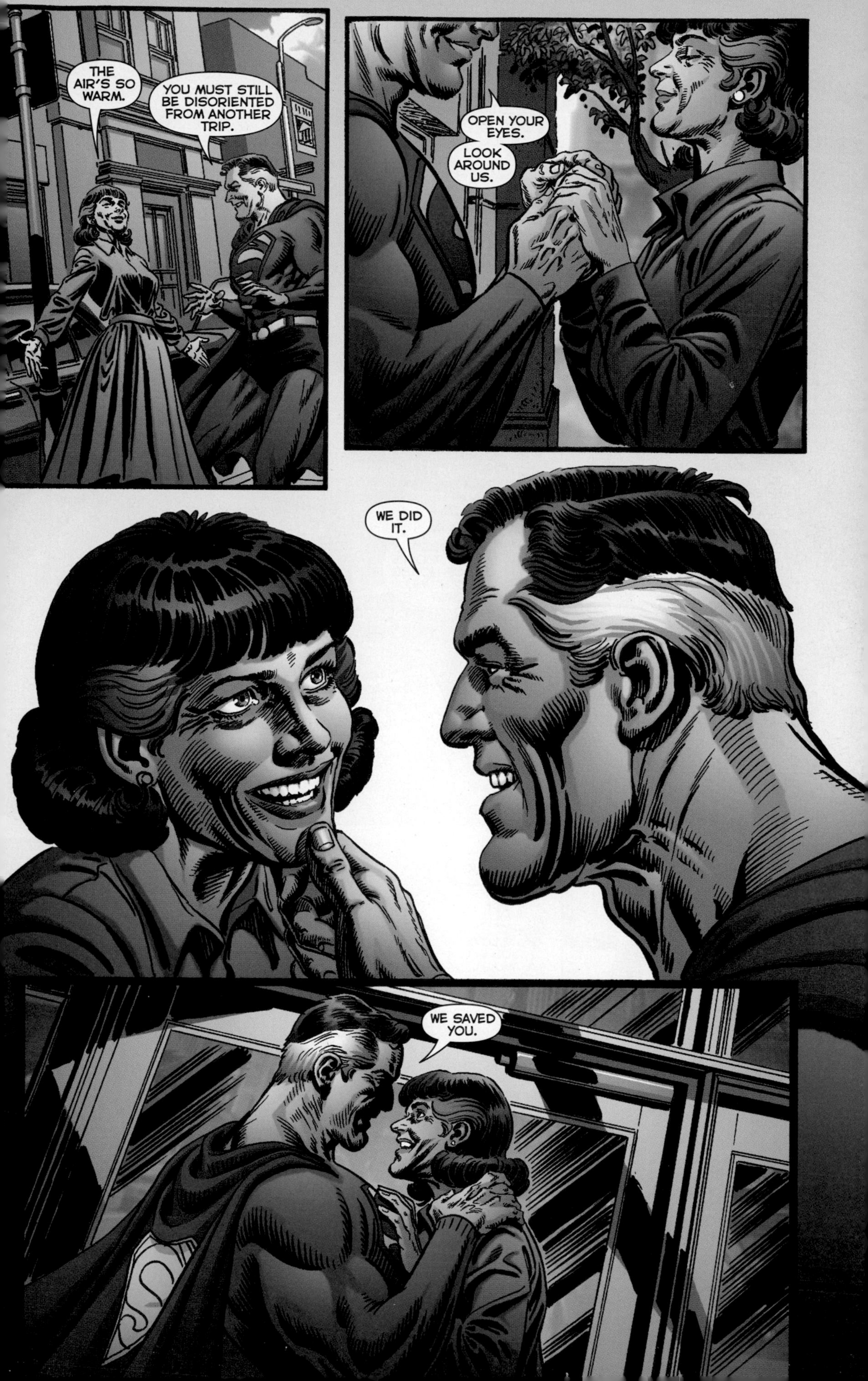
THE AIR'S SO WARM.
YOU MUST STILL BE DISORIENTED FROM ANOTHER TRIP.
OPEN YOUR EYES.
LOOK AROUND US.
WE DID IT.
WE SAVED YOU.

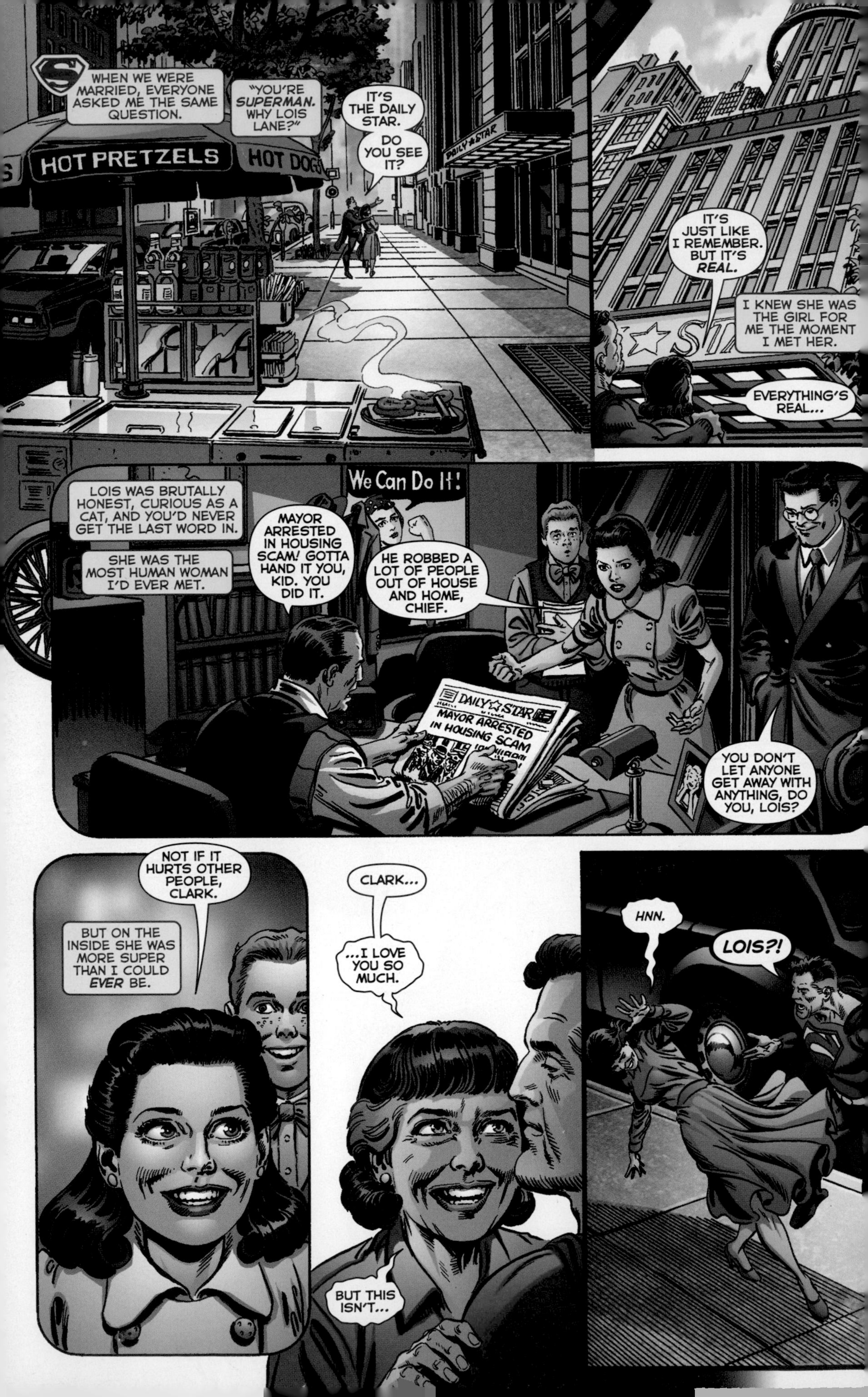
WHEN WE WERE MARRIED, EVERYONE ASKED ME THE SAME QUESTION.
"YOU'RE SUPERMAN. WHY LOIS LANE?"
HOT PRETZELS
HOT DOG
IT'S THE DAILY STAR.
DO YOU SEE IT?
DAILY STAR
IT'S JUST LIKE I REMEMBER. BUT IT'S REAL.
I KNEW SHE WAS THE GIRL FOR ME THE MOMENT I MET HER.
EVERYTHING'S REAL...
LOIS WAS BRUTALLY HONEST, CURIOUS AS A CAT, AND YOU'D NEVER GET THE LAST WORD IN.
SHE WAS THE MOST HUMAN WOMAN I'D EVER MET.
We Can Do It!
MAYOR ARRESTED IN HOUSING SCAM! GOTTA HAND IT YOU, KID. YOU DID IT.
HE ROBBED A LOT OF PEOPLE OUT OF HOUSE AND HOME, CHIEF.
DAILY STAR
MAYOR ARRESTED IN HOUSING SCAM
YOU DON'T LET ANYONE GET AWAY WITH ANYTHING, DO YOU, LOIS?
NOT IF IT HURTS OTHER PEOPLE, CLARK.
BUT ON THE INSIDE SHE WAS MORE SUPER THAN I COULD EVER BE.
CLARK...
...I LOVE YOU SO MUCH.
BUT THIS ISN'T...
HNN.
LOIS?!

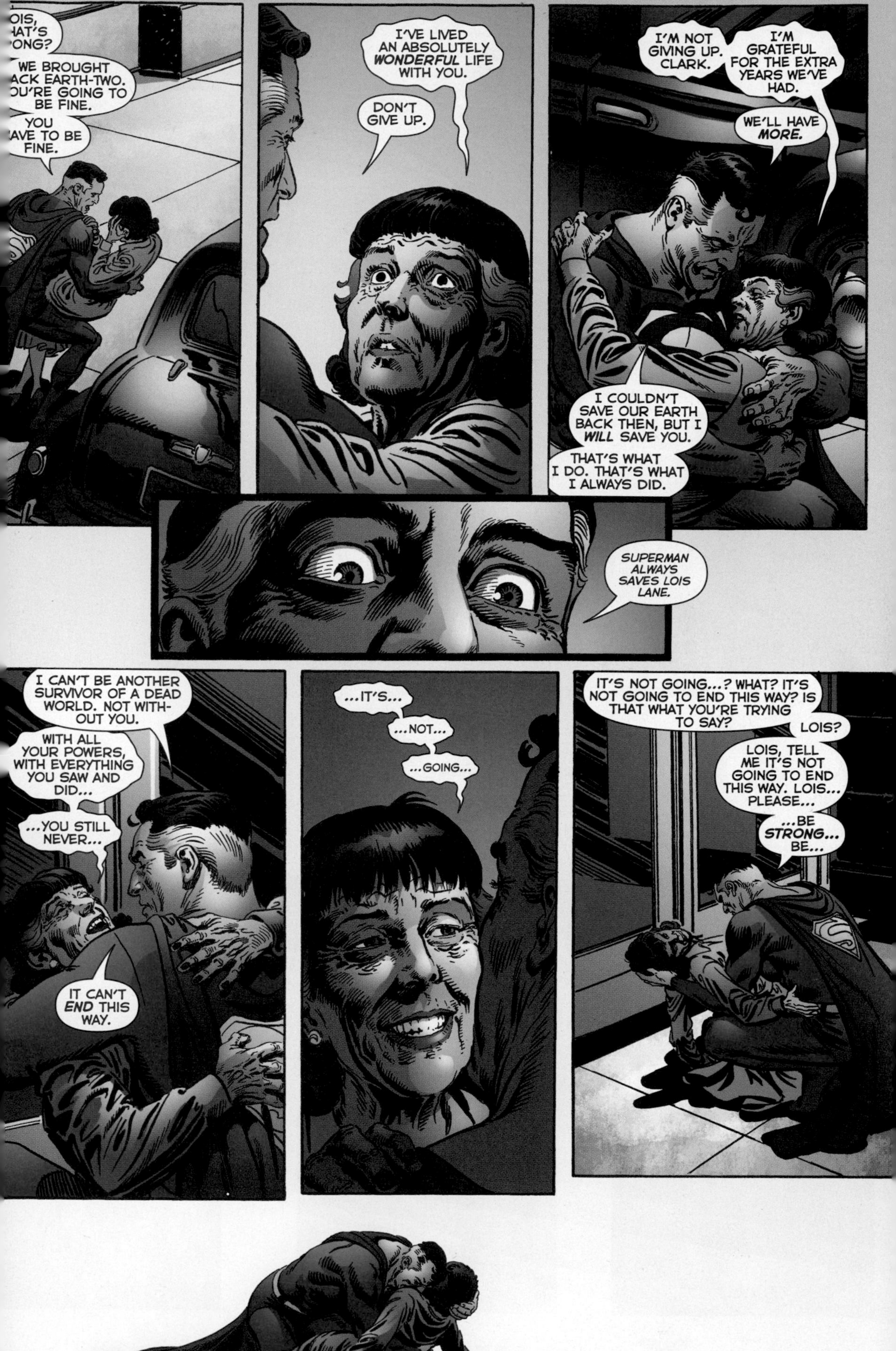

OIS, HAT'S ONG?
WE BROUGHT ACK EARTH-TWO. OU'RE GOING TO BE FINE.
YOU AVE TO BE FINE.
I'VE LIVED AN ABSOLUTELY WONDERFUL LIFE WITH YOU.
DON'T GIVE UP.
I'M NOT GIVING UP. CLARK.
I'M GRATEFUL FOR THE EXTRA YEARS WE'VE HAD.
WE'LL HAVE MORE.
I COULDN'T SAVE OUR EARTH BACK THEN, BUT I WILL SAVE YOU.
THAT'S WHAT I DO. THAT'S WHAT I ALWAYS DID.
SUPERMAN ALWAYS SAVES LOIS LANE.
I CAN'T BE ANOTHER SURVIVOR OF A DEAD WORLD. NOT WITH-OUT YOU.
WITH ALL YOUR POWERS, WITH EVERYTHING YOU SAW AND DID...
...YOU STILL NEVER...
IT CAN'T END THIS WAY.
...IT'S...
...NOT...
...GOING...
IT'S NOT GOING...? WHAT? IT'S NOT GOING TO END THIS WAY? IS THAT WHAT YOU'RE TRYING TO SAY?
LOIS?
LOIS, TELL ME IT'S NOT GOING TO END THIS WAY. LOIS... PLEASE...
...BE STRONG... BE...

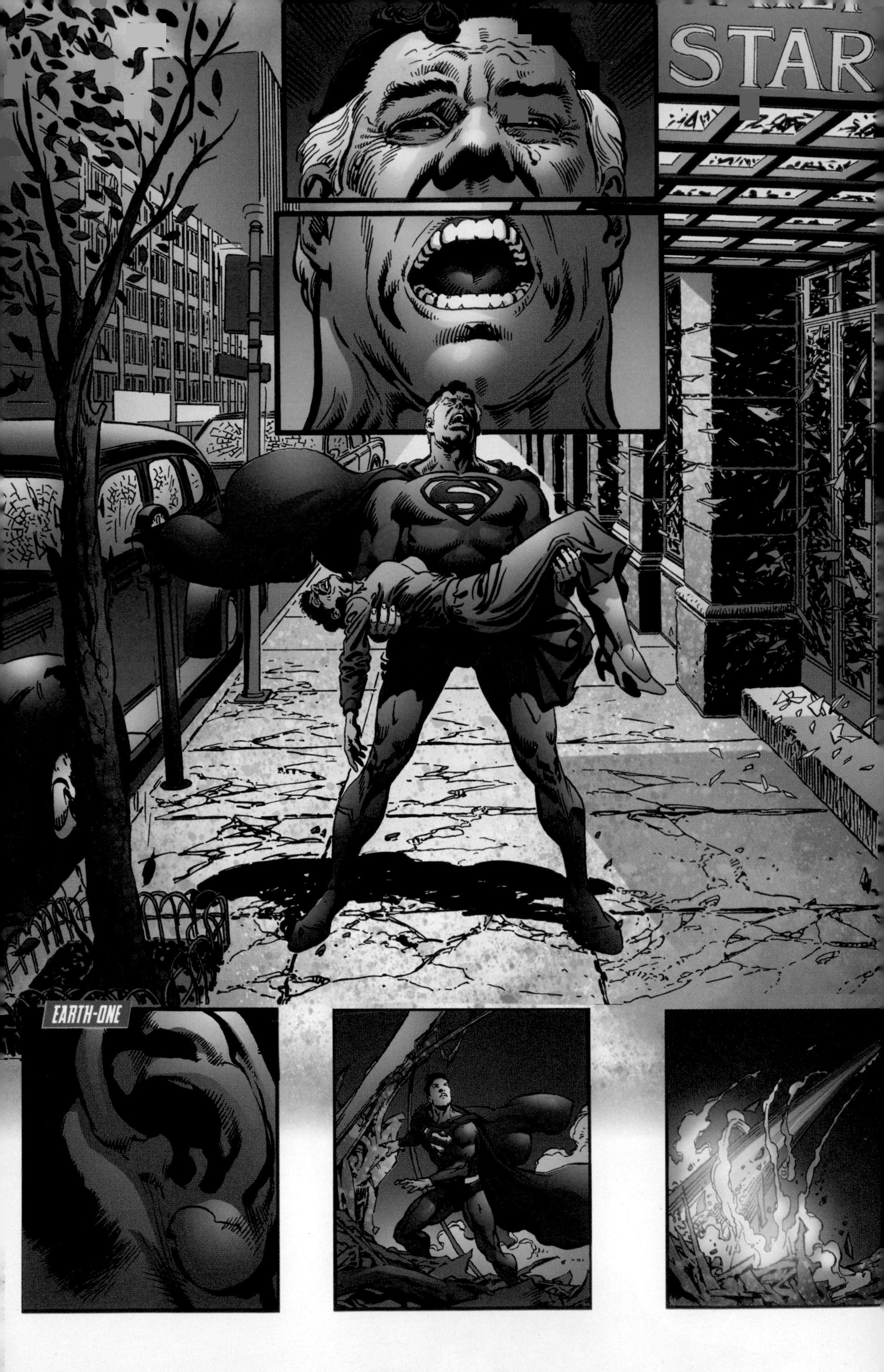
STAR
EARTH-ONE

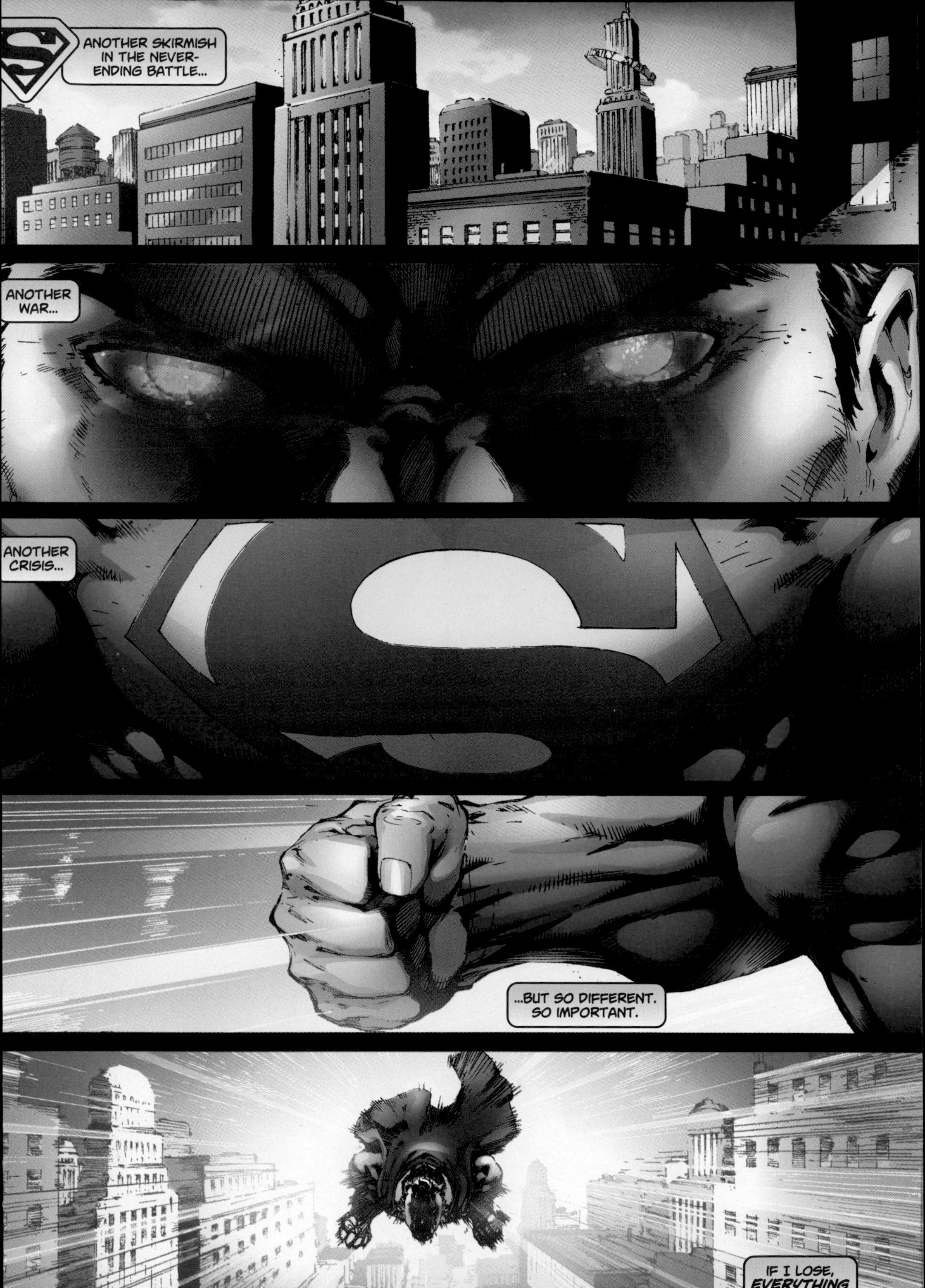
ANOTHER SKIRMISH IN THE NEVER-ENDING BATTLE...
ANOTHER WAR...
ANOTHER CRISIS...
...BUT SO DIFFERENT. SO IMPORTANT.
IF I LOSE, *EVERYTHING* DIES.

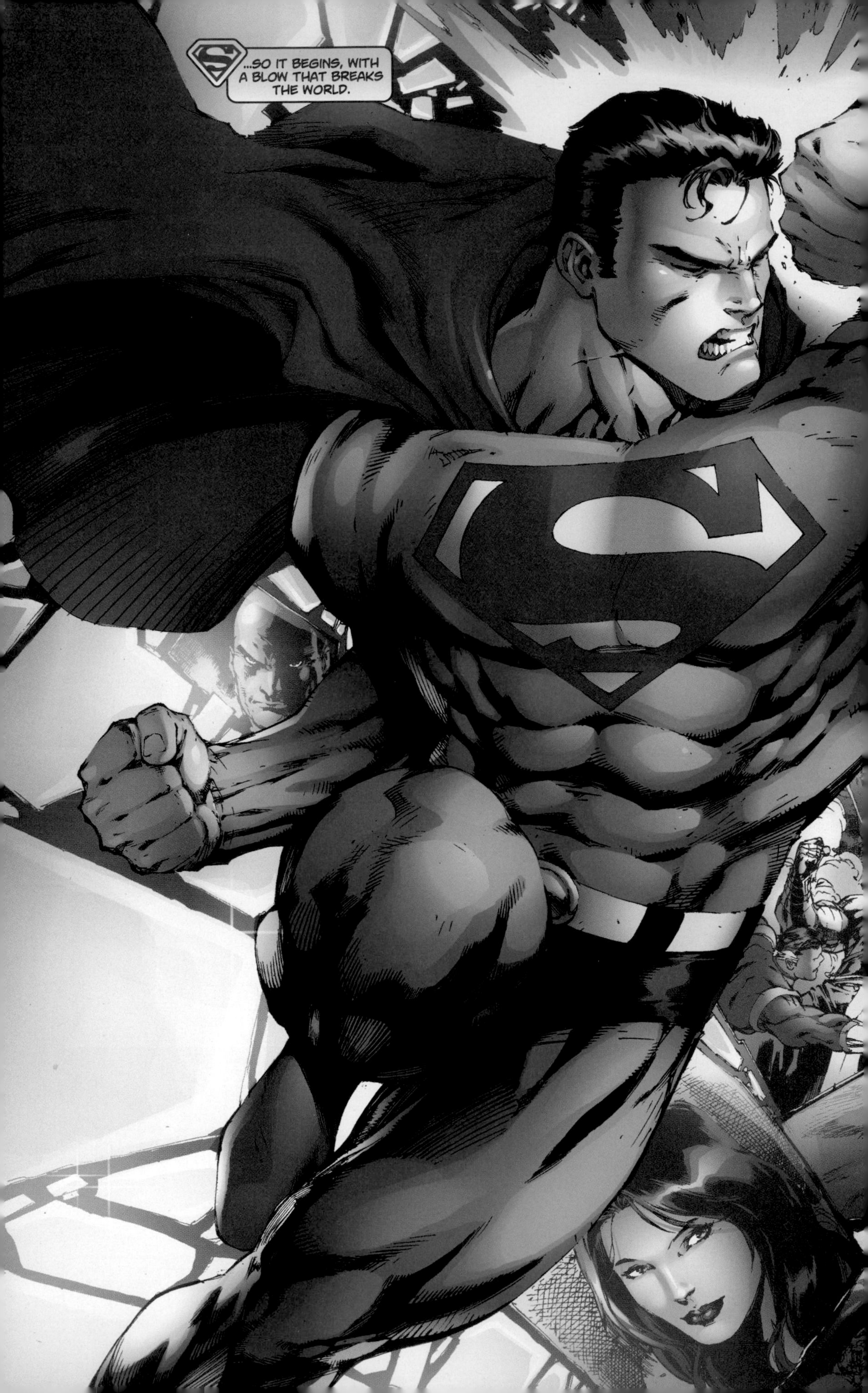
...SO IT BEGINS, WITH A BLOW THAT BREAKS THE WORLD.

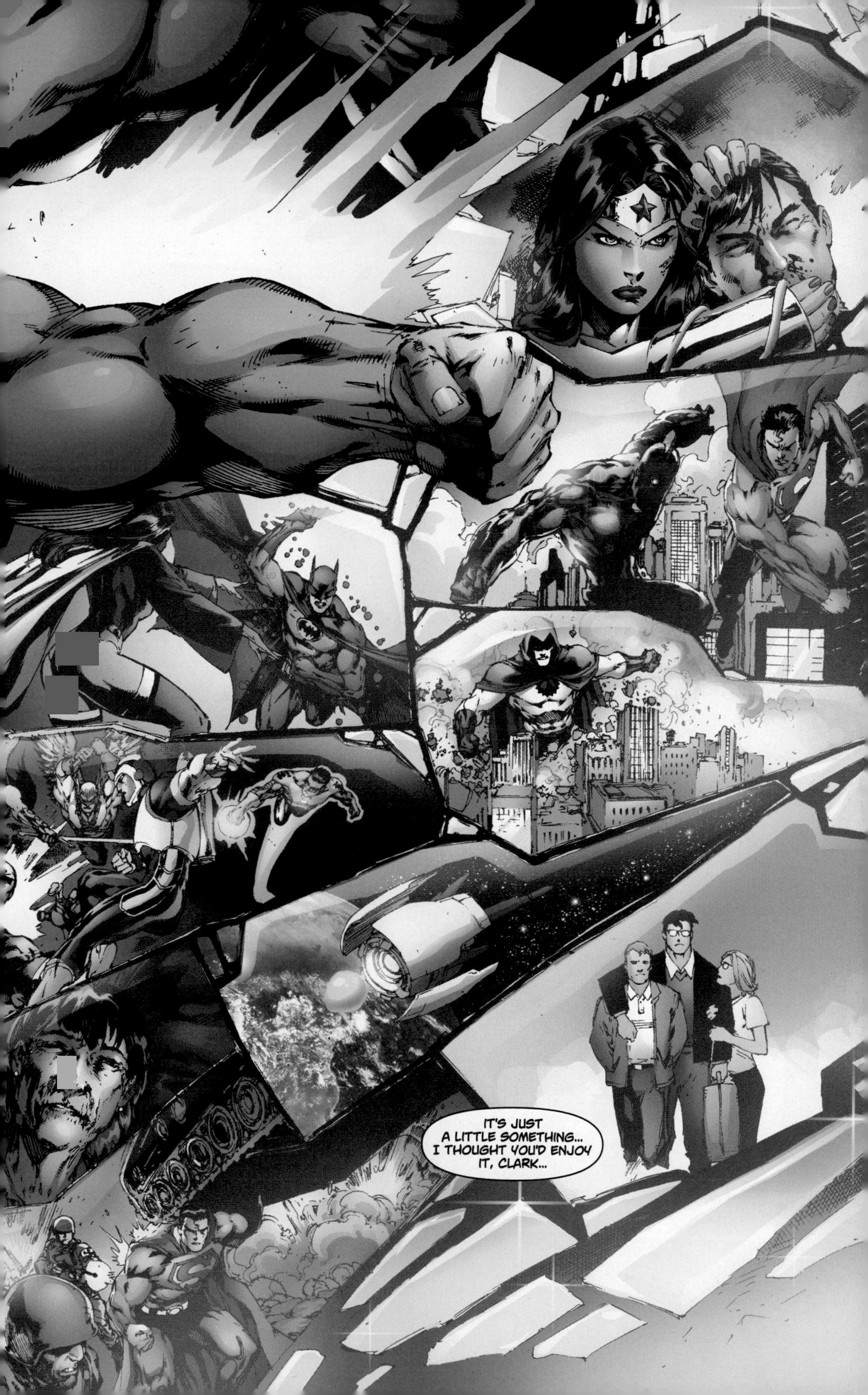
IT'S JUST A LITTLE SOMETHING... I THOUGHT YOU'D ENJOY IT, CLARK...

LOOK AT THAT ROCKET GO!
Clark drew this on a table napkin one night.
It's the Planet Krypton (where he's from) blowing up!

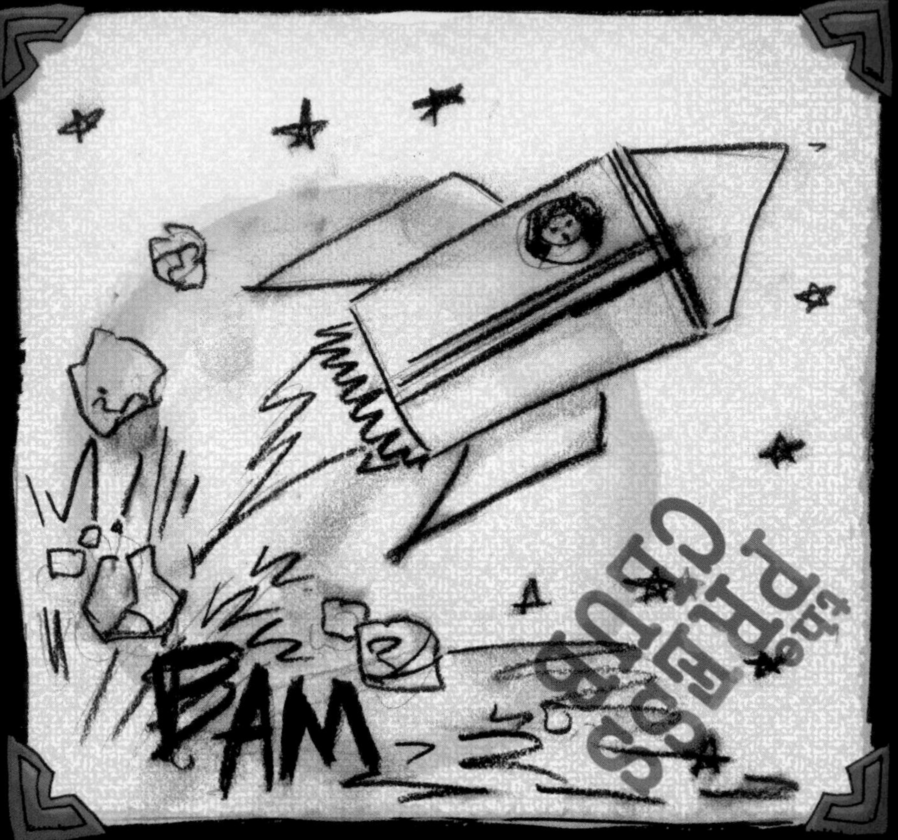
BAM
the PRESS CLUB

Ma Kent took this picture right after they rescued Baby Kal-L.
Of course, they didn't know he was from another planet at the time!

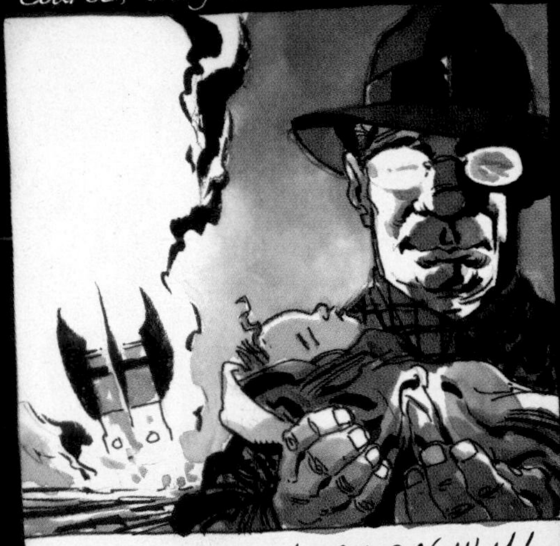

NOT A SCRATCH ON HIM!

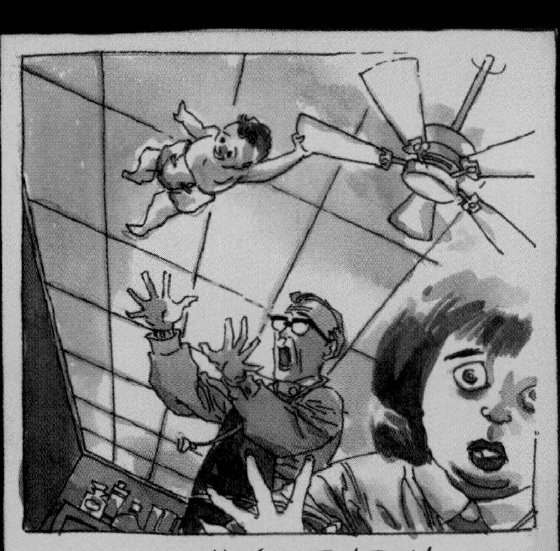

FLYING BABY!

The Kents took the baby to the Orphanage Asylum (where else?). Ma always said the doctors looked relieved to have Clark out of there. A nurse took this photo - but Pa got a hold of it when she tried to sell it to a newspaper!

PA WARNS CLARK TO BE CAREFUL!

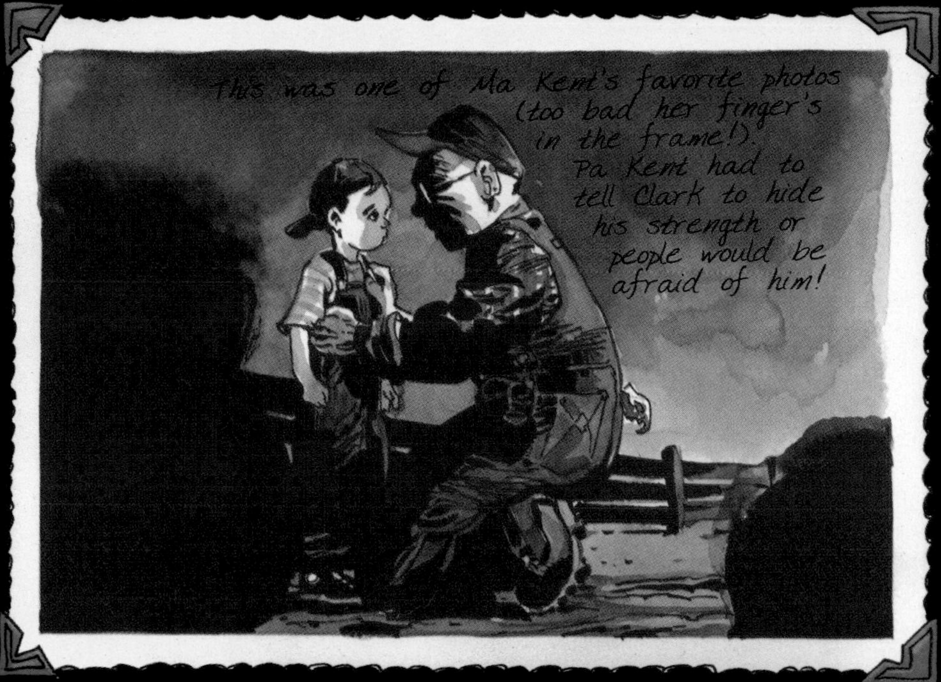
This was one of Ma Kent's favorite photos (too bad her finger's in the frame!). Pa Kent had to tell Clark to hide his strength or people would be afraid of him!

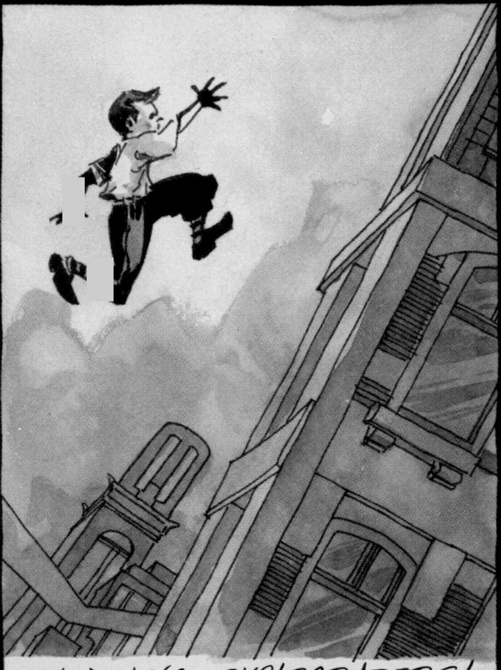

HURDLING SKYSCRAPERS!

By the [redacted] Clark was a teenager, he [redacted] would go into Metropolis [redacted] so Clark could [redacted] over buildings! Good thing they never got caught!

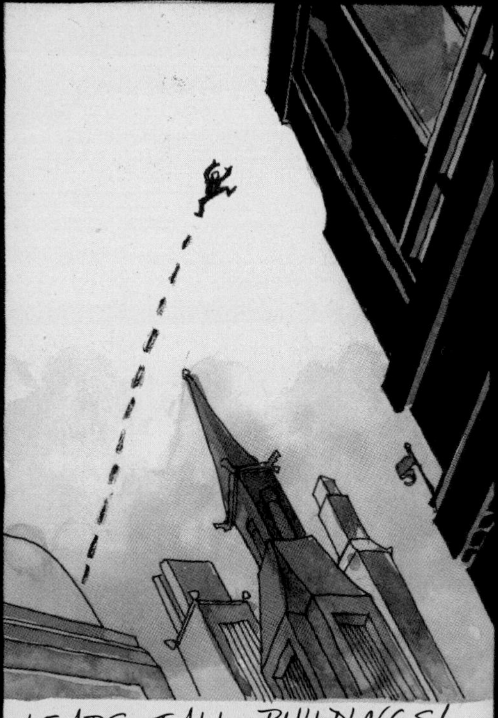

LEAPS TALL BUILDINGS!

Wow! What The Daily Star would've paid for this shot Pa took of young Clark. He could leap almost an eighth of a mile. I guess people didn't know then to look up in the sky!

WHAT A MAN!

Ma took this photo and the next one of her boy doing some amazing things. Good thing he didn't drop their car!

Clark had always been strong, but now he also had speed. Imagine if he ever played football? Whew!

FASTER THAN A SPEEDING TRAIN!

Clark said the doctor tried SIX TIMES to stick a needle in him. Look at Clark laughing! No secret identity worries yet. A nurse took this photo and gave it to Clark. (I think she had a crush on him.)

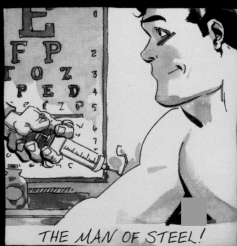

THE MAN OF STEEL!

R.I.P. THE KENTS

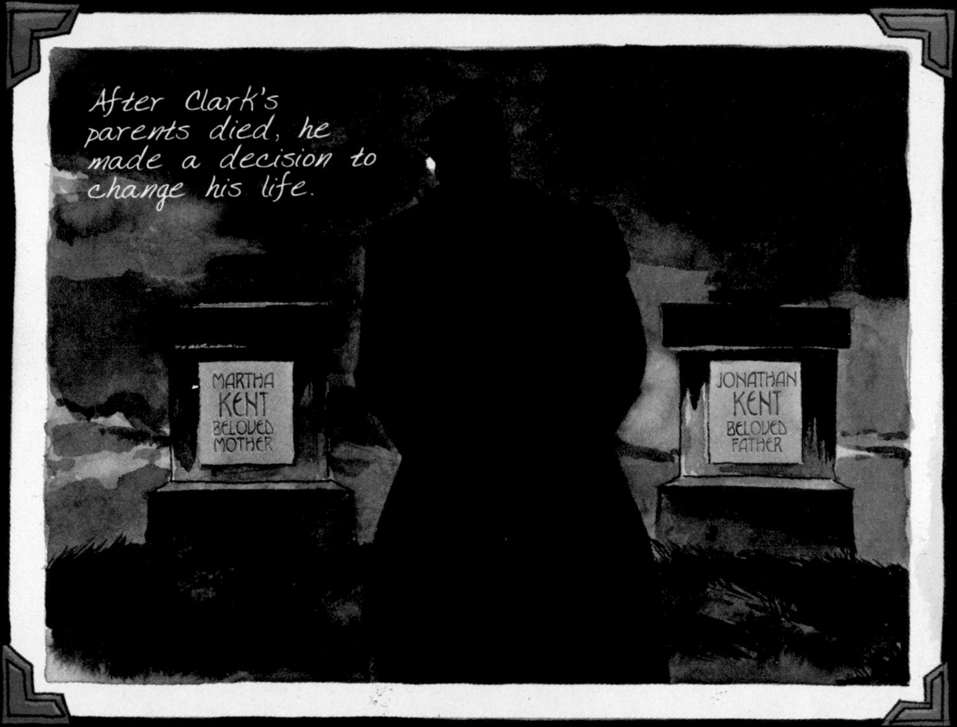
After Clark's parents died, he made a decision to change his life.
MARTHA KENT BELOVED MOTHER
JONATHAN KENT BELOVED FATHER

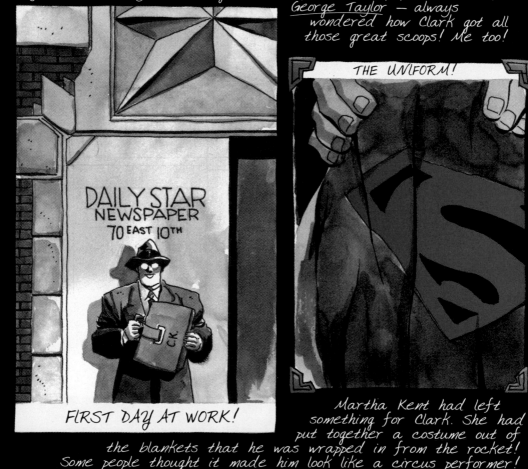

(Clark had someone on the street take this shot with Clark's camera!)

He got a job at The Daily Star. A great metropolitan newspaper. The Chief- George Taylor — always wondered how Clark got all those great scoops! Me too!

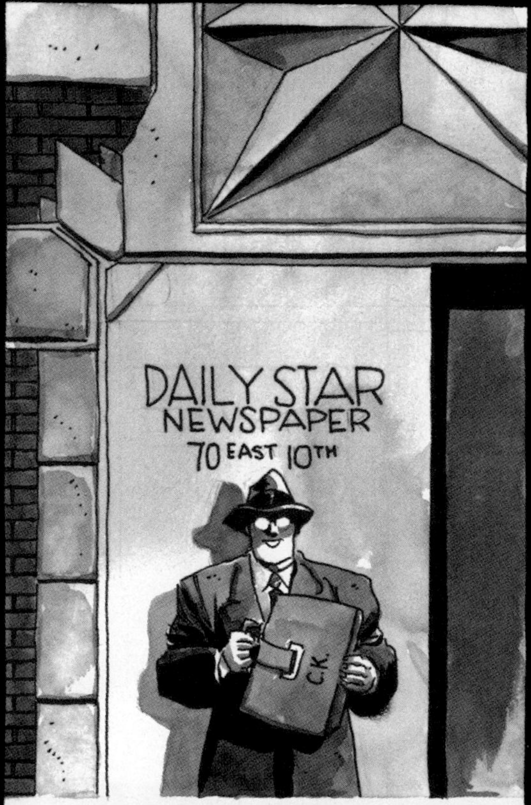
DAILY STAR NEWSPAPER 70 EAST 10TH
C.K.

FIRST DAY AT WORK!

THE UNIFORM!

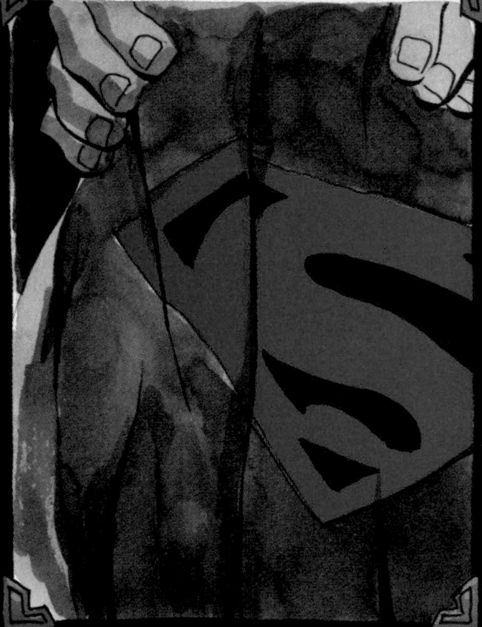

Martha Kent had left something for Clark. She had put together a costume out of the blankets that he was wrapped in from the rocket! Some people thought it made him look like a circus performer!

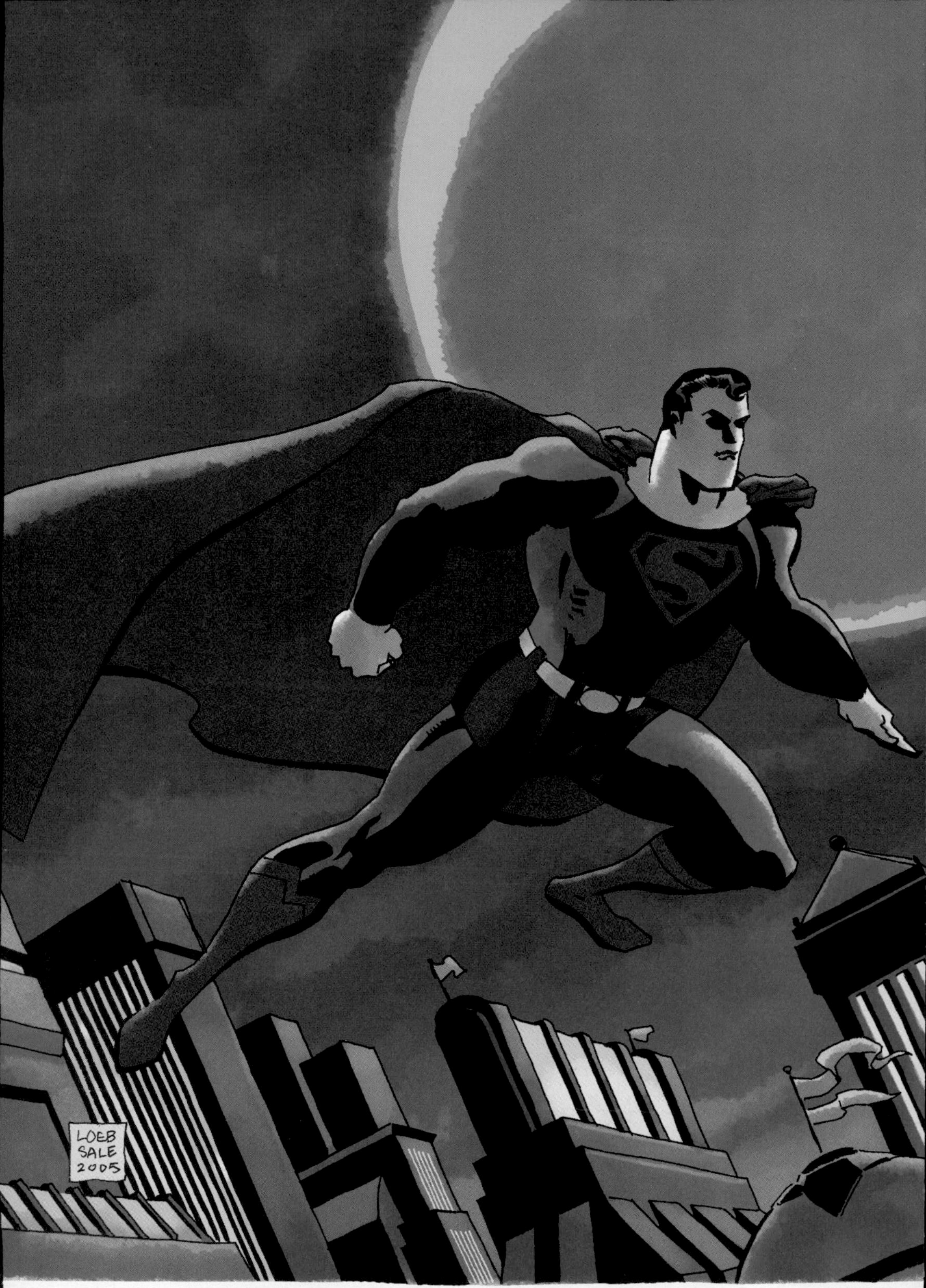
LOEB
SALE
2005

CHAMPION OF THE OPPRESSED!

I took this photo. One of the earliest ones of Superman in action.
He really is the greatest hero of them all!

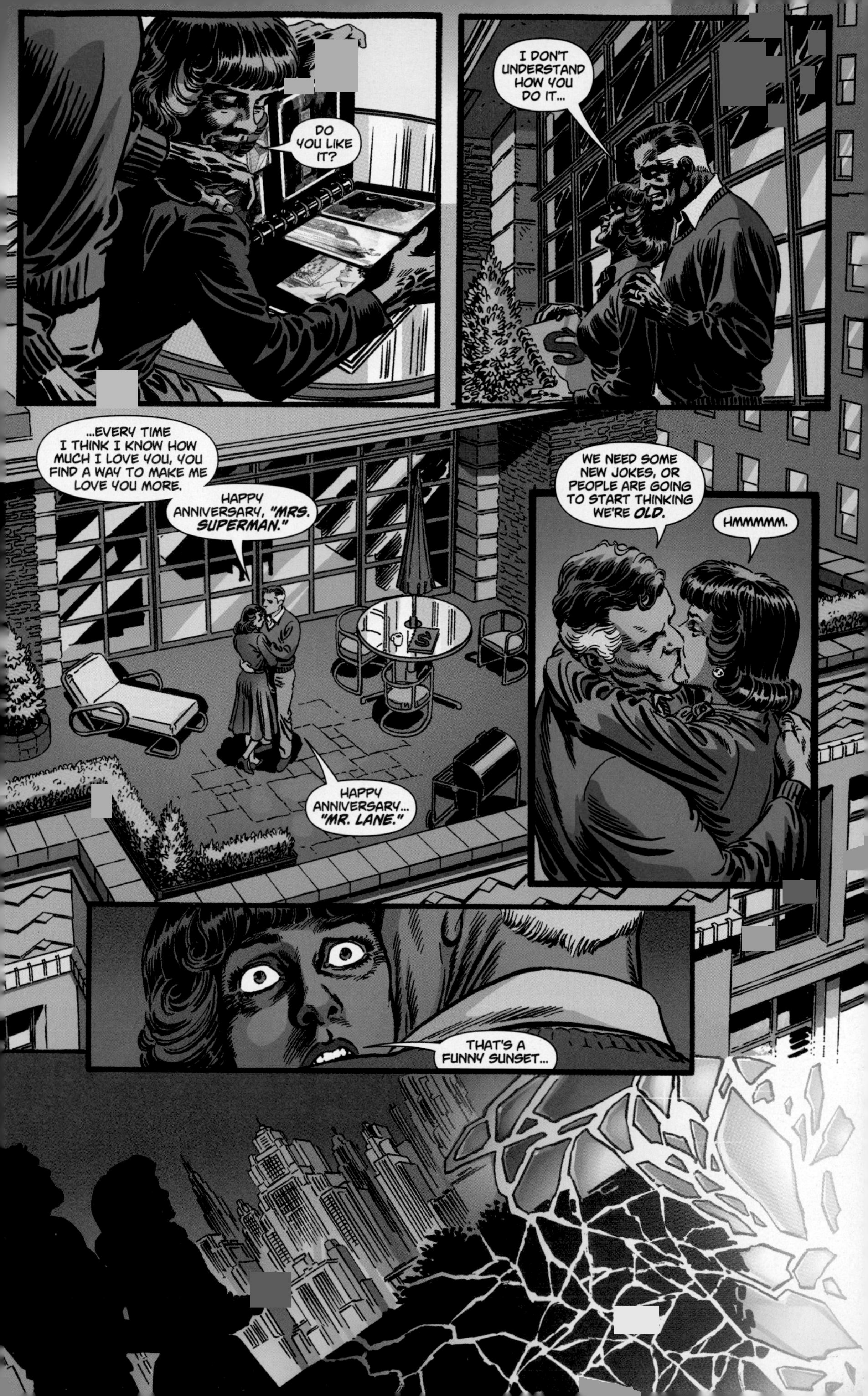
DO YOU LIKE IT?
I DON'T UNDERSTAND HOW YOU DO IT...
...EVERY TIME I THINK I KNOW HOW MUCH I LOVE YOU, YOU FIND A WAY TO MAKE ME LOVE YOU MORE.
HAPPY ANNIVERSARY, *"MRS. SUPERMAN."*
HAPPY ANNIVERSARY... *"MR. LANE."*
WE NEED SOME NEW JOKES, OR PEOPLE ARE GOING TO START THINKING WE'RE *OLD*.
HMMMMM.
THAT'S A FUNNY SUNSET...

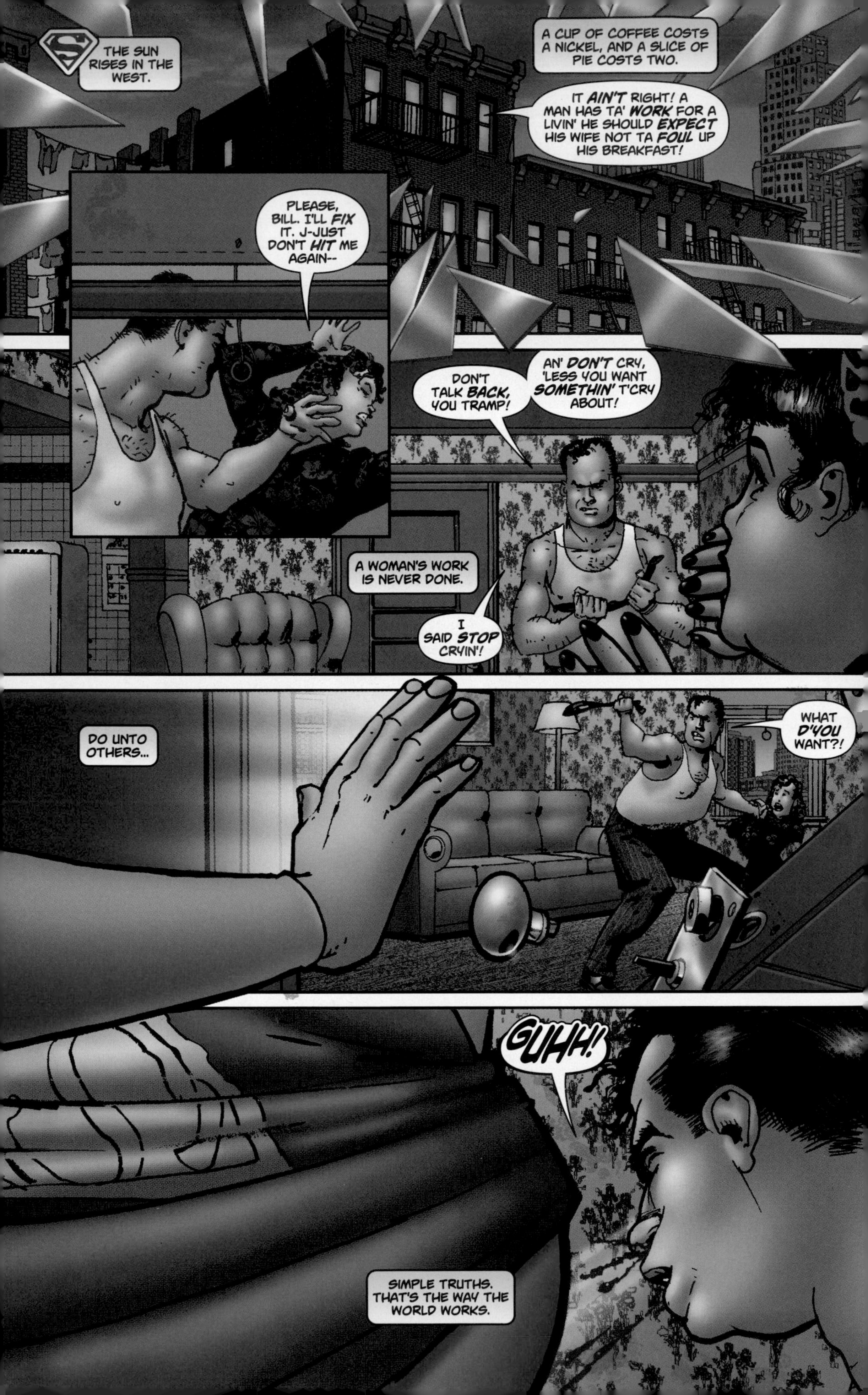
THE SUN RISES IN THE WEST.
A CUP OF COFFEE COSTS A NICKEL, AND A SLICE OF PIE COSTS TWO.
IT AIN'T RIGHT! A MAN HAS TA' WORK FOR A LIVIN' HE SHOULD EXPECT HIS WIFE NOT TA FOUL UP HIS BREAKFAST!
PLEASE, BILL. I'LL FIX IT. J-JUST DON'T HIT ME AGAIN--
DON'T TALK BACK, YOU TRAMP!
AN' DON'T CRY, 'LESS YOU WANT SOMETHIN' T'CRY ABOUT!
A WOMAN'S WORK IS NEVER DONE.
I SAID STOP CRYIN'!
DO UNTO OTHERS...
WHAT D'YOU WANT?!
GUHH!
SIMPLE TRUTHS. THAT'S THE WAY THE WORLD WORKS.

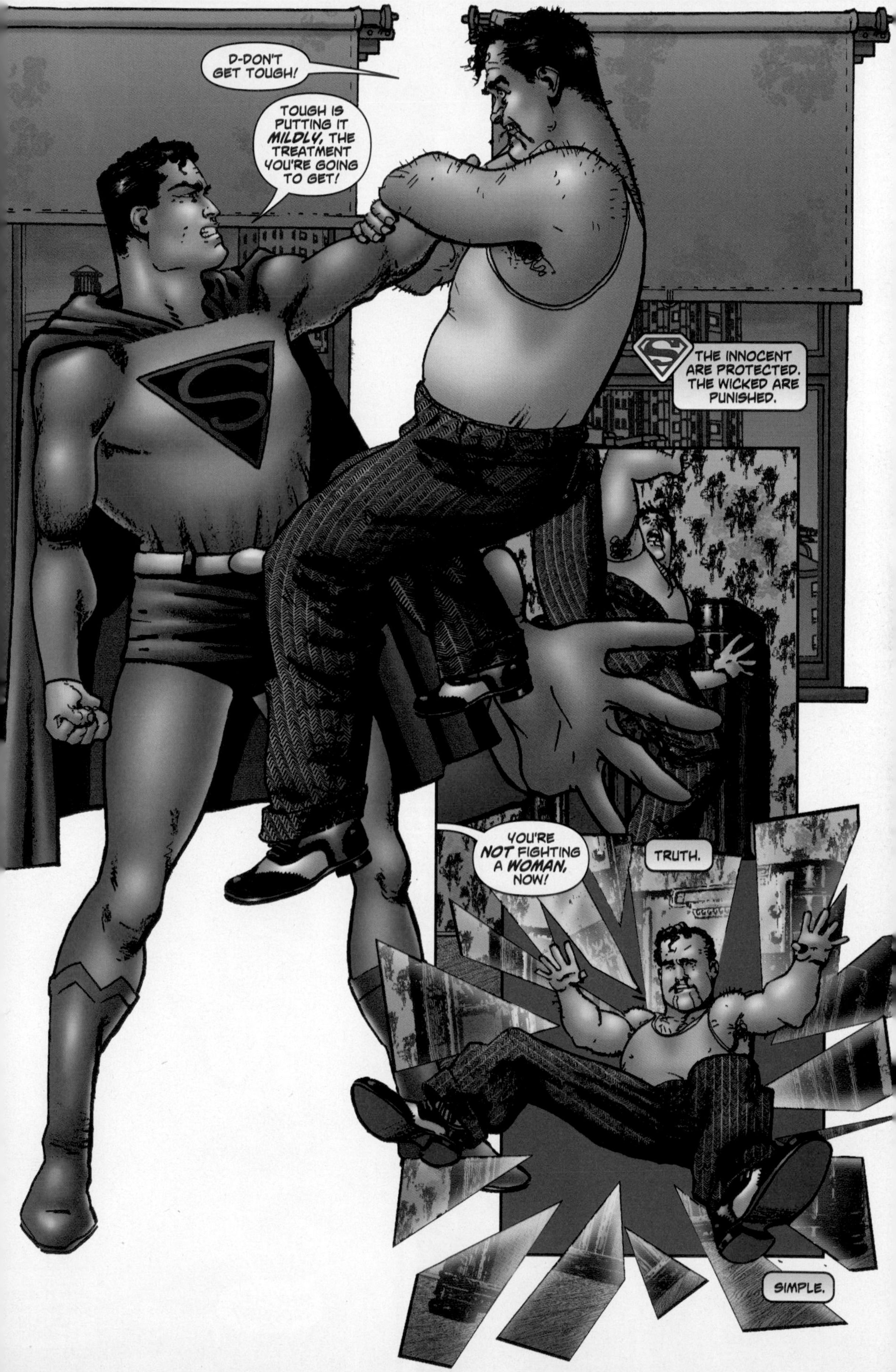

D-DON'T GET TOUGH!
TOUGH IS PUTTING IT MILDLY, THE TREATMENT YOU'RE GOING TO GET!
THE INNOCENT ARE PROTECTED. THE WICKED ARE PUNISHED.
YOU'RE NOT FIGHTING A WOMAN, NOW!
TRUTH.
SIMPLE.

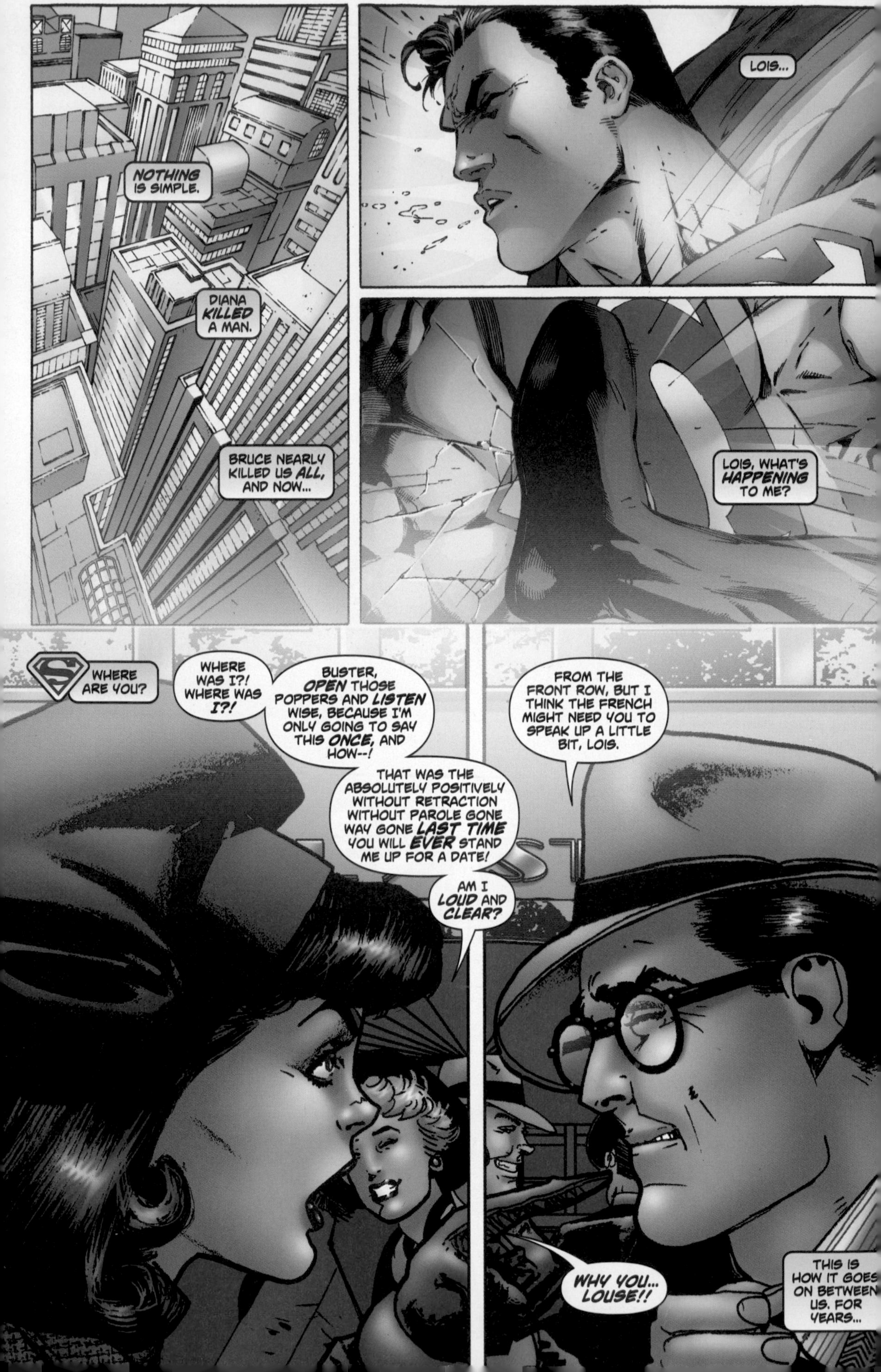
NOTHING IS SIMPLE.
DIANA KILLED A MAN.
BRUCE NEARLY KILLED US ALL, AND NOW...
LOIS...
LOIS, WHAT'S HAPPENING TO ME?
WHERE ARE YOU?
WHERE WAS I?! WHERE WAS I?!
BUSTER, OPEN THOSE POPPERS AND LISTEN WISE, BECAUSE I'M ONLY GOING TO SAY THIS ONCE, AND HOW--!
THAT WAS THE ABSOLUTELY POSITIVELY WITHOUT RETRACTION WITHOUT PAROLE GONE WAY GONE LAST TIME YOU WILL EVER STAND ME UP FOR A DATE!
AM I LOUD AND CLEAR?
FROM THE FRONT ROW, BUT I THINK THE FRENCH MIGHT NEED YOU TO SPEAK UP A LITTLE BIT, LOIS.
WHY YOU... LOUSE!!
THIS IS HOW IT GOES ON BETWEEN US. FOR YEARS...

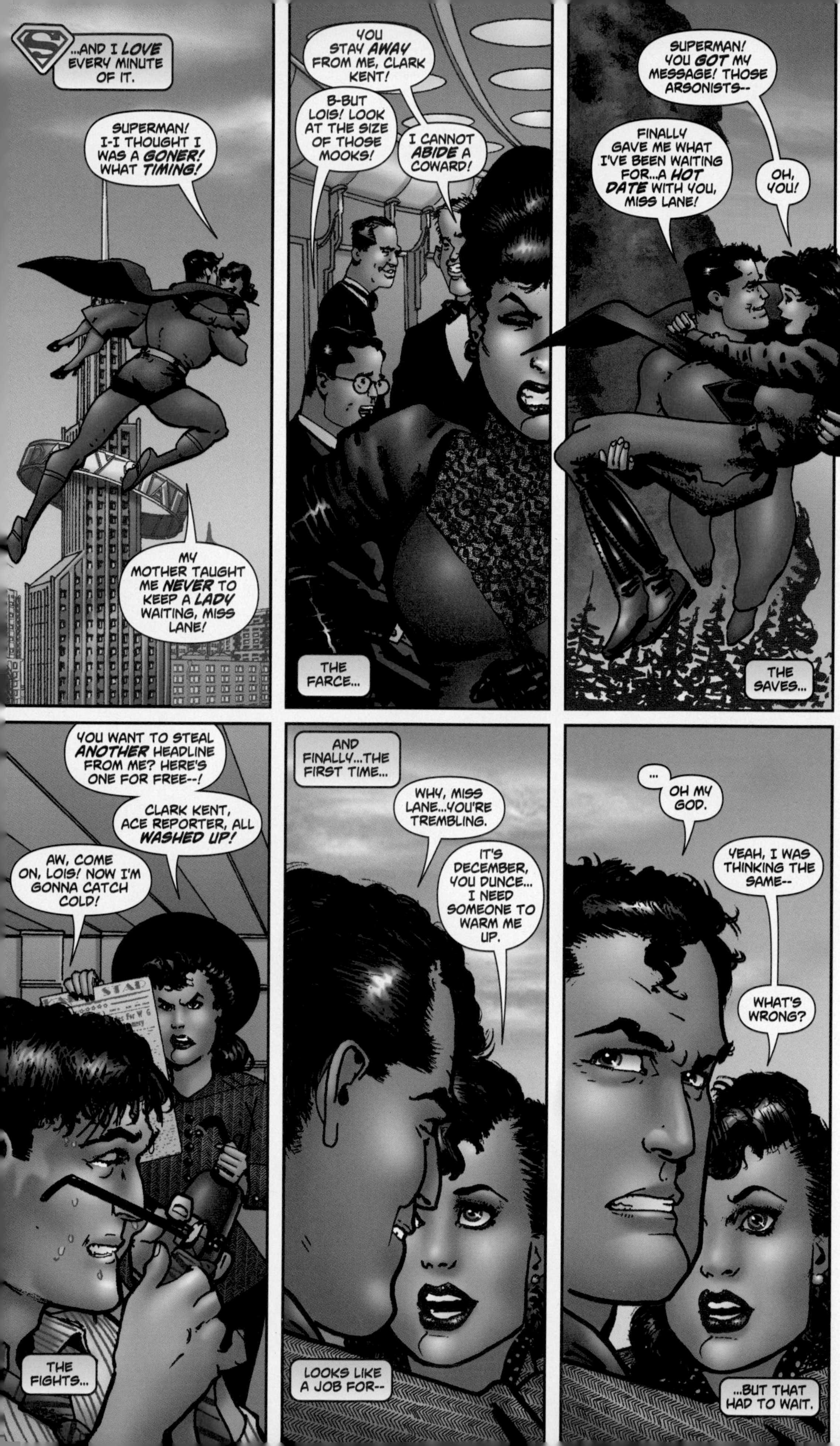
...AND I LOVE EVERY MINUTE OF IT.
SUPERMAN! I-I THOUGHT I WAS A GONER! WHAT TIMING!
MY MOTHER TAUGHT ME NEVER TO KEEP A LADY WAITING, MISS LANE!
YOU STAY AWAY FROM ME, CLARK KENT!
B-BUT LOIS! LOOK AT THE SIZE OF THOSE MOOKS!
I CANNOT ABIDE A COWARD!
THE FARCE...
SUPERMAN! YOU GOT MY MESSAGE! THOSE ARSONISTS--
FINALLY GAVE ME WHAT I'VE BEEN WAITING FOR...A HOT DATE WITH YOU, MISS LANE!
OH, YOU!
THE SAVES...
YOU WANT TO STEAL ANOTHER HEADLINE FROM ME? HERE'S ONE FOR FREE--!
CLARK KENT, ACE REPORTER, ALL WASHED UP!
AW, COME ON, LOIS! NOW I'M GONNA CATCH COLD!
STAR
THE FIGHTS...
AND FINALLY...THE FIRST TIME...
WHY, MISS LANE...YOU'RE TREMBLING.
IT'S DECEMBER, YOU DUNCE... I NEED SOMEONE TO WARM ME UP.
LOOKS LIKE A JOB FOR--
...
OH MY GOD.
YEAH, I WAS THINKING THE SAME--
WHAT'S WRONG?
...BUT THAT HAD TO WAIT.

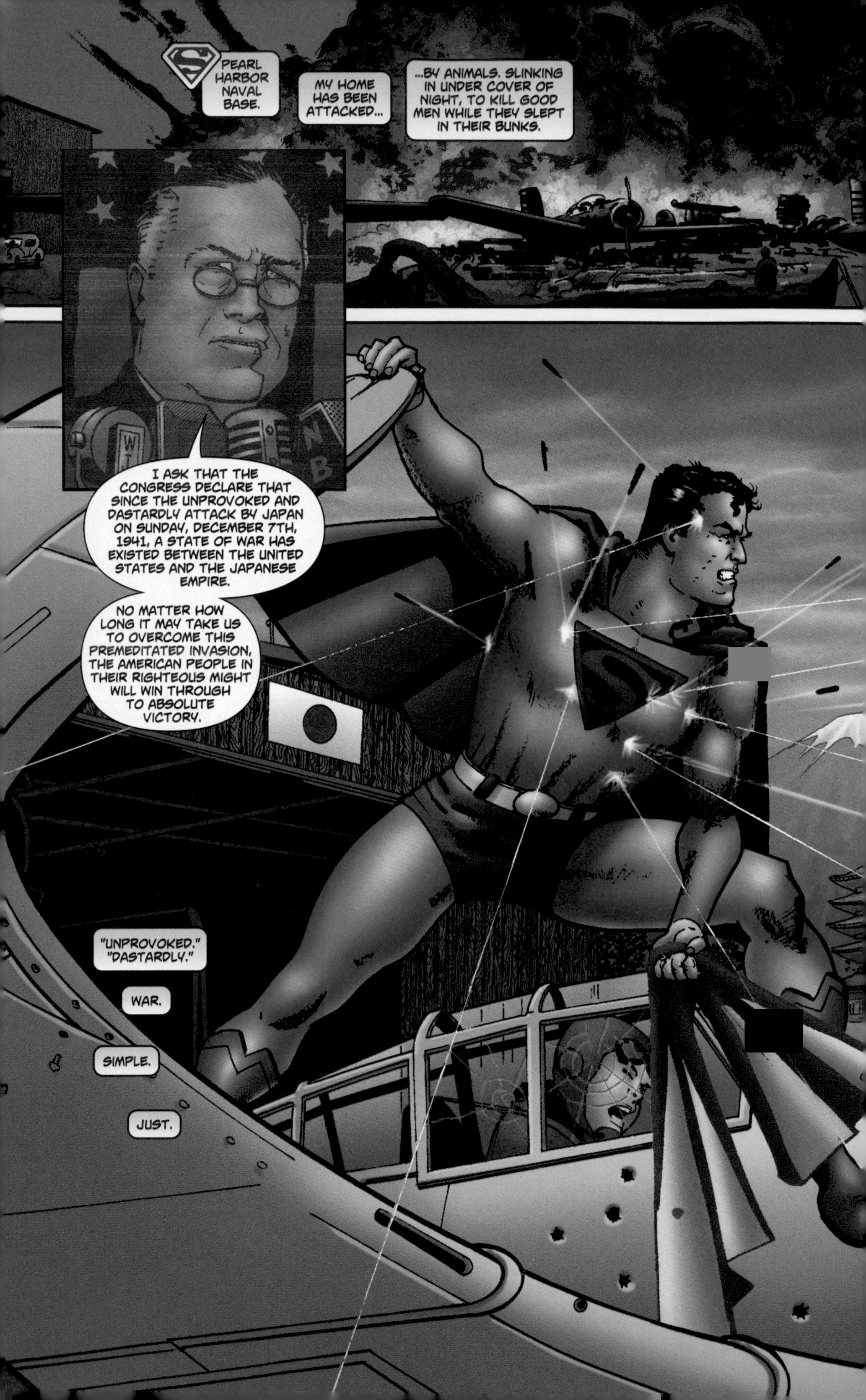
PEARL HARBOR NAVAL BASE.
MY HOME HAS BEEN ATTACKED...
...BY ANIMALS. SLINKING IN UNDER COVER OF NIGHT, TO KILL GOOD MEN WHILE THEY SLEPT IN THEIR BUNKS.
W
N B
I ASK THAT THE CONGRESS DECLARE THAT SINCE THE UNPROVOKED AND DASTARDLY ATTACK BY JAPAN ON SUNDAY, DECEMBER 7TH, 1941, A STATE OF WAR HAS EXISTED BETWEEN THE UNITED STATES AND THE JAPANESE EMPIRE.
NO MATTER HOW LONG IT MAY TAKE US TO OVERCOME THIS PREMEDITATED INVASION, THE AMERICAN PEOPLE IN THEIR RIGHTEOUS MIGHT WILL WIN THROUGH TO ABSOLUTE VICTORY.
"UNPROVOKED." "DASTARDLY."
WAR.
SIMPLE.
JUST.

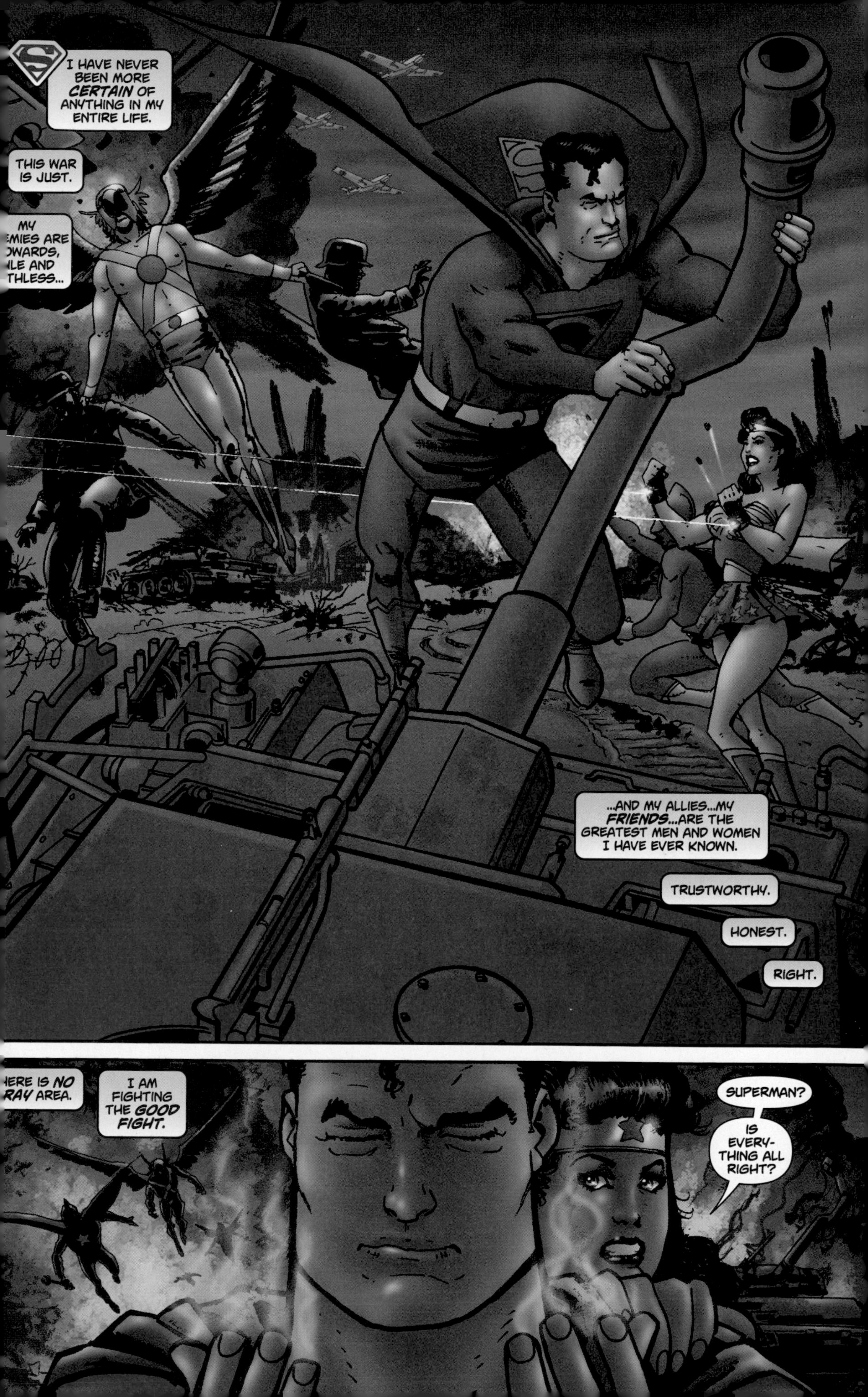
I HAVE NEVER BEEN MORE CERTAIN OF ANYTHING IN MY ENTIRE LIFE.
THIS WAR IS JUST.
MY EMIES ARE OWARDS, ILE AND THLESS...
...AND MY ALLIES...MY FRIENDS...ARE THE GREATEST MEN AND WOMEN I HAVE EVER KNOWN.
TRUSTWORTHY.
HONEST.
RIGHT.
HERE IS NO RAY AREA.
I AM FIGHTING THE GOOD FIGHT.
SUPERMAN?
IS EVERY-THING ALL RIGHT?

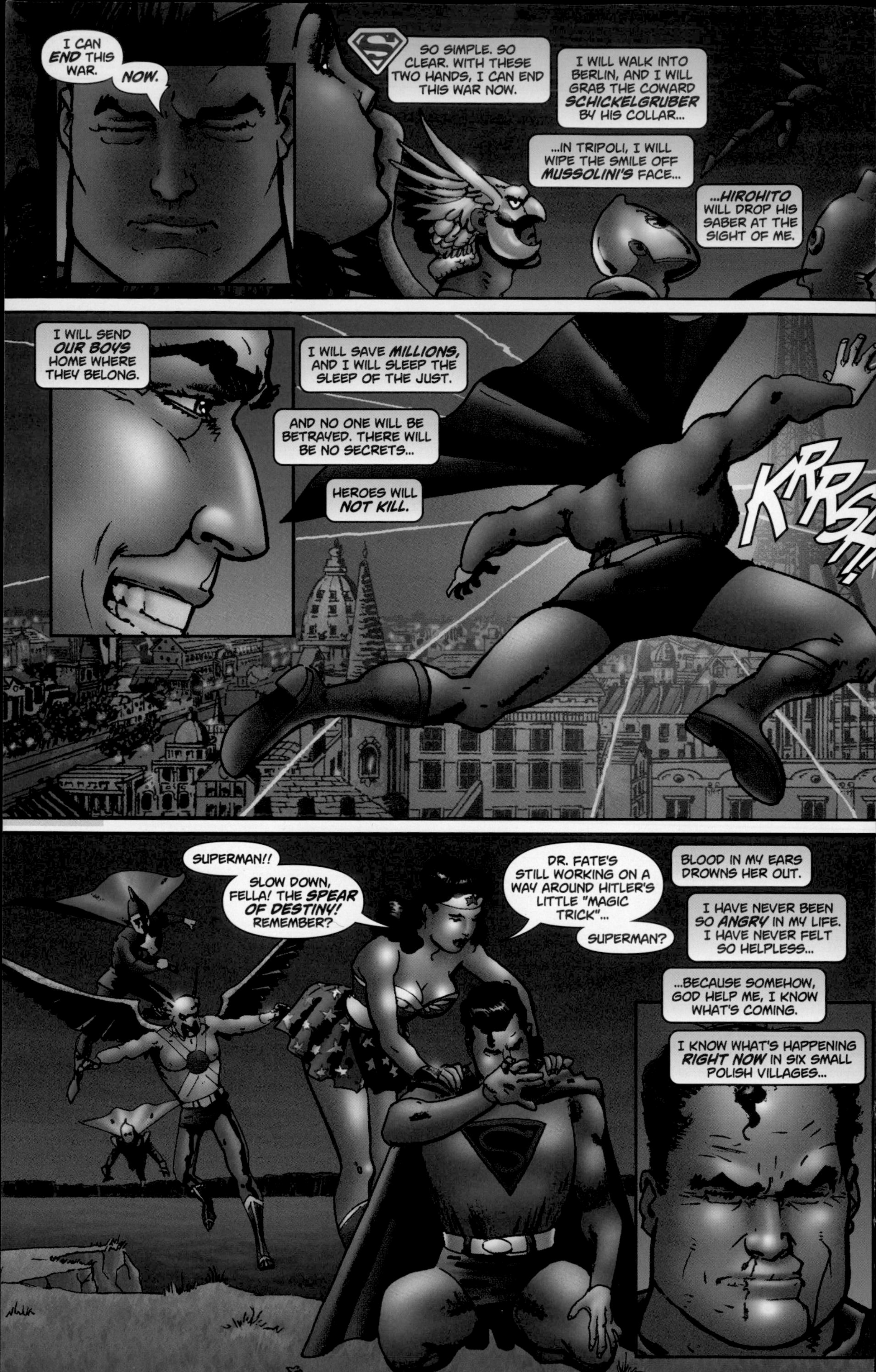
I CAN END THIS WAR.
NOW.
SO SIMPLE. SO CLEAR. WITH THESE TWO HANDS, I CAN END THIS WAR NOW.
I WILL WALK INTO BERLIN, AND I WILL GRAB THE COWARD SCHICKELGRUBER BY HIS COLLAR...
...IN TRIPOLI, I WILL WIPE THE SMILE OFF MUSSOLINI'S FACE...
...HIROHITO WILL DROP HIS SABER AT THE SIGHT OF ME.
I WILL SEND OUR BOYS HOME WHERE THEY BELONG.
I WILL SAVE MILLIONS, AND I WILL SLEEP THE SLEEP OF THE JUST.
AND NO ONE WILL BE BETRAYED. THERE WILL BE NO SECRETS...
HEROES WILL NOT KILL.
KRRSH!!
SUPERMAN!!
SLOW DOWN, FELLA! THE SPEAR OF DESTINY! REMEMBER?
DR. FATE'S STILL WORKING ON A WAY AROUND HITLER'S LITTLE "MAGIC TRICK"...
SUPERMAN?
BLOOD IN MY EARS DROWNS HER OUT.
I HAVE NEVER BEEN SO ANGRY IN MY LIFE. I HAVE NEVER FELT SO HELPLESS...
...BECAUSE SOMEHOW, GOD HELP ME, I KNOW WHAT'S COMING.
I KNOW WHAT'S HAPPENING RIGHT NOW IN SIX SMALL POLISH VILLAGES...

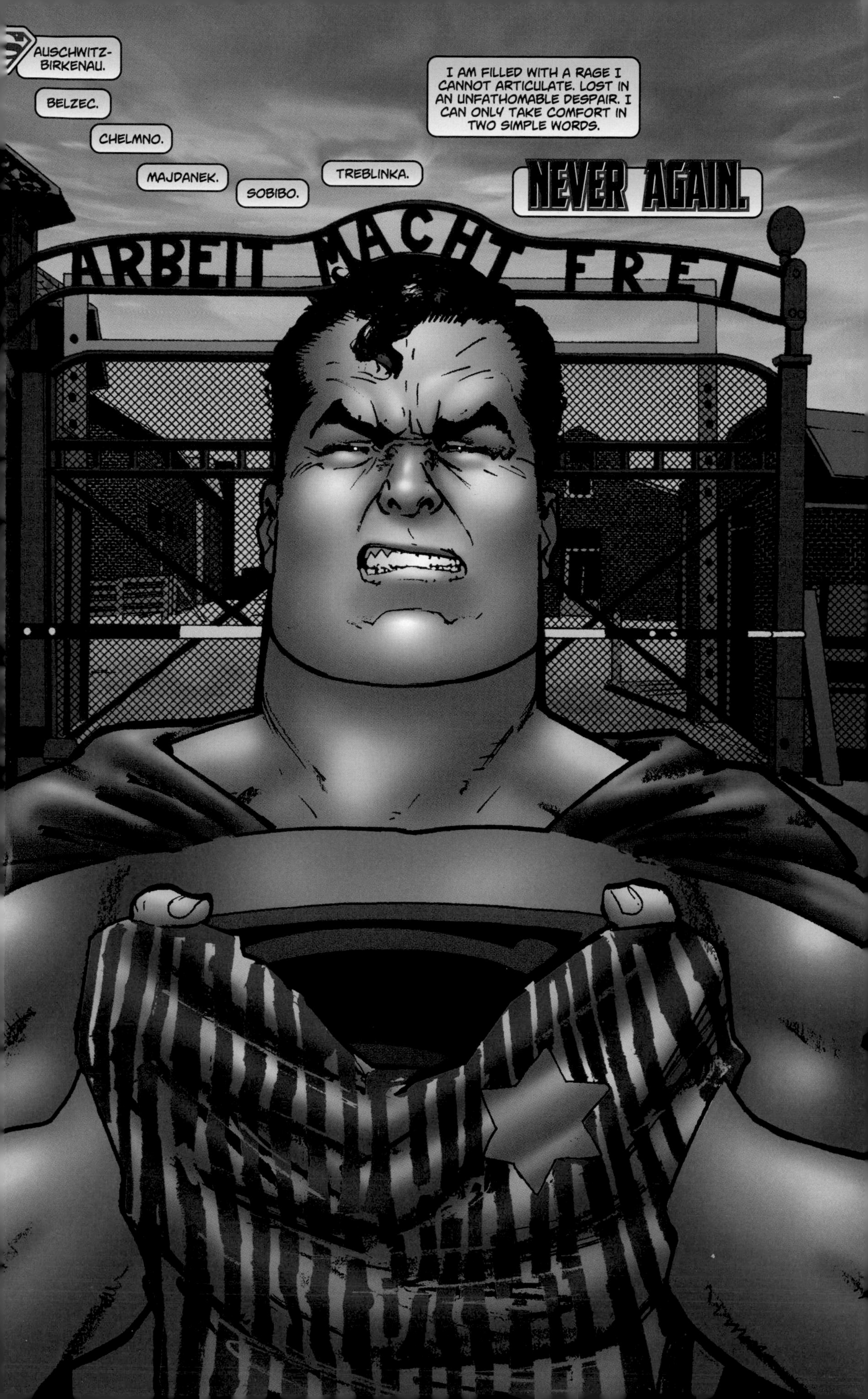
AUSCHWITZ-BIRKENAU.
BELZEC.
CHELMNO.
MAJDANEK.
SOBIBO.
TREBLINKA.
I AM FILLED WITH A RAGE I CANNOT ARTICULATE. LOST IN AN UNFATHOMABLE DESPAIR. I CAN ONLY TAKE COMFORT IN TWO SIMPLE WORDS.
NEVER AGAIN.
ARBEIT MACHT FREI

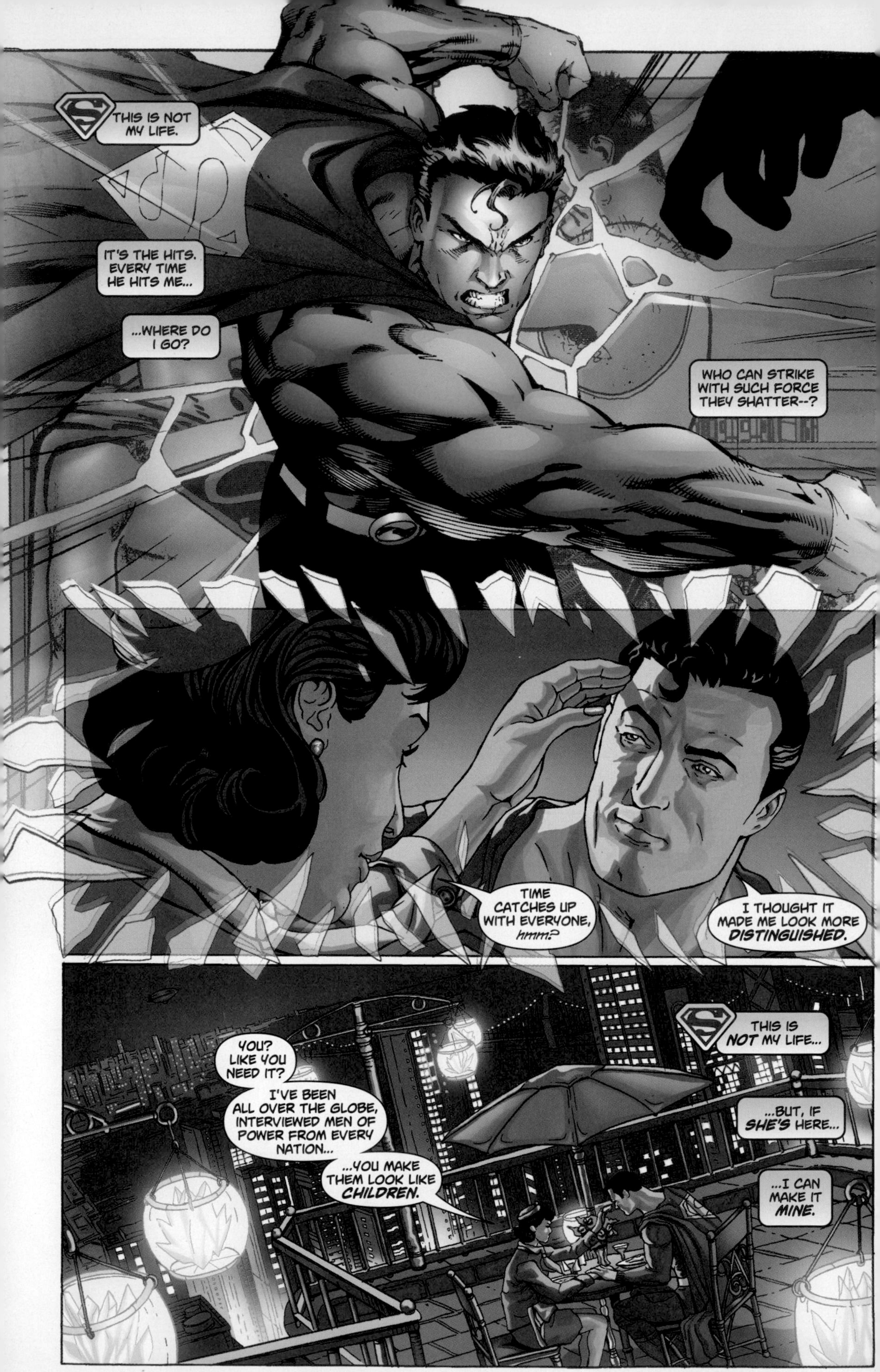

THIS IS NOT MY LIFE.
IT'S THE HITS. EVERY TIME HE HITS ME...
...WHERE DO I GO?
WHO CAN STRIKE WITH SUCH FORCE THEY SHATTER--?
TIME CATCHES UP WITH EVERYONE, *hmm?*
I THOUGHT IT MADE ME LOOK MORE **DISTINGUISHED**.
YOU? LIKE YOU NEED IT?
I'VE BEEN ALL OVER THE GLOBE, INTERVIEWED MEN OF POWER FROM EVERY NATION...
...YOU MAKE THEM LOOK LIKE **CHILDREN**.
THIS IS **NOT** MY LIFE...
...BUT, IF **SHE'S** HERE...
...I CAN MAKE IT **MINE**.

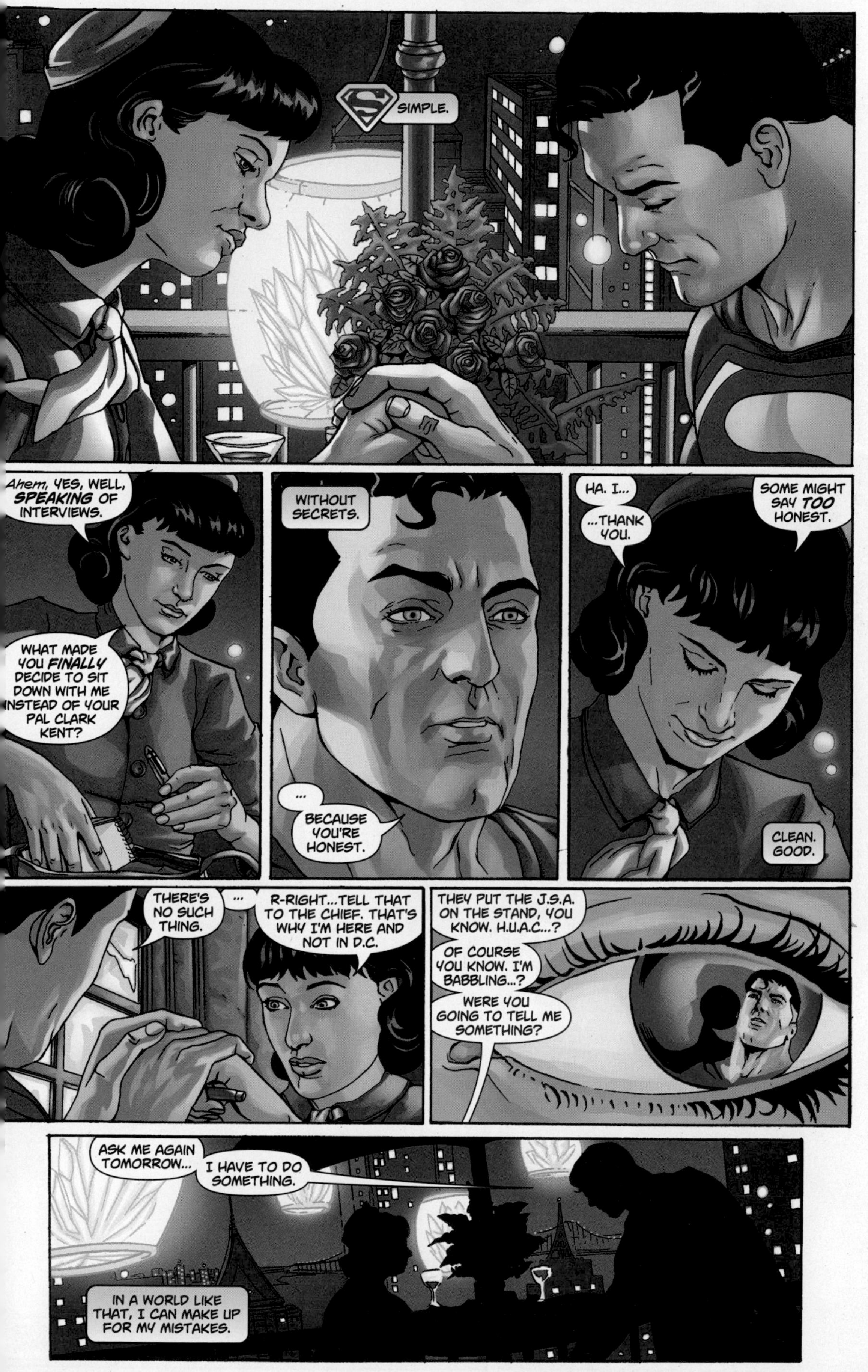
SIMPLE.
Ahem, YES, WELL, SPEAKING OF INTERVIEWS.
WHAT MADE YOU FINALLY DECIDE TO SIT DOWN WITH ME INSTEAD OF YOUR PAL CLARK KENT?
WITHOUT SECRETS.
... BECAUSE YOU'RE HONEST.
HA. I...
...THANK YOU.
SOME MIGHT SAY TOO HONEST.
CLEAN. GOOD.
THERE'S NO SUCH THING.
...
R-RIGHT...TELL THAT TO THE CHIEF. THAT'S WHY I'M HERE AND NOT IN D.C.
THEY PUT THE J.S.A. ON THE STAND, YOU KNOW. H.U.A.C...?
OF COURSE YOU KNOW. I'M BABBLING...?
WERE YOU GOING TO TELL ME SOMETHING?
ASK ME AGAIN TOMORROW...
I HAVE TO DO SOMETHING.
IN A WORLD LIKE THAT, I CAN MAKE UP FOR MY MISTAKES.

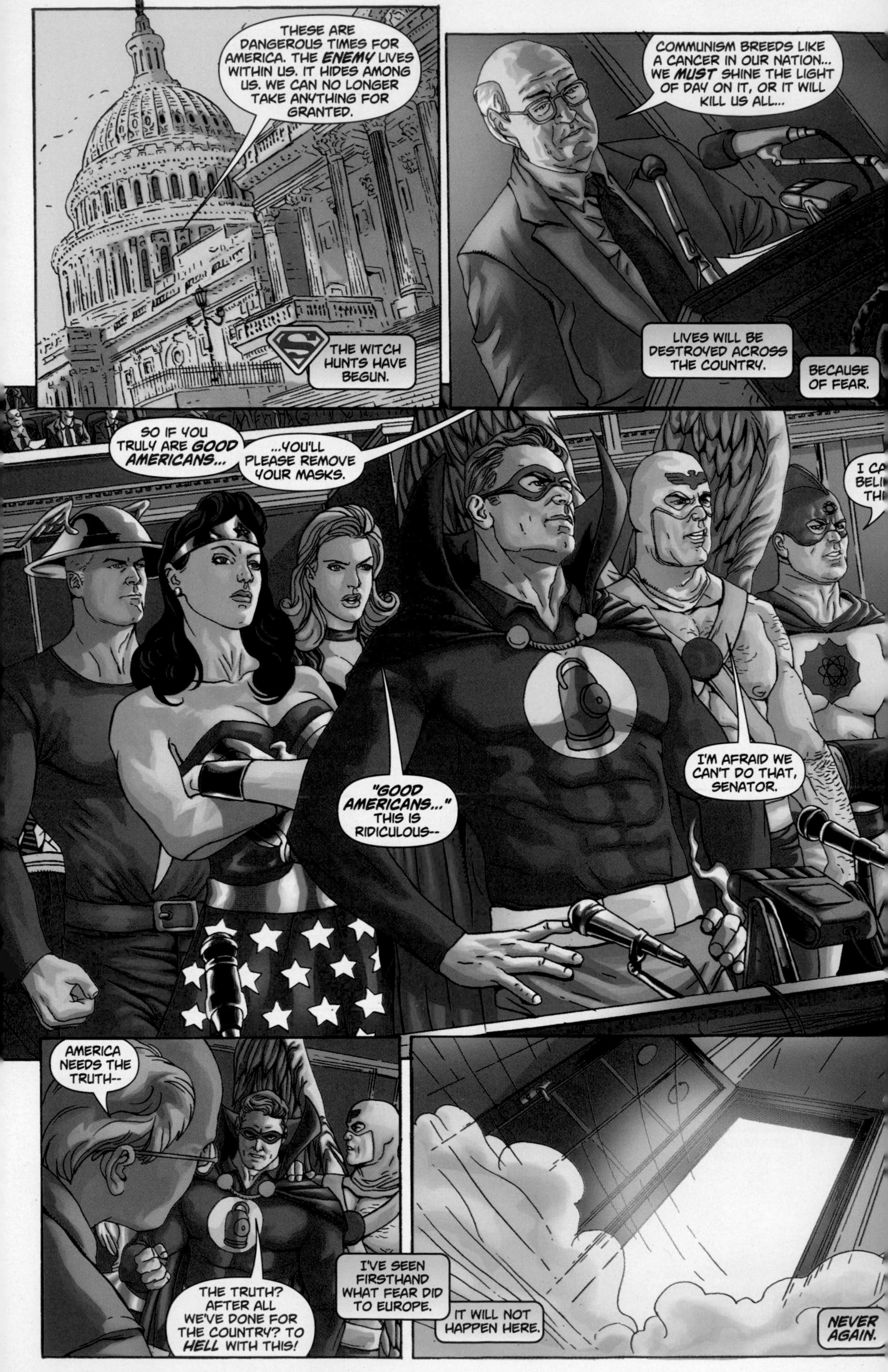
THESE ARE DANGEROUS TIMES FOR AMERICA. THE ENEMY LIVES WITHIN US. IT HIDES AMONG US. WE CAN NO LONGER TAKE ANYTHING FOR GRANTED.
THE WITCH HUNTS HAVE BEGUN.
COMMUNISM BREEDS LIKE A CANCER IN OUR NATION... WE MUST SHINE THE LIGHT OF DAY ON IT, OR IT WILL KILL US ALL...
LIVES WILL BE DESTROYED ACROSS THE COUNTRY.
BECAUSE OF FEAR.
SO IF YOU TRULY ARE GOOD AMERICANS...
...YOU'LL PLEASE REMOVE YOUR MASKS.
I CA BELI THI
"GOOD AMERICANS..." THIS IS RIDICULOUS--
I'M AFRAID WE CAN'T DO THAT, SENATOR.
AMERICA NEEDS THE TRUTH--
THE TRUTH? AFTER ALL WE'VE DONE FOR THE COUNTRY? TO HELL WITH THIS!
I'VE SEEN FIRSTHAND WHAT FEAR DID TO EUROPE.
IT WILL NOT HAPPEN HERE.
NEVER AGAIN.

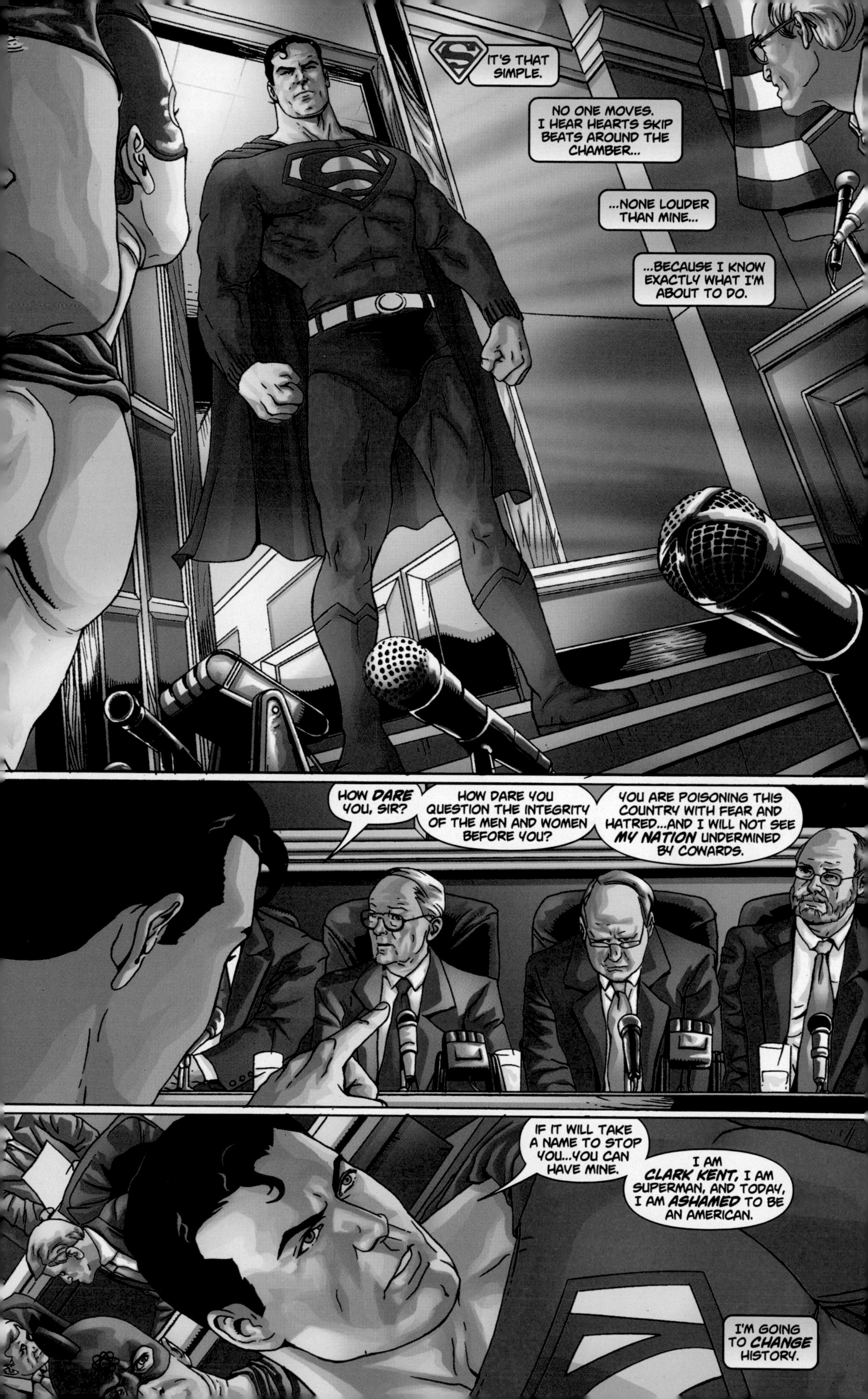
IT'S THAT SIMPLE.
NO ONE MOVES. I HEAR HEARTS SKIP BEATS AROUND THE CHAMBER...
...NONE LOUDER THAN MINE...
...BECAUSE I KNOW EXACTLY WHAT I'M ABOUT TO DO.
HOW DARE YOU, SIR?
HOW DARE YOU QUESTION THE INTEGRITY OF THE MEN AND WOMEN BEFORE YOU?
YOU ARE POISONING THIS COUNTRY WITH FEAR AND HATRED...AND I WILL NOT SEE MY NATION UNDERMINED BY COWARDS.
IF IT WILL TAKE A NAME TO STOP YOU...YOU CAN HAVE MINE.
I AM CLARK KENT, I AM SUPERMAN, AND TODAY, I AM ASHAMED TO BE AN AMERICAN.
I'M GOING TO CHANGE HISTORY.

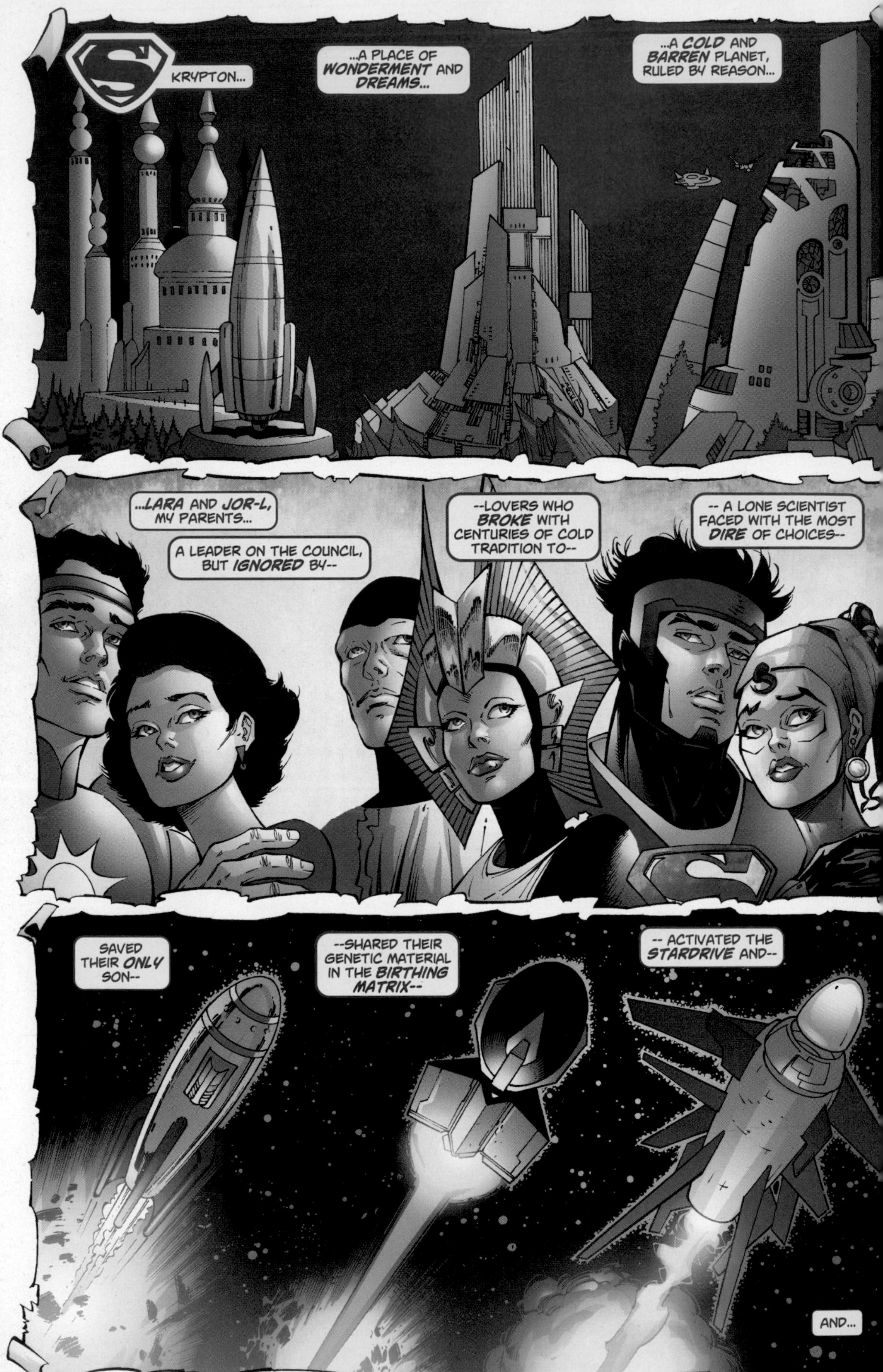
KRYPTON...
...A PLACE OF WONDERMENT AND DREAMS...
...A COLD AND BARREN PLANET, RULED BY REASON...
...LARA AND JOR-L, MY PARENTS...
A LEADER ON THE COUNCIL, BUT IGNORED BY--
--LOVERS WHO BROKE WITH CENTURIES OF COLD TRADITION TO--
-- A LONE SCIENTIST FACED WITH THE MOST DIRE OF CHOICES--
SAVED THEIR ONLY SON--
--SHARED THEIR GENETIC MATERIAL IN THE BIRTHING MATRIX--
-- ACTIVATED THE STARDRIVE AND--
AND...

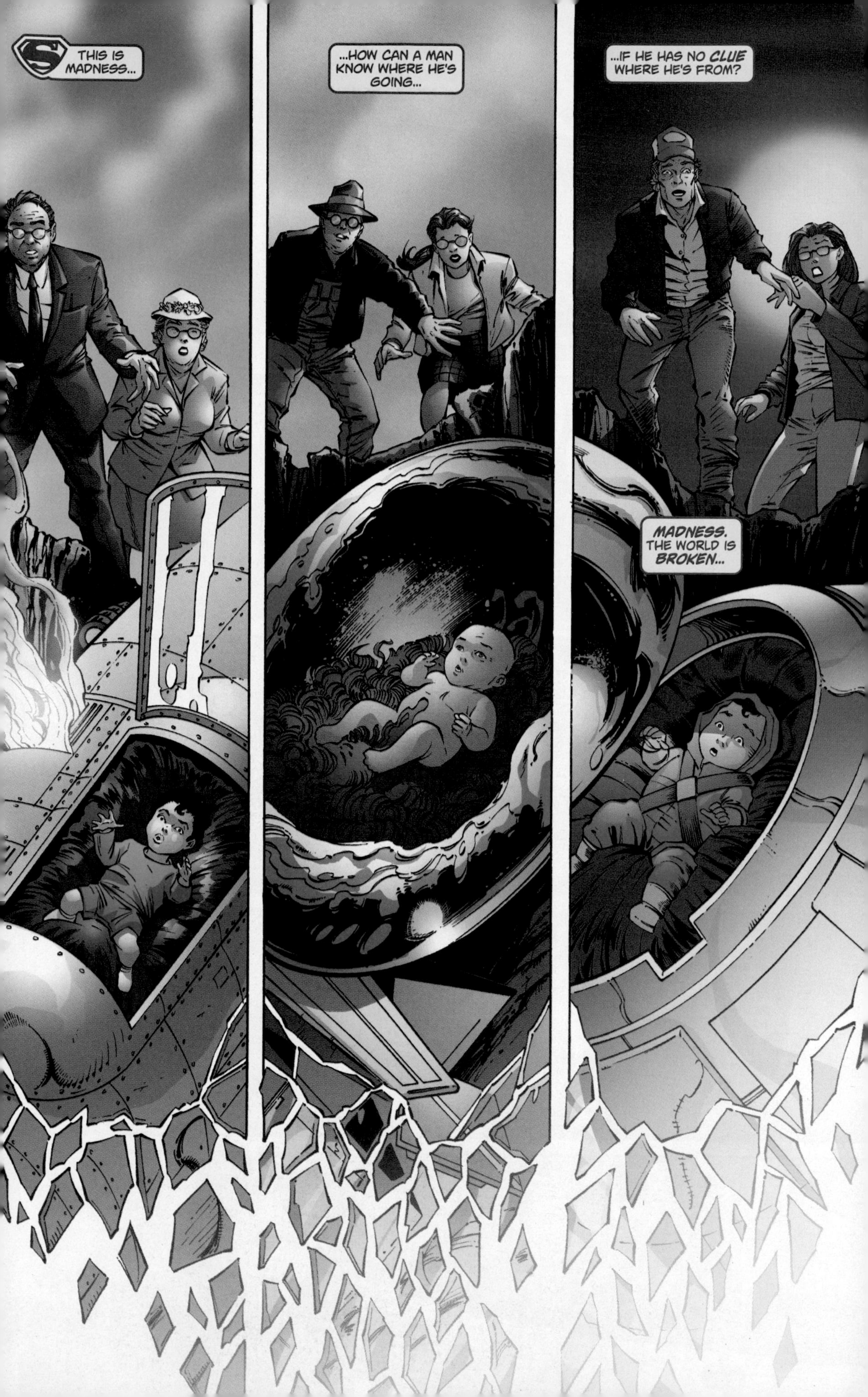
THIS IS MADNESS...
...HOW CAN A MAN KNOW WHERE HE'S GOING...
...IF HE HAS NO CLUE WHERE HE'S FROM?
MADNESS. THE WORLD IS BROKEN...

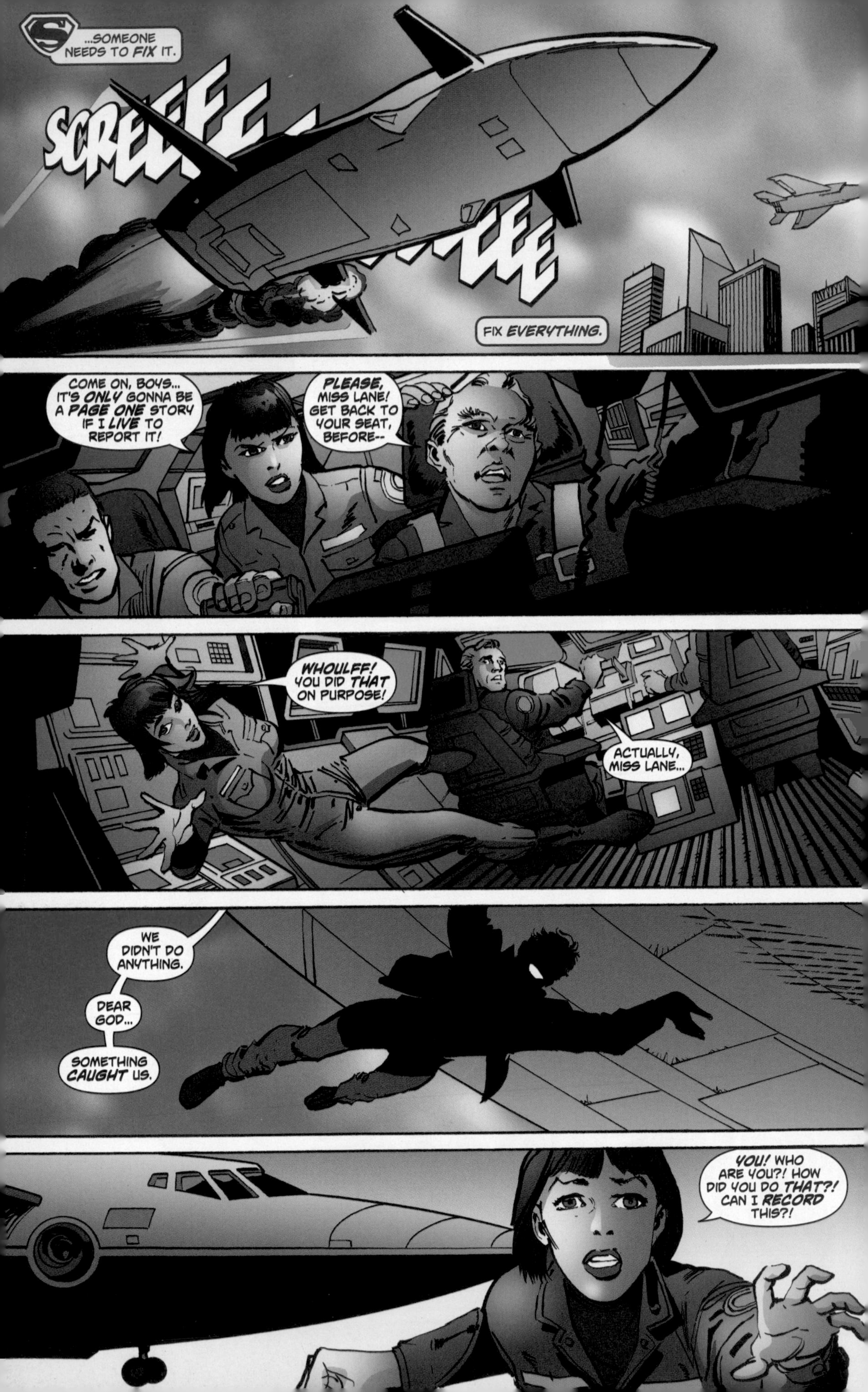
...SOMEONE NEEDS TO FIX IT.
SCREEEE EEEE
FIX EVERYTHING.
COME ON, BOYS... IT'S ONLY GONNA BE A PAGE ONE STORY IF I LIVE TO REPORT IT!
PLEASE, MISS LANE! GET BACK TO YOUR SEAT, BEFORE--
WHOULFF! YOU DID THAT ON PURPOSE!
ACTUALLY, MISS LANE...
WE DIDN'T DO ANYTHING.
DEAR GOD...
SOMETHING CAUGHT US.
YOU! WHO ARE YOU?! HOW DID YOU DO THAT?! CAN I RECORD THIS?!

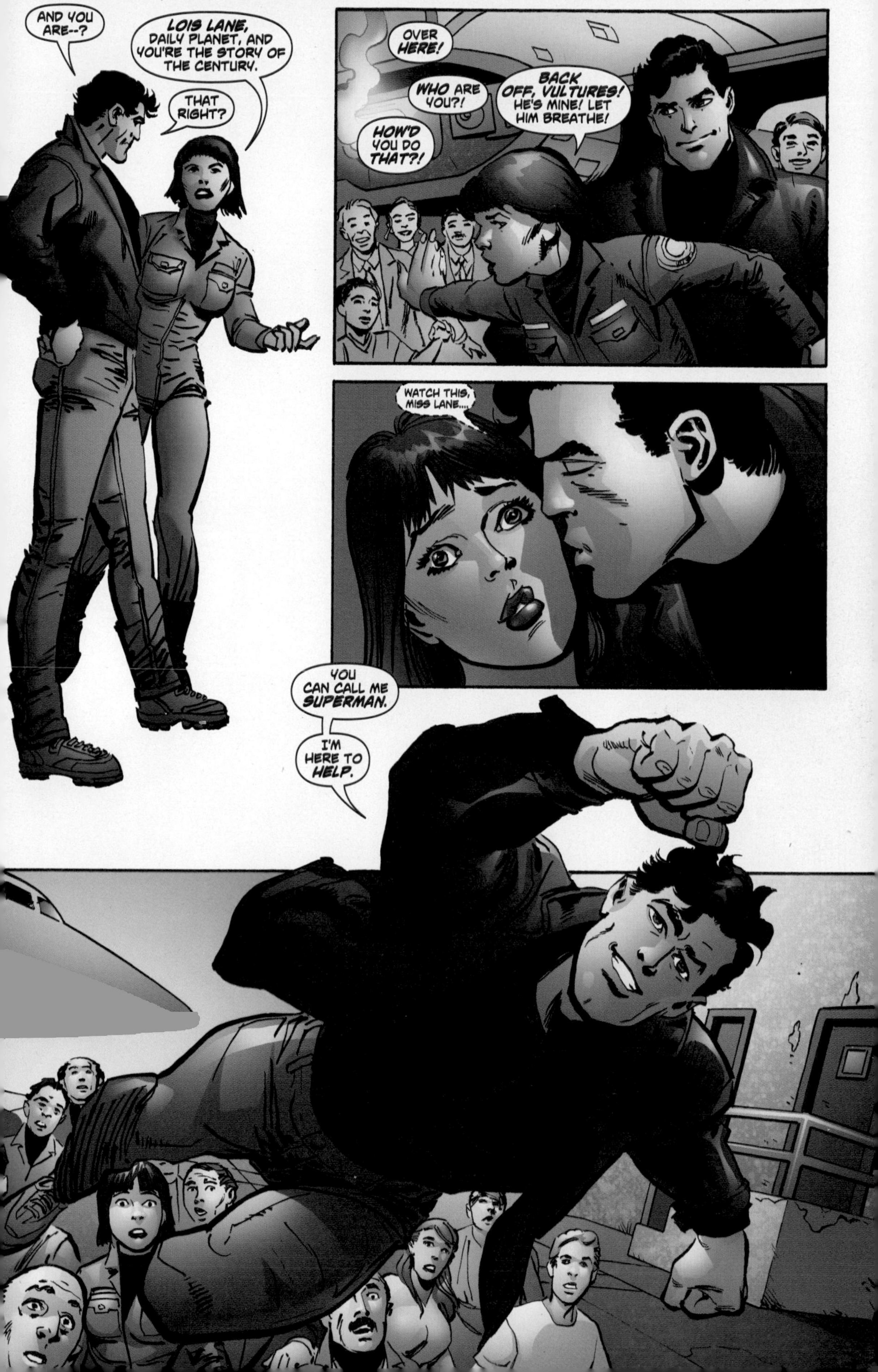
AND YOU ARE--?
LOIS LANE, DAILY PLANET, AND YOU'RE THE STORY OF THE CENTURY.
THAT RIGHT?
OVER HERE!
WHO ARE YOU?!
HOW'D YOU DO THAT?!
BACK OFF, VULTURES! HE'S MINE! LET HIM BREATHE!
WATCH THIS, MISS LANE...
YOU CAN CALL ME SUPERMAN.
I'M HERE TO HELP.

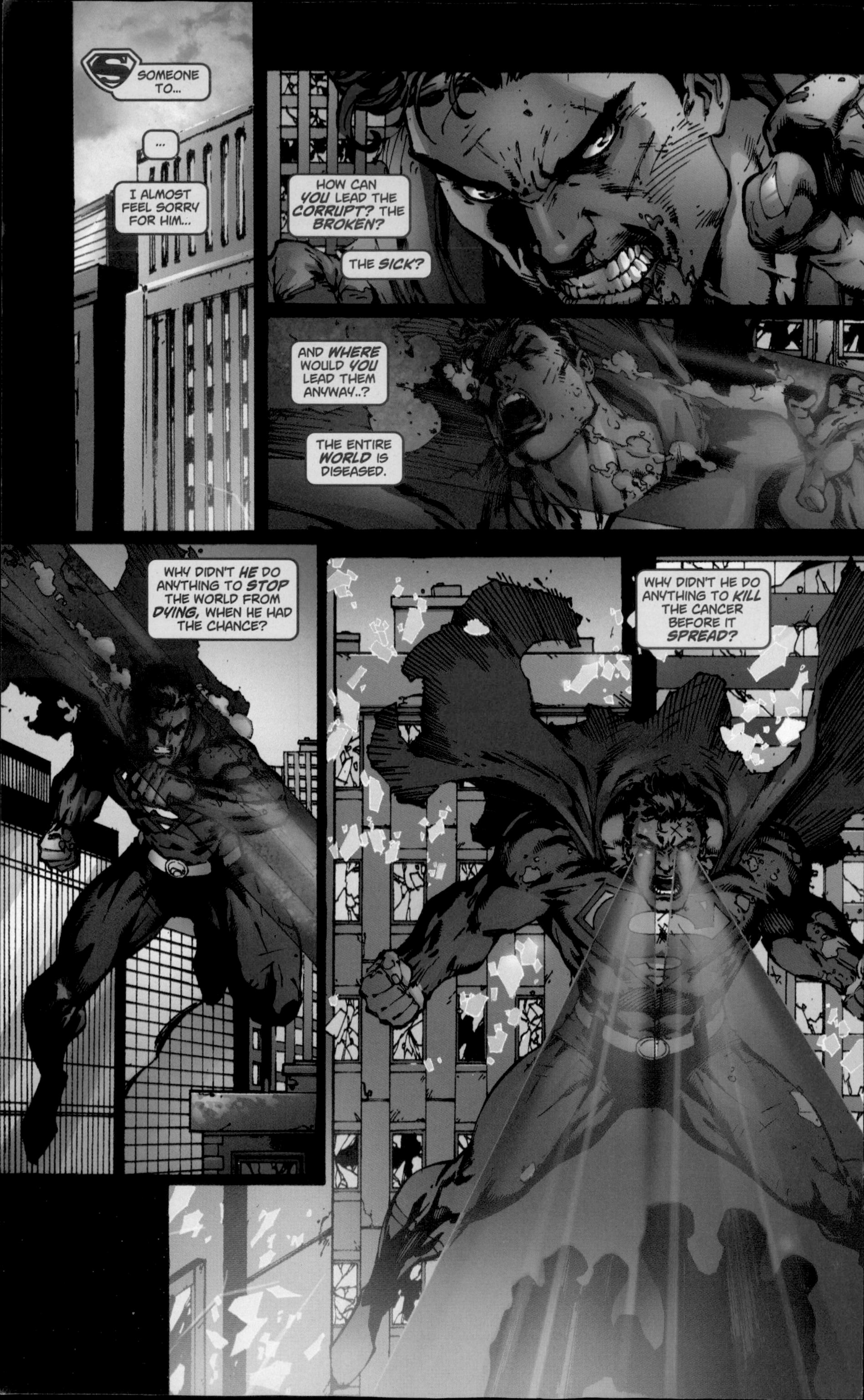
SOMEONE TO...
...
I ALMOST FEEL SORRY FOR HIM...
HOW CAN YOU LEAD THE CORRUPT? THE BROKEN?
THE SICK?
AND WHERE WOULD YOU LEAD THEM ANYWAY..?
THE ENTIRE WORLD IS DISEASED.
WHY DIDN'T HE DO ANYTHING TO STOP THE WORLD FROM DYING, WHEN HE HAD THE CHANCE?
WHY DIDN'T HE DO ANYTHING TO KILL THE CANCER BEFORE IT SPREAD?

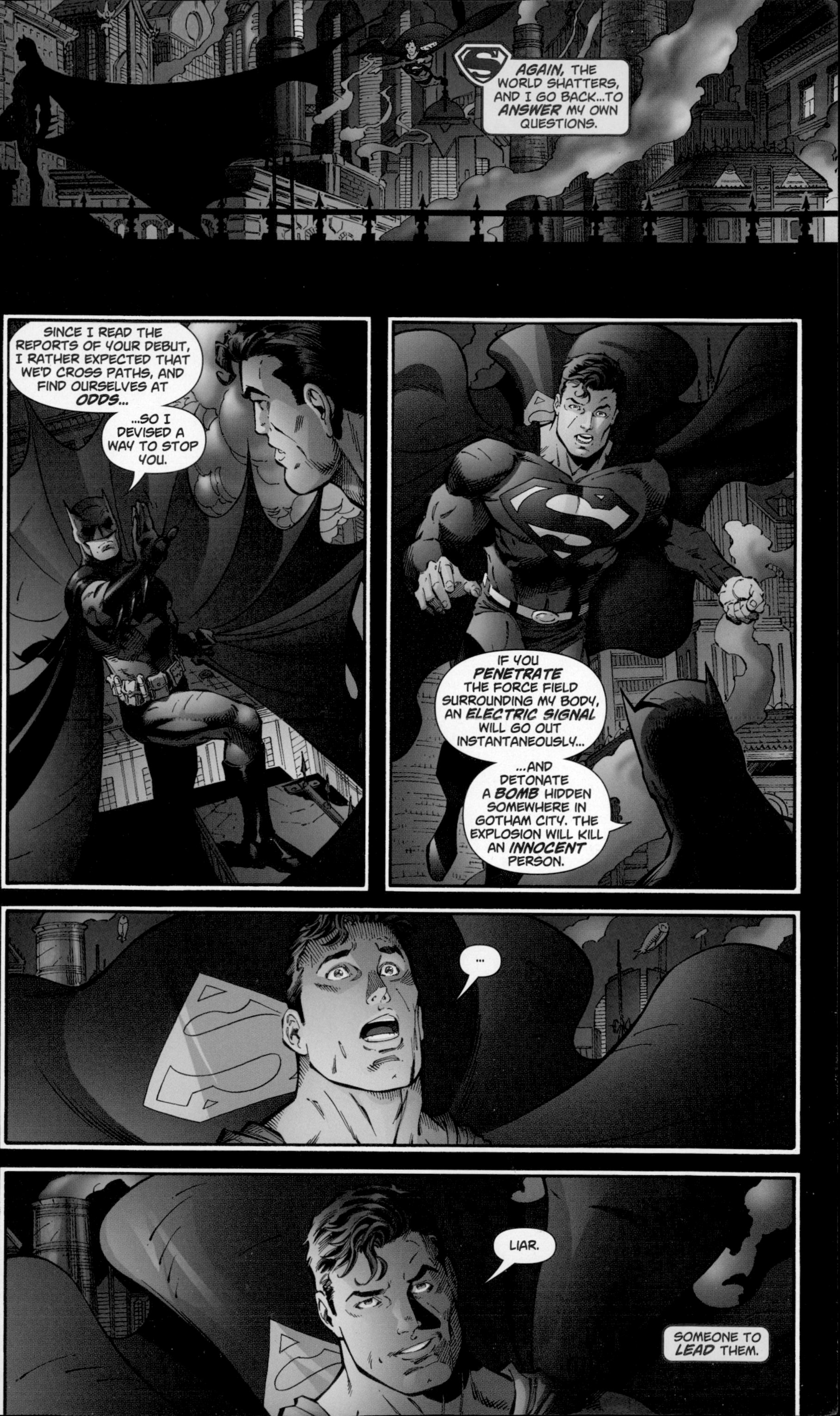
AGAIN, THE WORLD SHATTERS, AND I GO BACK...TO ANSWER MY OWN QUESTIONS.
SINCE I READ THE REPORTS OF YOUR DEBUT, I RATHER EXPECTED THAT WE'D CROSS PATHS, AND FIND OURSELVES AT ODDS...
...SO I DEVISED A WAY TO STOP YOU.
IF YOU PENETRATE THE FORCE FIELD SURROUNDING MY BODY, AN ELECTRIC SIGNAL WILL GO OUT INSTANTANEOUSLY...
...AND DETONATE A BOMB HIDDEN SOMEWHERE IN GOTHAM CITY. THE EXPLOSION WILL KILL AN INNOCENT PERSON.
...
LIAR.
SOMEONE TO LEAD THEM.

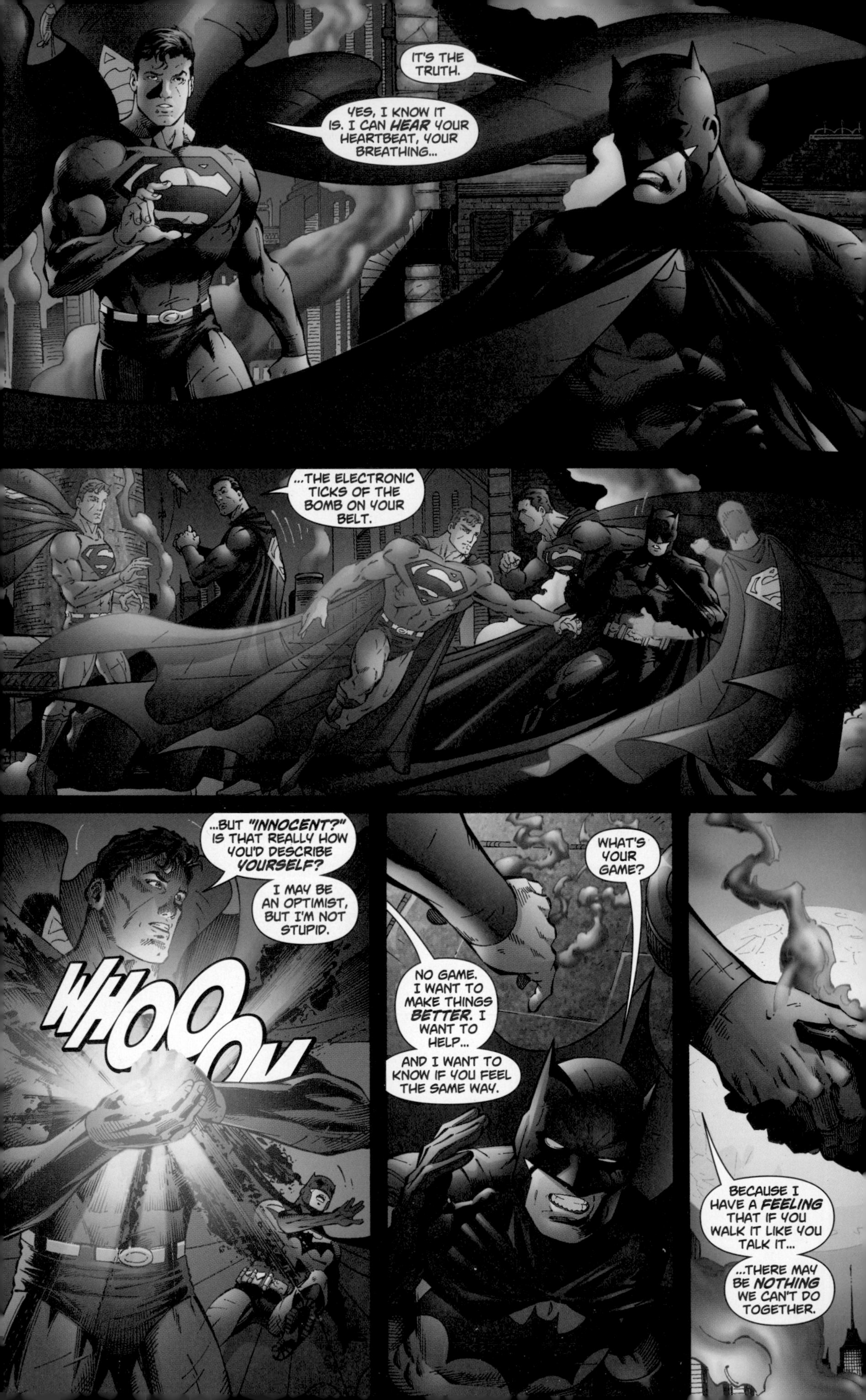
IT'S THE TRUTH.
YES, I KNOW IT IS. I CAN HEAR YOUR HEARTBEAT, YOUR BREATHING...
...THE ELECTRONIC TICKS OF THE BOMB ON YOUR BELT.
...BUT "INNOCENT?" IS THAT REALLY HOW YOU'D DESCRIBE YOURSELF?
I MAY BE AN OPTIMIST, BUT I'M NOT STUPID.
WHOOOM
WHAT'S YOUR GAME?
NO GAME. I WANT TO MAKE THINGS BETTER. I WANT TO HELP...
AND I WANT TO KNOW IF YOU FEEL THE SAME WAY.
BECAUSE I HAVE A FEELING THAT IF YOU WALK IT LIKE YOU TALK IT...
...THERE MAY BE NOTHING WE CAN'T DO TOGETHER.

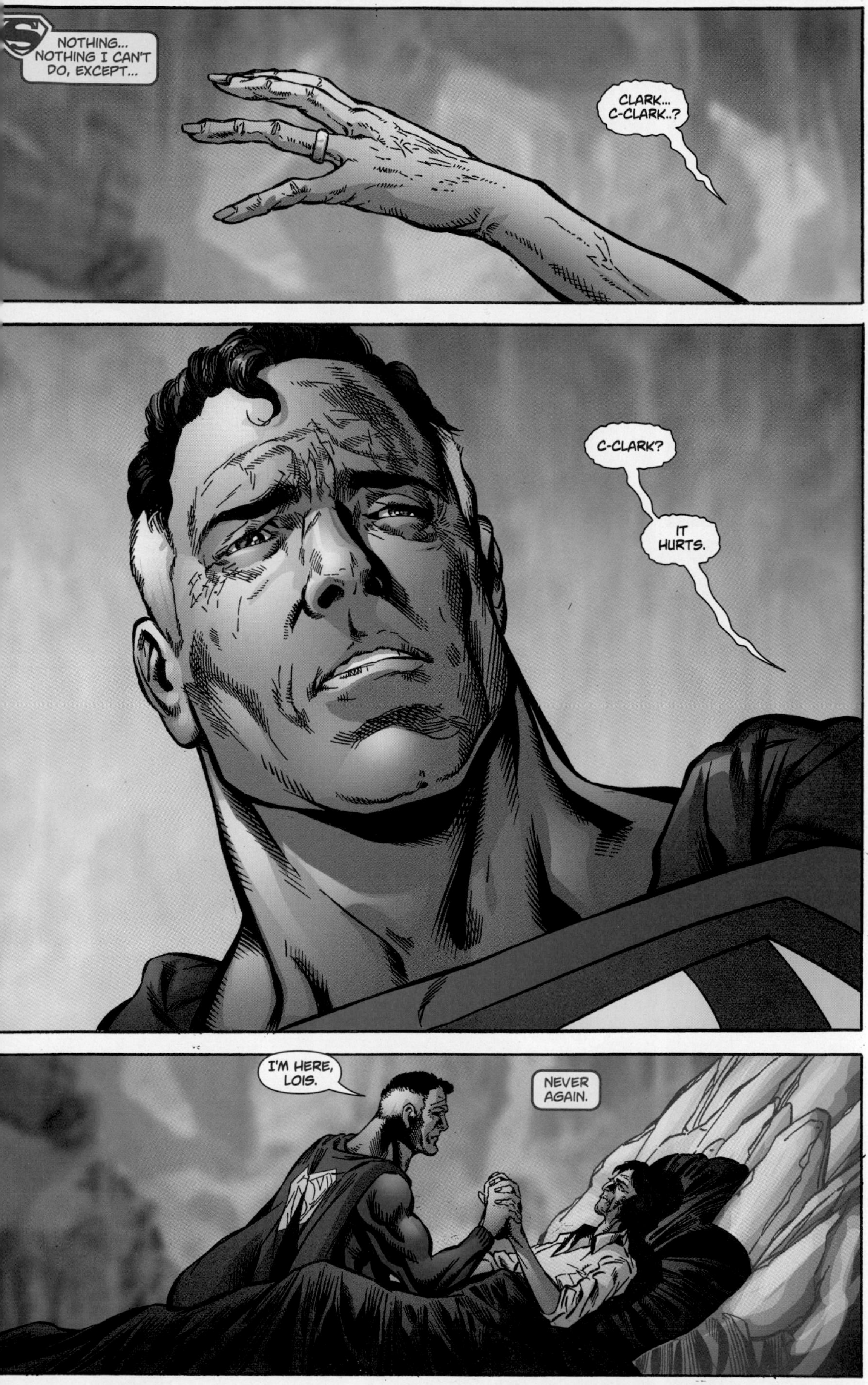
NOTHING... NOTHING I CAN'T DO, EXCEPT...
CLARK... C-CLARK..?
C-CLARK?
IT HURTS.
I'M HERE, LOIS.
NEVER AGAIN.

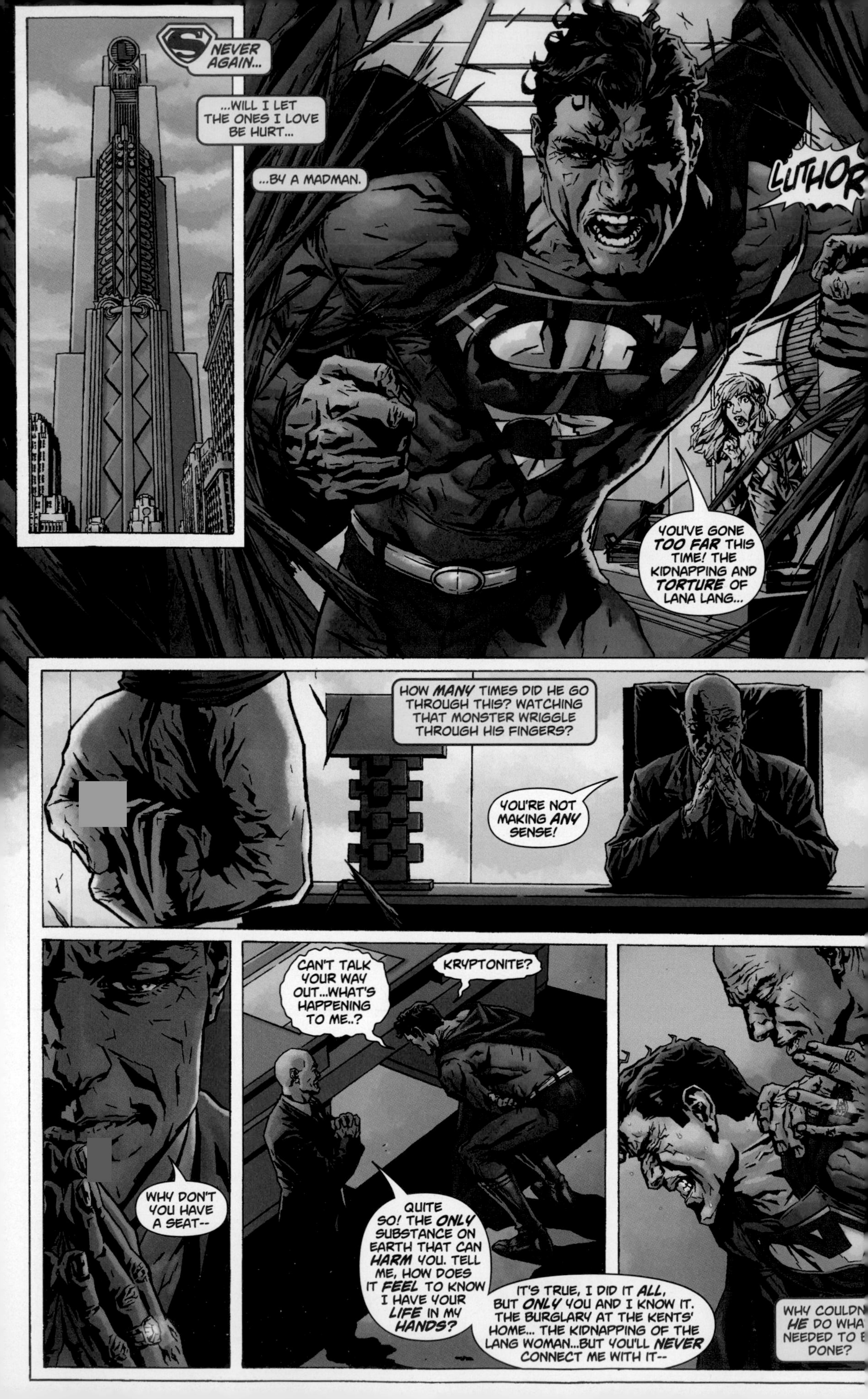
NEVER AGAIN...
...WILL I LET THE ONES I LOVE BE HURT...
...BY A MADMAN.
LUTHOR
YOU'VE GONE TOO FAR THIS TIME! THE KIDNAPPING AND TORTURE OF LANA LANG...
HOW MANY TIMES DID HE GO THROUGH THIS? WATCHING THAT MONSTER WRIGGLE THROUGH HIS FINGERS?
YOU'RE NOT MAKING ANY SENSE!
WHY DON'T YOU HAVE A SEAT--
CAN'T TALK YOUR WAY OUT...WHAT'S HAPPENING TO ME..?
KRYPTONITE?
QUITE SO! THE ONLY SUBSTANCE ON EARTH THAT CAN HARM YOU. TELL ME, HOW DOES IT FEEL TO KNOW I HAVE YOUR LIFE IN MY HANDS?
IT'S TRUE, I DID IT ALL, BUT ONLY YOU AND I KNOW IT. THE BURGLARY AT THE KENTS' HOME... THE KIDNAPPING OF THE LANG WOMAN...BUT YOU'LL NEVER CONNECT ME WITH IT--
WHY COULDN HE DO WHA NEEDED TO B DONE?

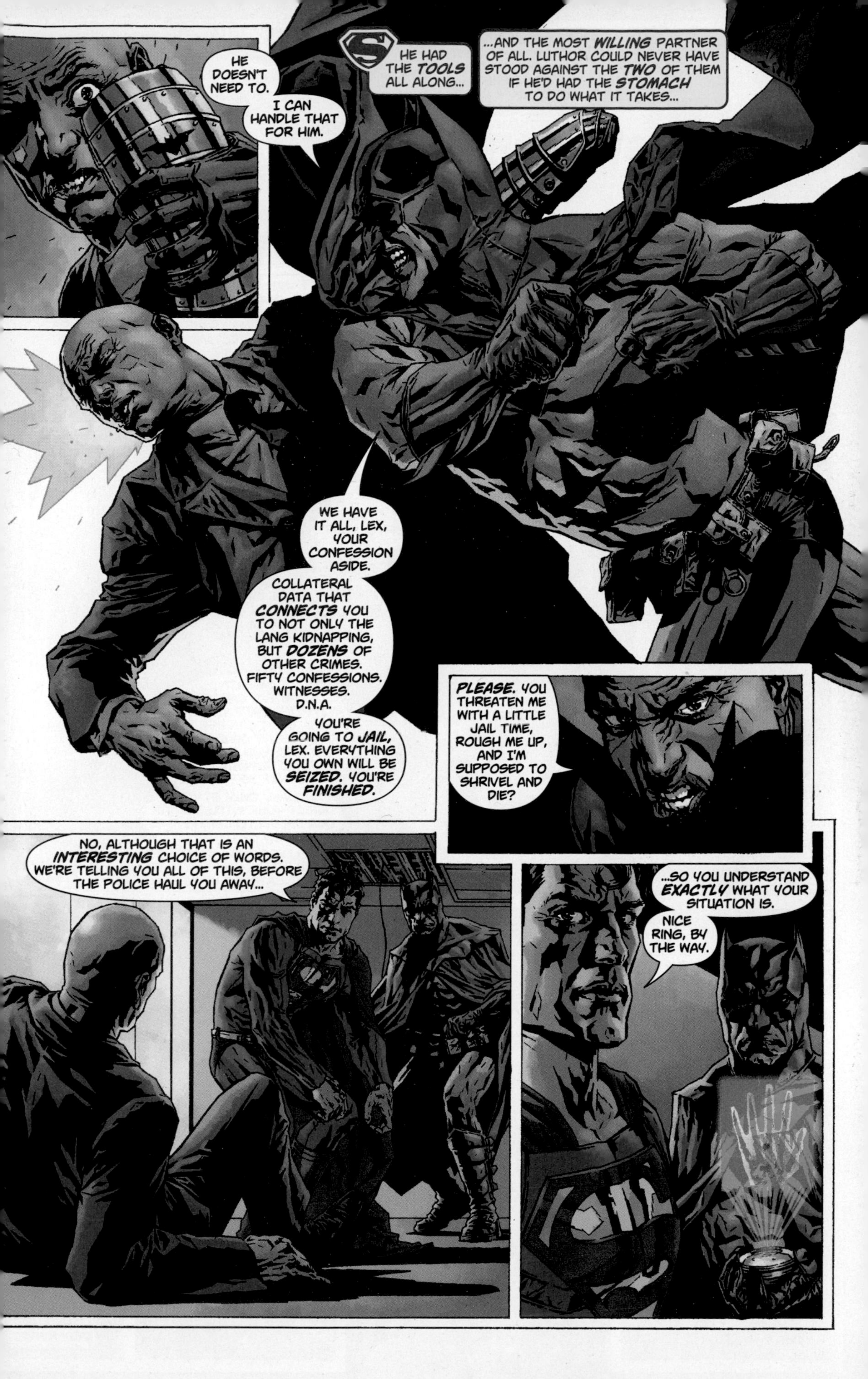
HE DOESN'T NEED TO.
I CAN HANDLE THAT FOR HIM.
HE HAD THE TOOLS ALL ALONG...
...AND THE MOST WILLING PARTNER OF ALL. LUTHOR COULD NEVER HAVE STOOD AGAINST THE TWO OF THEM IF HE'D HAD THE STOMACH TO DO WHAT IT TAKES...
WE HAVE IT ALL, LEX, YOUR CONFESSION ASIDE.
COLLATERAL DATA THAT CONNECTS YOU TO NOT ONLY THE LANG KIDNAPPING, BUT DOZENS OF OTHER CRIMES. FIFTY CONFESSIONS. WITNESSES. D.N.A.
YOU'RE GOING TO JAIL, LEX. EVERYTHING YOU OWN WILL BE SEIZED. YOU'RE FINISHED.
PLEASE. YOU THREATEN ME WITH A LITTLE JAIL TIME, ROUGH ME UP, AND I'M SUPPOSED TO SHRIVEL AND DIE?
NO, ALTHOUGH THAT IS AN INTERESTING CHOICE OF WORDS. WE'RE TELLING YOU ALL OF THIS, BEFORE THE POLICE HAUL YOU AWAY...
...SO YOU UNDERSTAND EXACTLY WHAT YOUR SITUATION IS.
NICE RING, BY THE WAY.

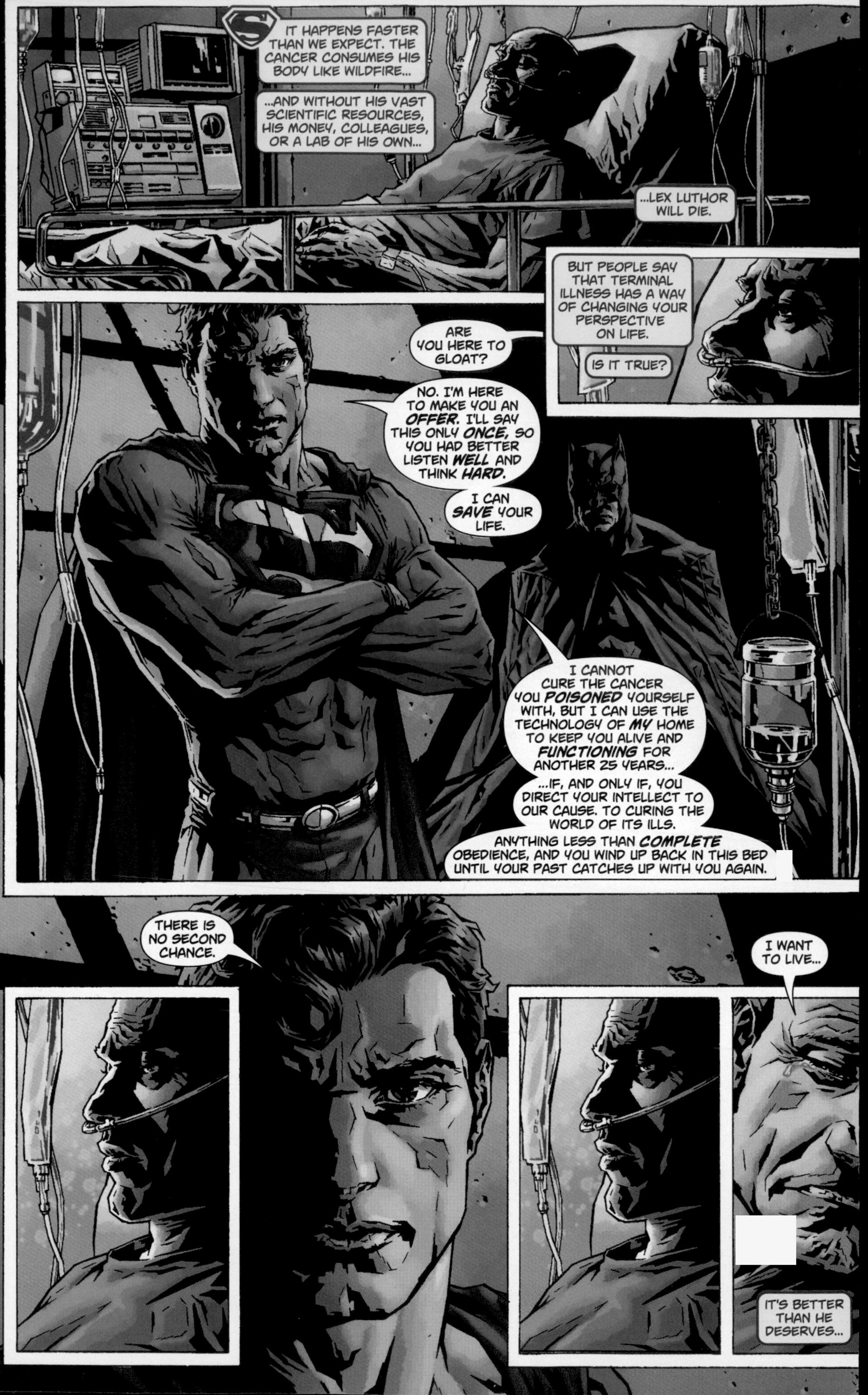
IT HAPPENS FASTER THAN WE EXPECT. THE CANCER CONSUMES HIS BODY LIKE WILDFIRE...
...AND WITHOUT HIS VAST SCIENTIFIC RESOURCES, HIS MONEY, COLLEAGUES, OR A LAB OF HIS OWN...
...LEX LUTHOR WILL DIE.
BUT PEOPLE SAY THAT TERMINAL ILLNESS HAS A WAY OF CHANGING YOUR PERSPECTIVE ON LIFE.
IS IT TRUE?
ARE YOU HERE TO GLOAT?
NO. I'M HERE TO MAKE YOU AN OFFER. I'LL SAY THIS ONLY ONCE, SO YOU HAD BETTER LISTEN WELL AND THINK HARD.
I CAN SAVE YOUR LIFE.
I CANNOT CURE THE CANCER YOU POISONED YOURSELF WITH, BUT I CAN USE THE TECHNOLOGY OF MY HOME TO KEEP YOU ALIVE AND FUNCTIONING FOR ANOTHER 25 YEARS...
...IF, AND ONLY IF, YOU DIRECT YOUR INTELLECT TO OUR CAUSE. TO CURING THE WORLD OF ITS ILLS.
ANYTHING LESS THAN COMPLETE OBEDIENCE, AND YOU WIND UP BACK IN THIS BED UNTIL YOUR PAST CATCHES UP WITH YOU AGAIN.
THERE IS NO SECOND CHANCE.
I WANT TO LIVE...
IT'S BETTER THAN HE DESERVES...

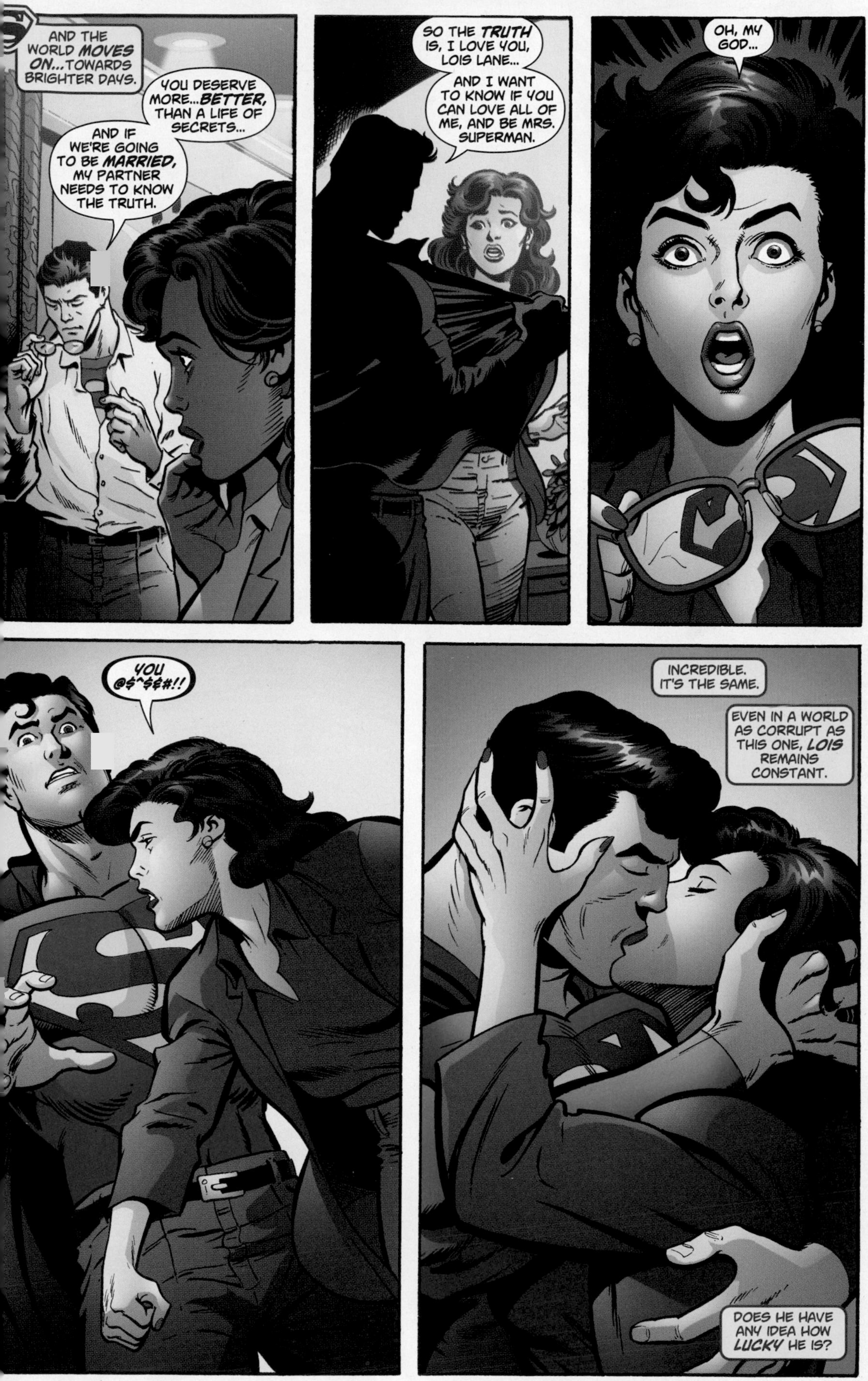

AND THE WORLD MOVES ON...TOWARDS BRIGHTER DAYS.
YOU DESERVE MORE...BETTER, THAN A LIFE OF SECRETS...
AND IF WE'RE GOING TO BE MARRIED, MY PARTNER NEEDS TO KNOW THE TRUTH.
SO THE TRUTH IS, I LOVE YOU, LOIS LANE...
AND I WANT TO KNOW IF YOU CAN LOVE ALL OF ME, AND BE MRS. SUPERMAN.
OH, MY GOD...
YOU @$^$&#!!
INCREDIBLE. IT'S THE SAME.
EVEN IN A WORLD AS CORRUPT AS THIS ONE, LOIS REMAINS CONSTANT.
DOES HE HAVE ANY IDEA HOW LUCKY HE IS?

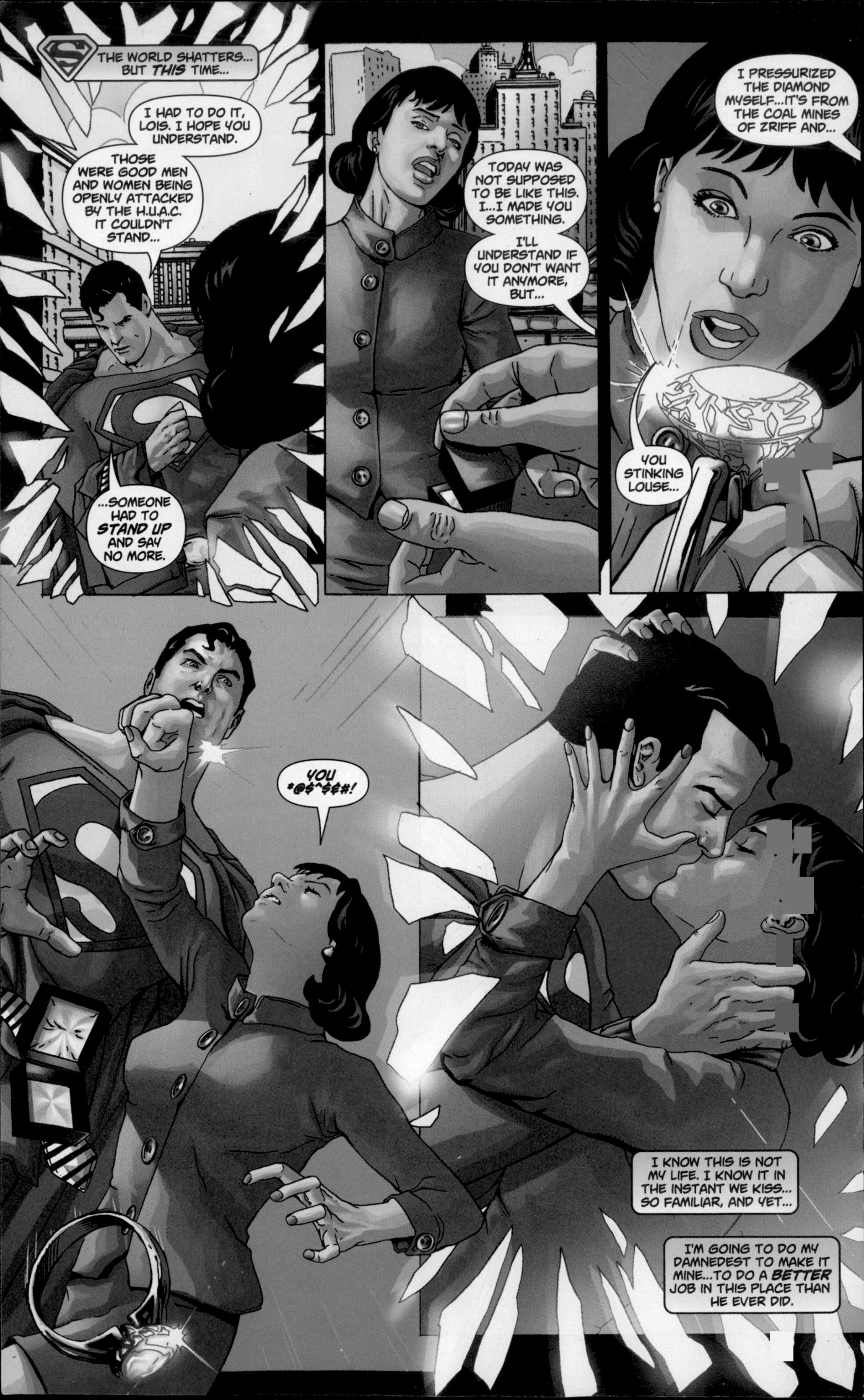
THE WORLD SHATTERS... BUT THIS TIME...
I HAD TO DO IT, LOIS. I HOPE YOU UNDERSTAND.
THOSE WERE GOOD MEN AND WOMEN BEING OPENLY ATTACKED BY THE H.U.A.C. IT COULDN'T STAND...
...SOMEONE HAD TO STAND UP AND SAY NO MORE.
TODAY WAS NOT SUPPOSED TO BE LIKE THIS. I...I MADE YOU SOMETHING.
I'LL UNDERSTAND IF YOU DON'T WANT IT ANYMORE, BUT...
I PRESSURIZED THE DIAMOND MYSELF...IT'S FROM THE COAL MINES OF ZRIFF AND...
YOU STINKING LOUSE...
YOU *@$^$¢#!
I KNOW THIS IS NOT MY LIFE. I KNOW IT IN THE INSTANT WE KISS... SO FAMILIAR, AND YET...
I'M GOING TO DO MY DAMNEDEST TO MAKE IT MINE...TO DO A BETTER JOB IN THIS PLACE THAN HE EVER DID.

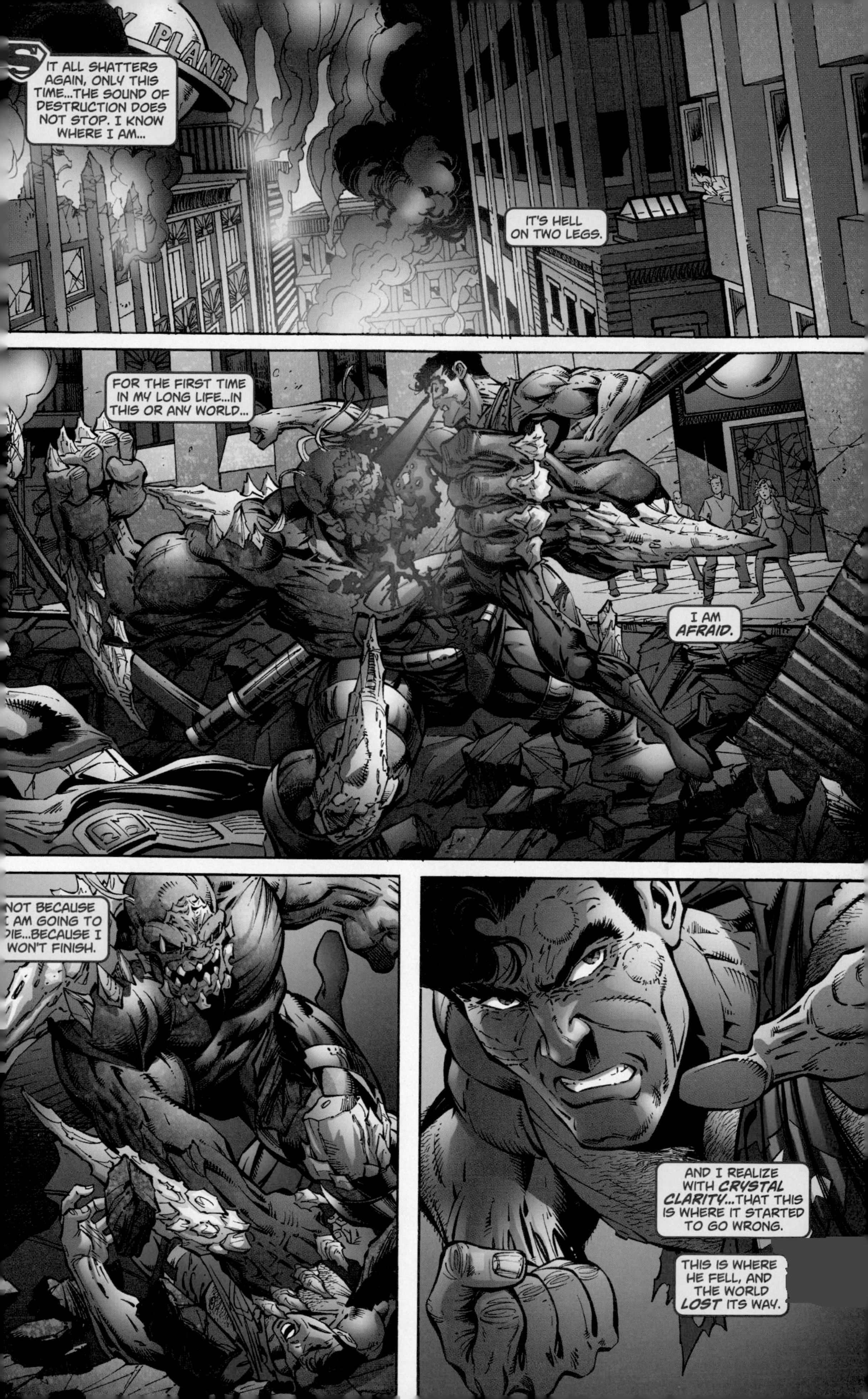
IT ALL SHATTERS AGAIN, ONLY THIS TIME...THE SOUND OF DESTRUCTION DOES NOT STOP. I KNOW WHERE I AM...
IT'S HELL ON TWO LEGS.
FOR THE FIRST TIME IN MY LONG LIFE...IN THIS OR ANY WORLD...
I AM AFRAID.
NOT BECAUSE I AM GOING TO DIE...BECAUSE I WON'T FINISH.
AND I REALIZE WITH CRYSTAL CLARITY...THAT THIS IS WHERE IT STARTED TO GO WRONG.
THIS IS WHERE HE FELL, AND THE WORLD LOST ITS WAY.

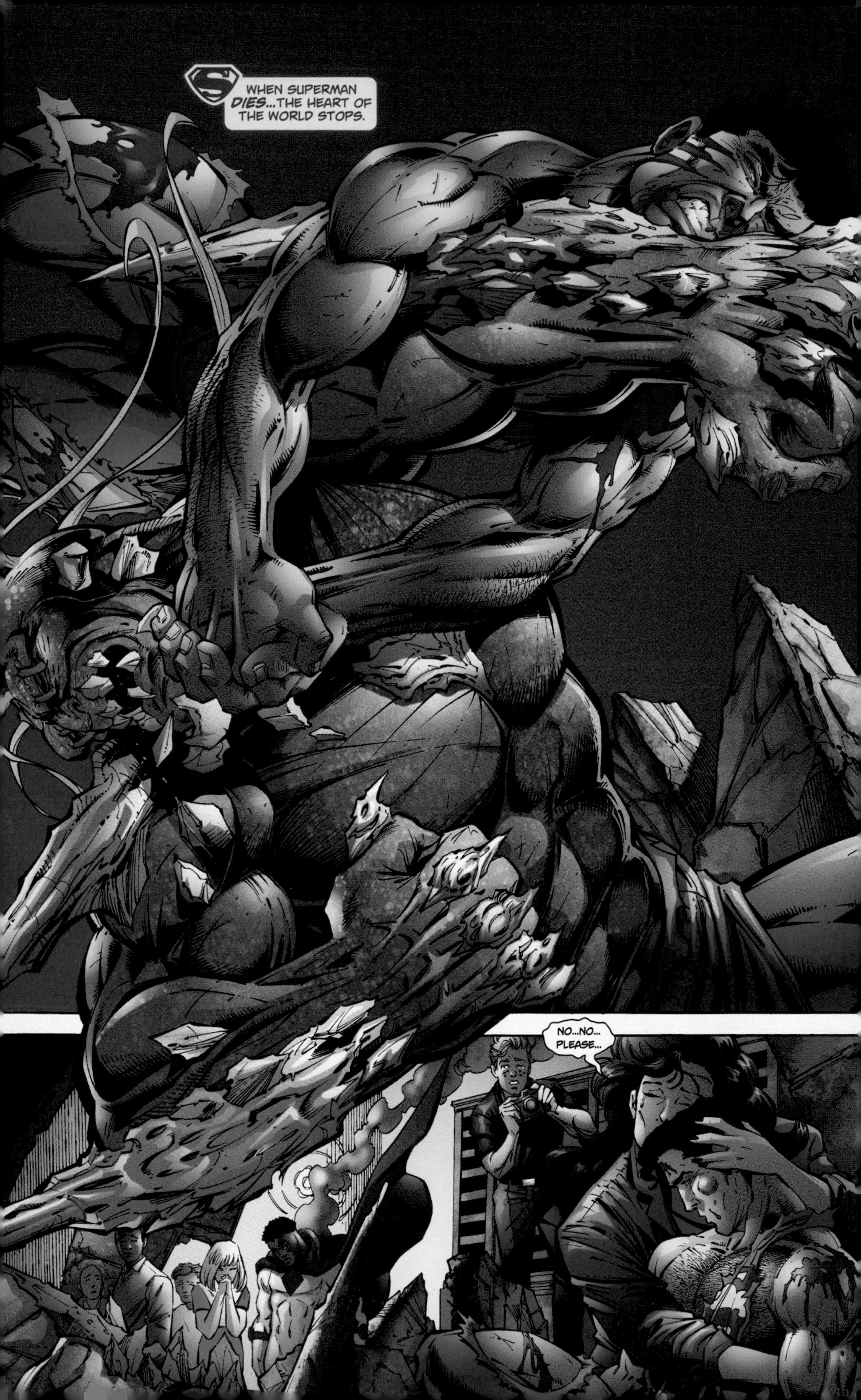
WHEN SUPERMAN DIES...THE HEART OF THE WORLD STOPS.
NO...NO... PLEASE...

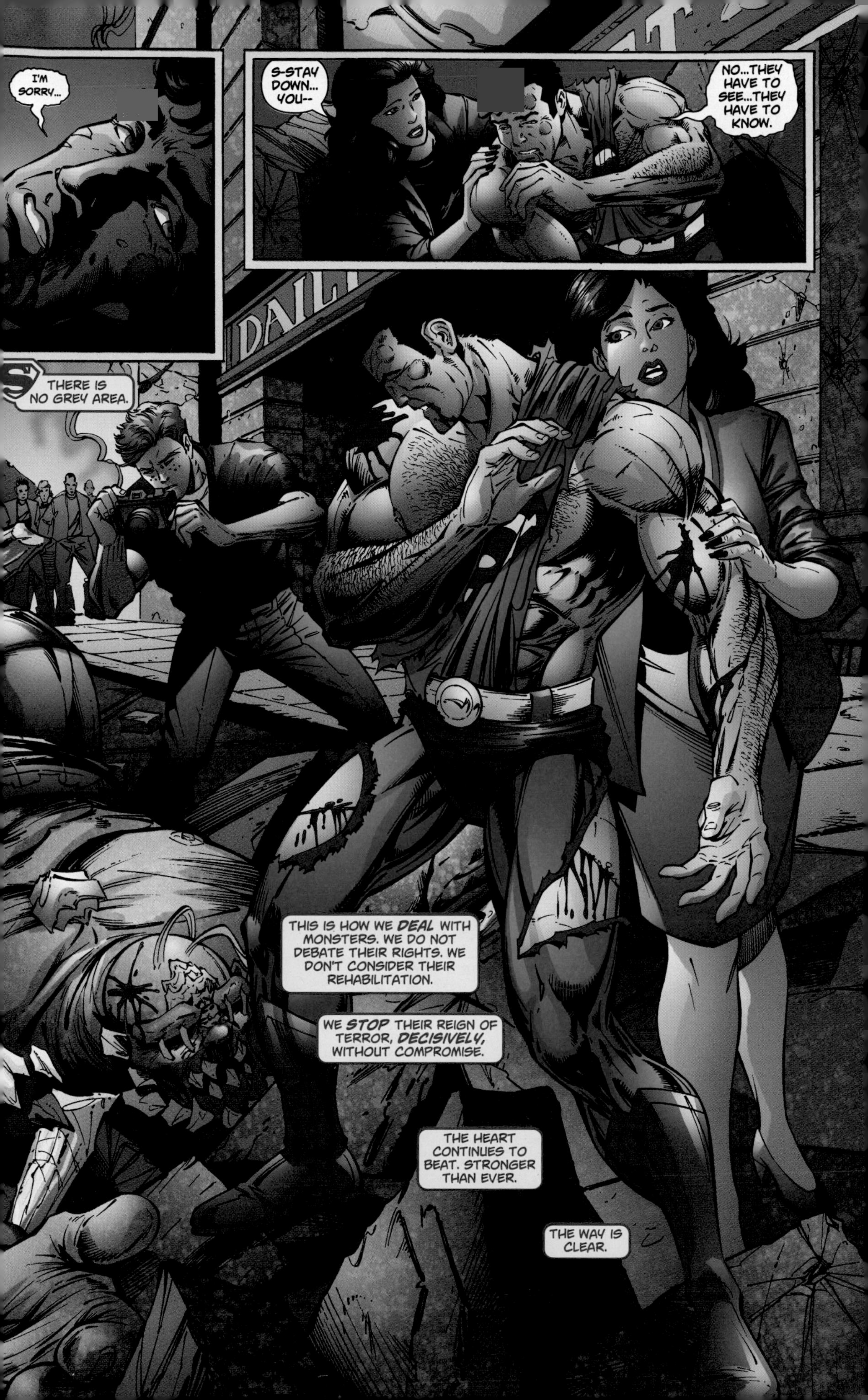

I'M SORRY...
[redacted]
S-STAY DOWN... YOU--
[redacted]
NO...THEY HAVE TO SEE...THEY HAVE TO KNOW.
THERE IS NO GREY AREA.
THIS IS HOW WE DEAL WITH MONSTERS. WE DO NOT DEBATE THEIR RIGHTS. WE DON'T CONSIDER THEIR REHABILITATION.
WE STOP THEIR REIGN OF TERROR, DECISIVELY, WITHOUT COMPROMISE.
THE HEART CONTINUES TO BEAT. STRONGER THAN EVER.
THE WAY IS CLEAR.

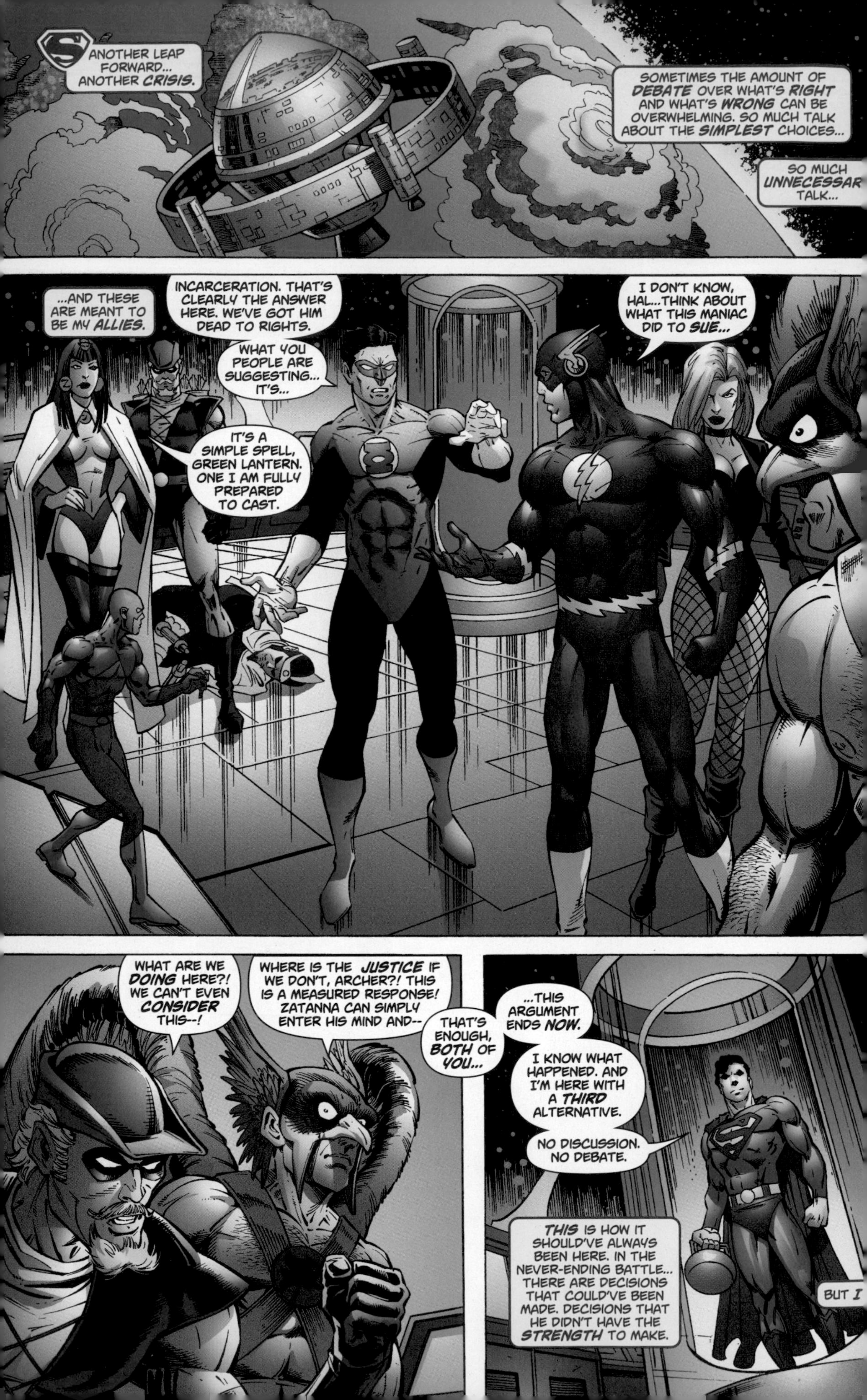

ANOTHER LEAP FORWARD... ANOTHER CRISIS.
SOMETIMES THE AMOUNT OF DEBATE OVER WHAT'S RIGHT AND WHAT'S WRONG CAN BE OVERWHELMING. SO MUCH TALK ABOUT THE SIMPLEST CHOICES...
SO MUCH UNNECESSAR
TALK...
...AND THESE ARE MEANT TO BE MY ALLIES.
INCARCERATION. THAT'S CLEARLY THE ANSWER HERE. WE'VE GOT HIM DEAD TO RIGHTS.
WHAT YOU PEOPLE ARE SUGGESTING... IT'S...
IT'S A SIMPLE SPELL, GREEN LANTERN. ONE I AM FULLY PREPARED TO CAST.
I DON'T KNOW, HAL...THINK ABOUT WHAT THIS MANIAC DID TO SUE...
WHAT ARE WE DOING HERE?! WE CAN'T EVEN CONSIDER THIS--!
WHERE IS THE JUSTICE IF WE DON'T, ARCHER?! THIS IS A MEASURED RESPONSE! ZATANNA CAN SIMPLY ENTER HIS MIND AND--
THAT'S ENOUGH, BOTH OF YOU...
...THIS ARGUMENT ENDS NOW.
I KNOW WHAT HAPPENED. AND I'M HERE WITH A THIRD ALTERNATIVE.
NO DISCUSSION. NO DEBATE.
THIS IS HOW IT SHOULD'VE ALWAYS BEEN HERE. IN THE NEVER-ENDING BATTLE... THERE ARE DECISIONS THAT COULD'VE BEEN MADE. DECISIONS THAT HE DIDN'T HAVE THE STRENGTH TO MAKE.
BUT I

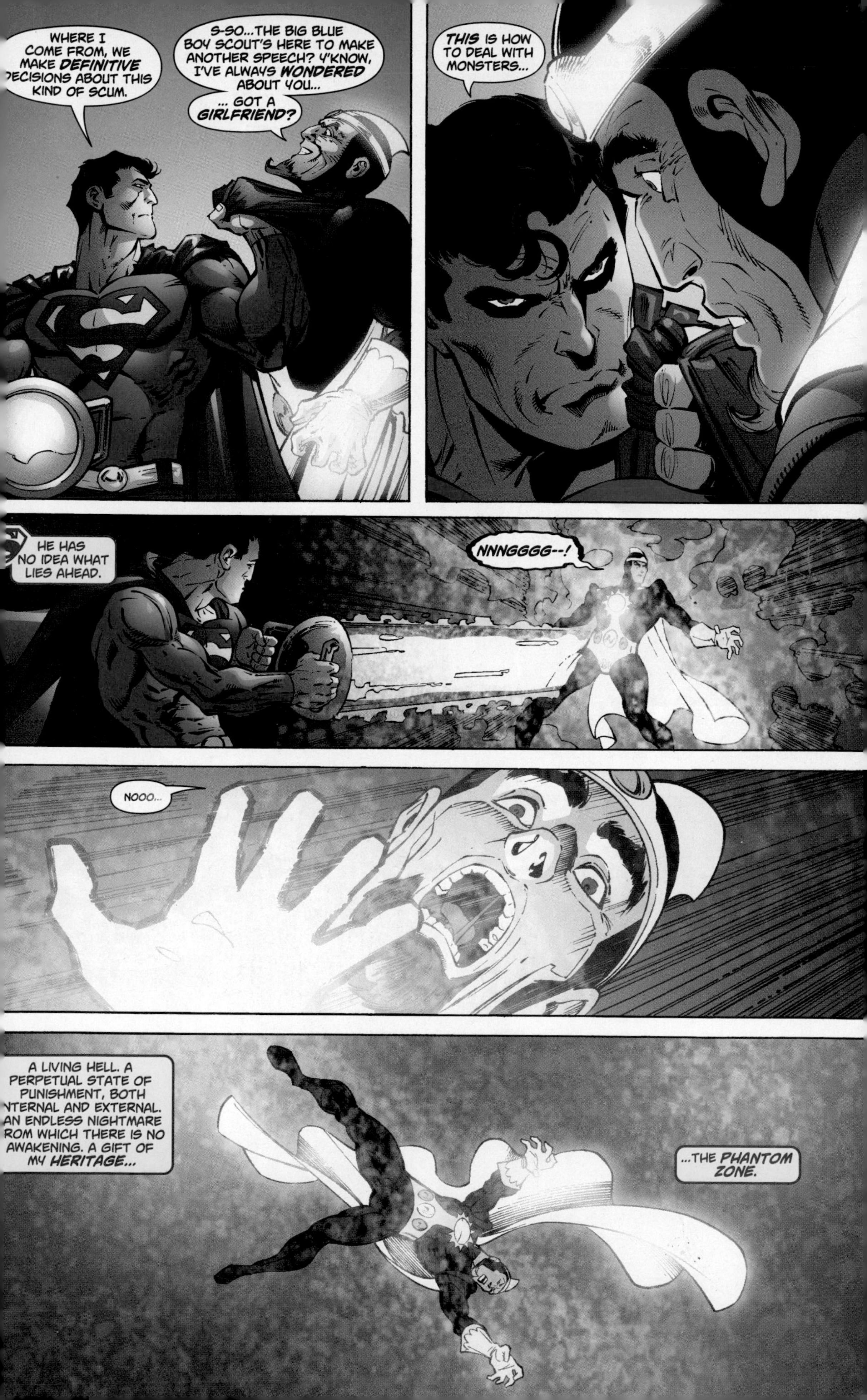

WHERE I COME FROM, WE MAKE DEFINITIVE DECISIONS ABOUT THIS KIND OF SCUM.
S-SO...THE BIG BLUE BOY SCOUT'S HERE TO MAKE ANOTHER SPEECH? Y'KNOW, I'VE ALWAYS WONDERED ABOUT YOU...
... GOT A GIRLFRIEND?
THIS IS HOW TO DEAL WITH MONSTERS...
HE HAS NO IDEA WHAT LIES AHEAD.
NNNGGGG--!
NOOO...
A LIVING HELL. A PERPETUAL STATE OF PUNISHMENT, BOTH INTERNAL AND EXTERNAL. AN ENDLESS NIGHTMARE FROM WHICH THERE IS NO AWAKENING. A GIFT OF MY HERITAGE...
...THE PHANTOM ZONE.

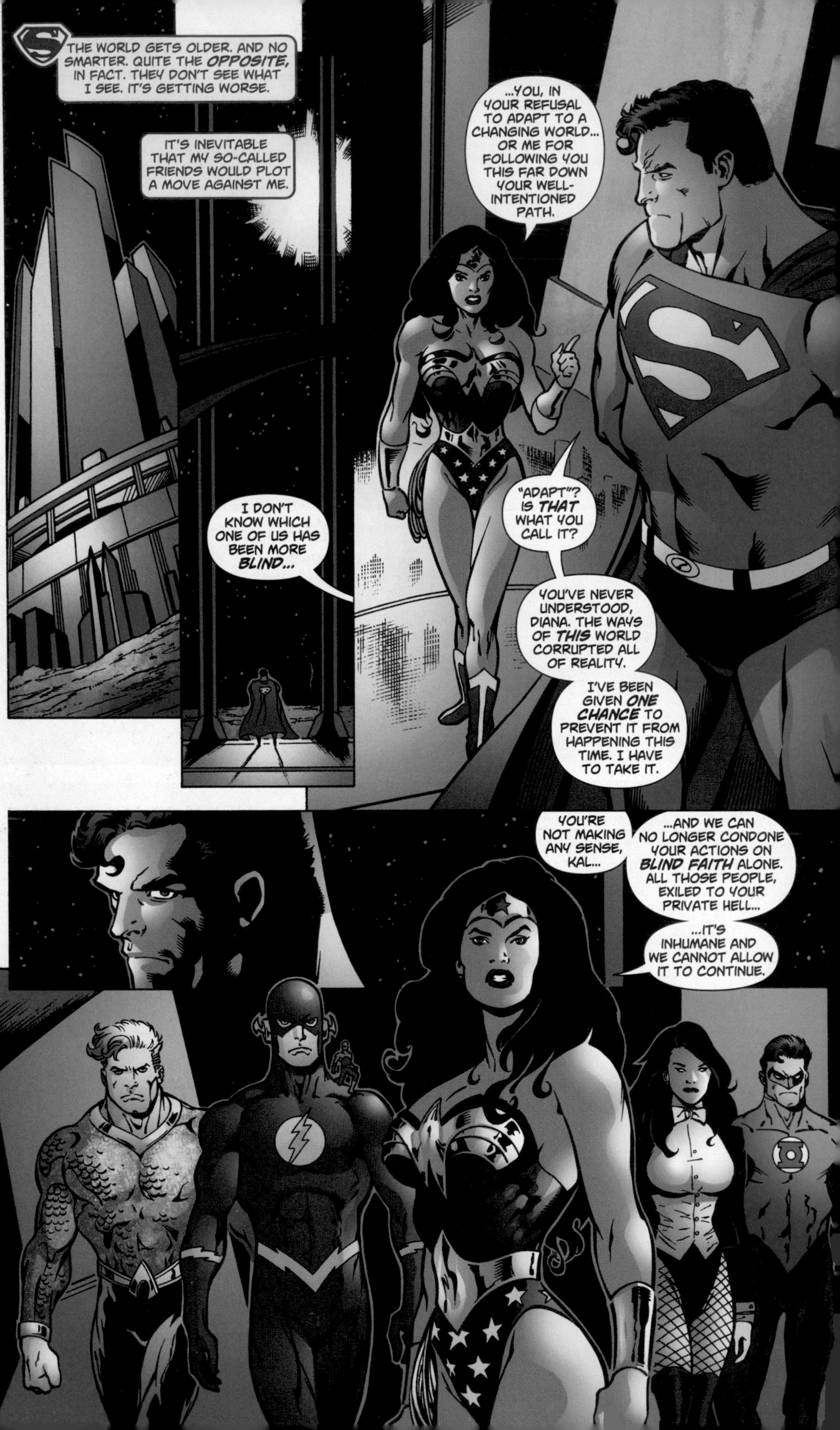
THE WORLD GETS OLDER. AND NO SMARTER. QUITE THE OPPOSITE, IN FACT. THEY DON'T SEE WHAT I SEE. IT'S GETTING WORSE.
IT'S INEVITABLE THAT MY SO-CALLED FRIENDS WOULD PLOT A MOVE AGAINST ME.
I DON'T KNOW WHICH ONE OF US HAS BEEN MORE BLIND...
...YOU, IN YOUR REFUSAL TO ADAPT TO A CHANGING WORLD... OR ME FOR FOLLOWING YOU THIS FAR DOWN YOUR WELL-INTENTIONED PATH.
"ADAPT"? IS THAT WHAT YOU CALL IT?
YOU'VE NEVER UNDERSTOOD, DIANA. THE WAYS OF THIS WORLD CORRUPTED ALL OF REALITY.
I'VE BEEN GIVEN ONE CHANCE TO PREVENT IT FROM HAPPENING THIS TIME. I HAVE TO TAKE IT.
YOU'RE NOT MAKING ANY SENSE, KAL...
...AND WE CAN NO LONGER CONDONE YOUR ACTIONS ON BLIND FAITH ALONE. ALL THOSE PEOPLE, EXILED TO YOUR PRIVATE HELL...
...IT'S INHUMANE AND WE CANNOT ALLOW IT TO CONTINUE.

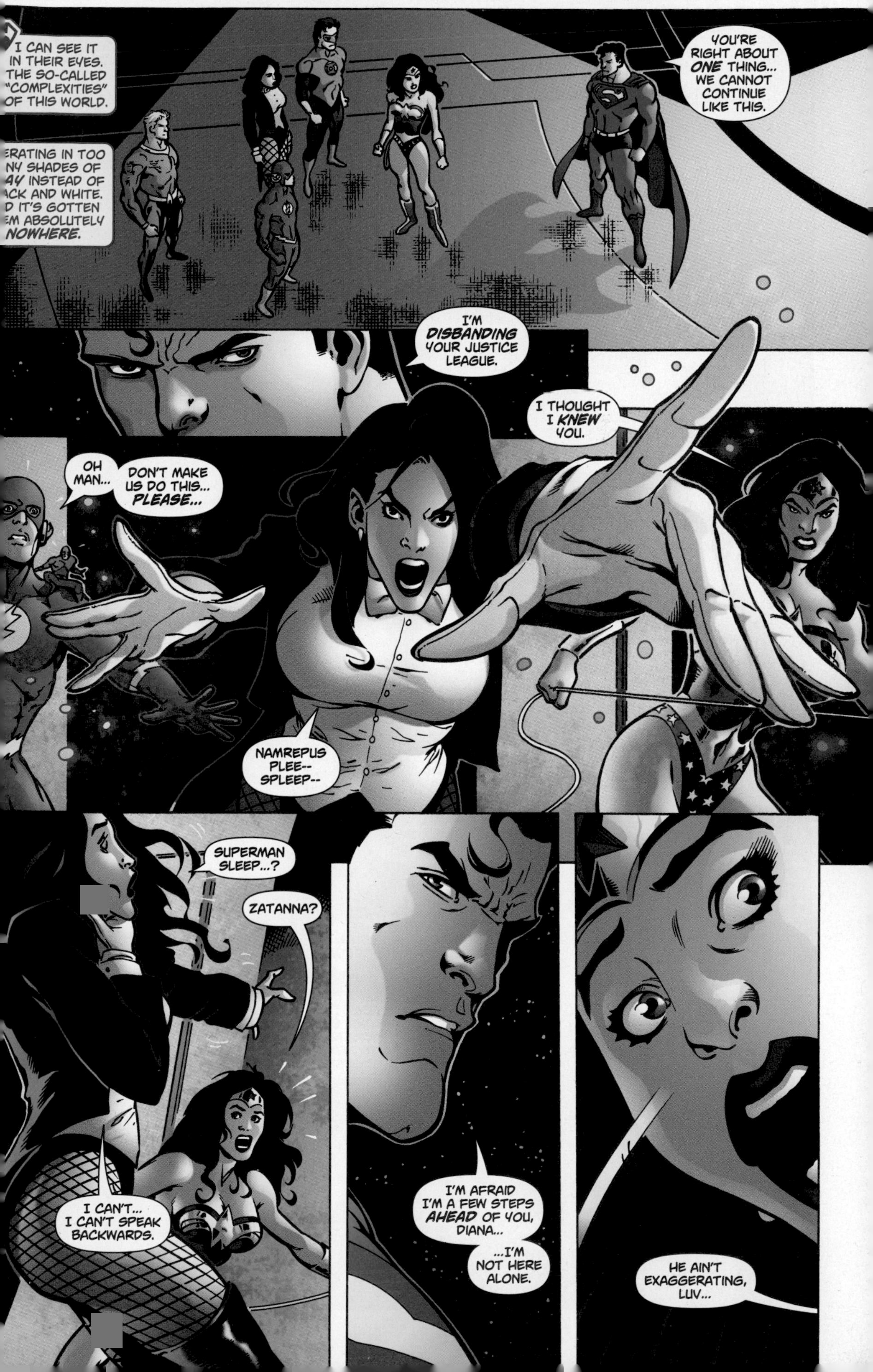
I CAN SEE IT IN THEIR EYES. THE SO-CALLED "COMPLEXITIES" OF THIS WORLD.
ERATING IN TOO NY SHADES OF AY INSTEAD OF ACK AND WHITE. D IT'S GOTTEN EM ABSOLUTELY NOWHERE.
YOU'RE RIGHT ABOUT ONE THING... WE CANNOT CONTINUE LIKE THIS.
I'M DISBANDING YOUR JUSTICE LEAGUE.
I THOUGHT I KNEW YOU.
OH MAN...
DON'T MAKE US DO THIS... PLEASE...
NAMREPUS PLEE-- SPLEEP--
SUPERMAN SLEEP...?
ZATANNA?
I CAN'T... I CAN'T SPEAK BACKWARDS.
I'M AFRAID I'M A FEW STEPS AHEAD OF YOU, DIANA...
...I'M NOT HERE ALONE.
HE AIN'T EXAGGERATING, LUV...

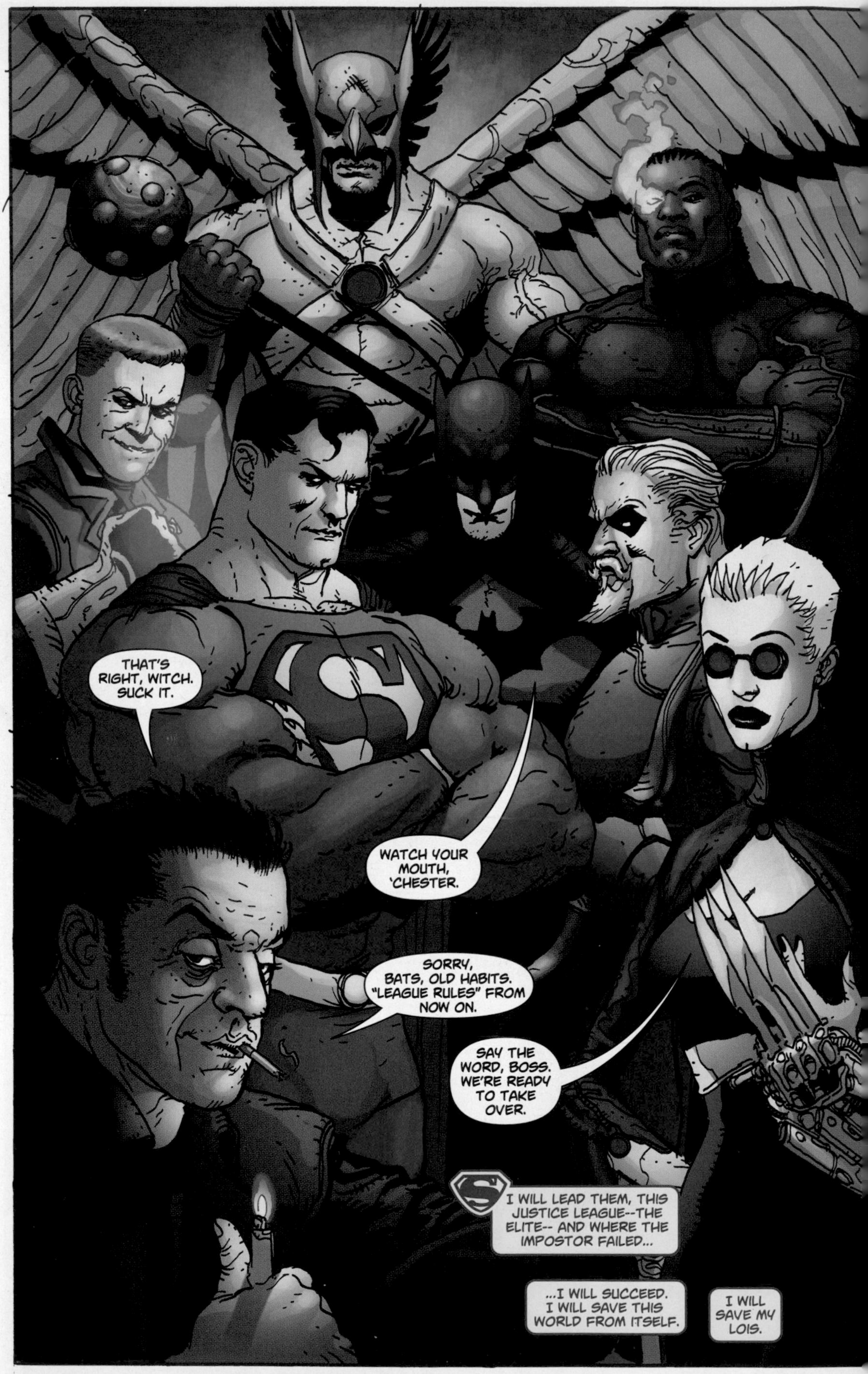

THAT'S RIGHT, WITCH. SUCK IT.
WATCH YOUR MOUTH, 'CHESTER.
SORRY, BATS, OLD HABITS. "LEAGUE RULES" FROM NOW ON.
SAY THE WORD, BOSS. WE'RE READY TO TAKE OVER.
I WILL LEAD THEM, THIS JUSTICE LEAGUE--THE ELITE-- AND WHERE THE IMPOSTOR FAILED...
...I WILL SUCCEED. I WILL SAVE THIS WORLD FROM ITSELF.
I WILL SAVE MY LOIS.

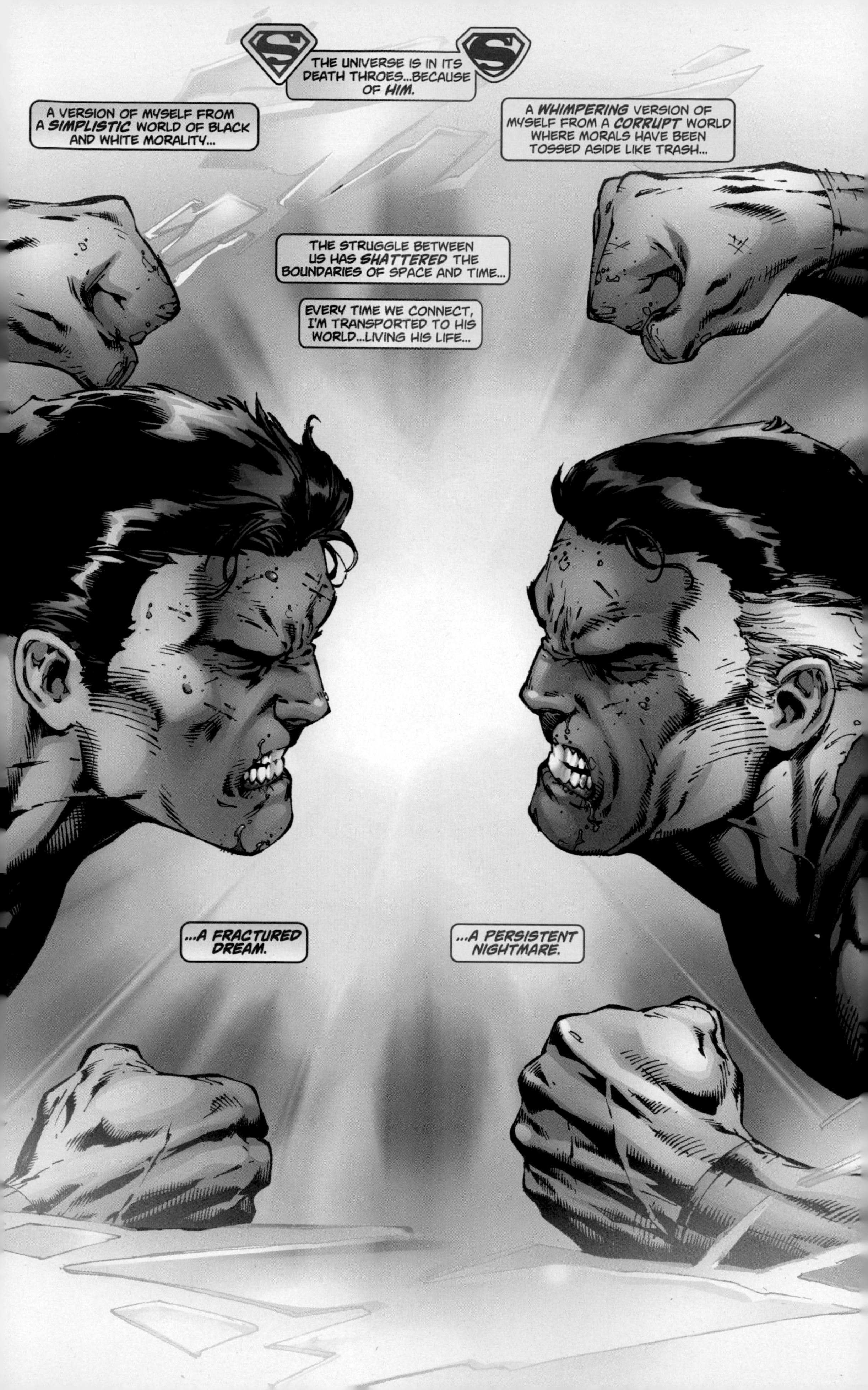
THE UNIVERSE IS IN ITS DEATH THROES...BECAUSE OF *HIM*.
A VERSION OF MYSELF FROM A *SIMPLISTIC* WORLD OF BLACK AND WHITE MORALITY...
A *WHIMPERING* VERSION OF MYSELF FROM A *CORRUPT* WORLD WHERE MORALS HAVE BEEN TOSSED ASIDE LIKE TRASH...
THE STRUGGLE BETWEEN US HAS *SHATTERED* THE BOUNDARIES OF SPACE AND TIME...
EVERY TIME WE CONNECT, I'M TRANSPORTED TO HIS WORLD...LIVING HIS LIFE...
...A FRACTURED DREAM.
...A PERSISTENT NIGHTMARE.

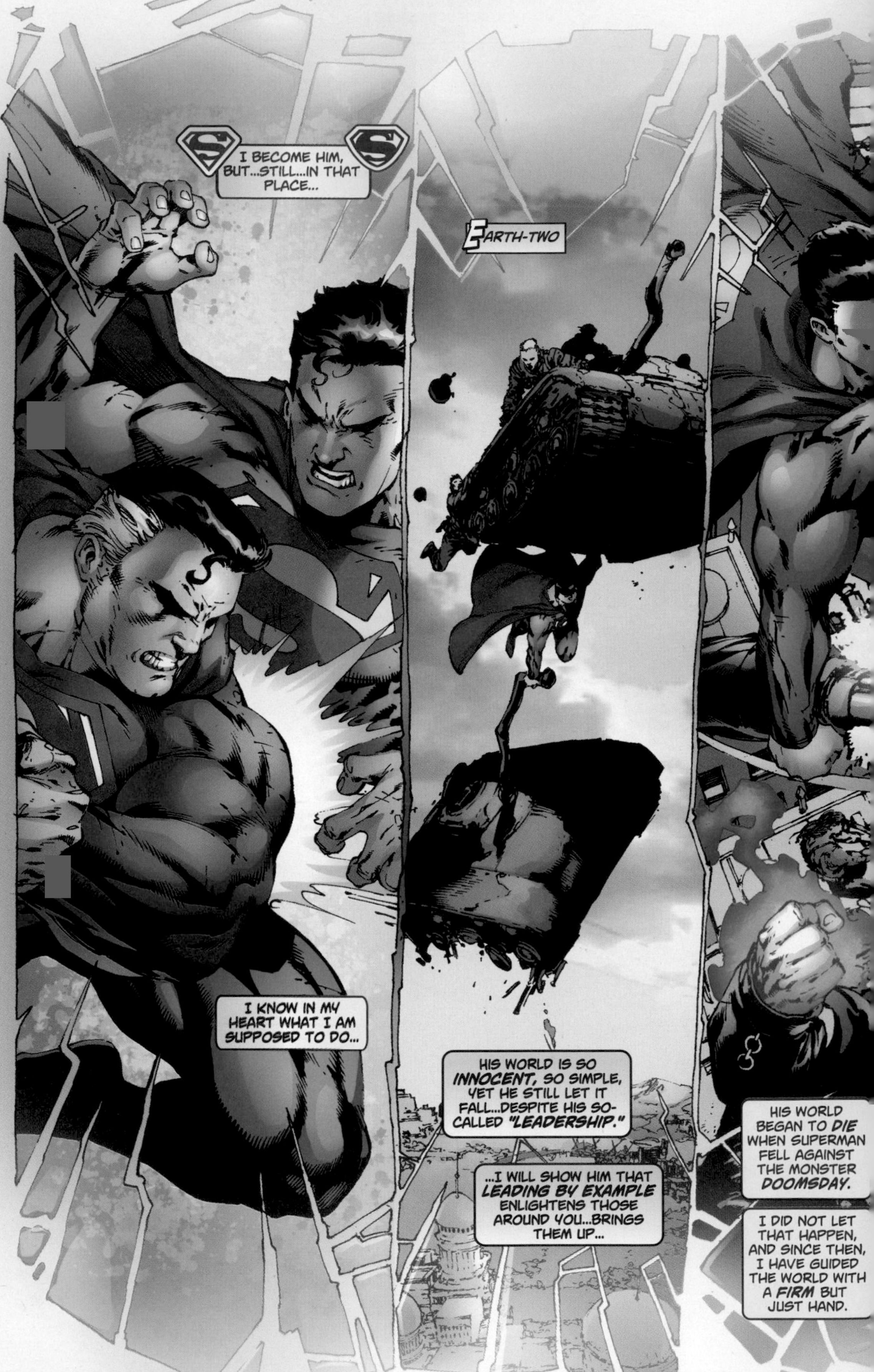
I BECOME HIM, BUT...STILL...IN THAT PLACE...
I KNOW IN MY HEART WHAT I AM SUPPOSED TO DO...
EARTH-TWO
HIS WORLD IS SO INNOCENT, SO SIMPLE, YET HE STILL LET IT FALL...DESPITE HIS SO-CALLED "LEADERSHIP."
...I WILL SHOW HIM THAT LEADING BY EXAMPLE ENLIGHTENS THOSE AROUND YOU...BRINGS THEM UP...
HIS WORLD BEGAN TO DIE WHEN SUPERMAN FELL AGAINST THE MONSTER DOOMSDAY.
I DID NOT LET THAT HAPPEN, AND SINCE THEN, I HAVE GUIDED THE WORLD WITH A FIRM BUT JUST HAND.

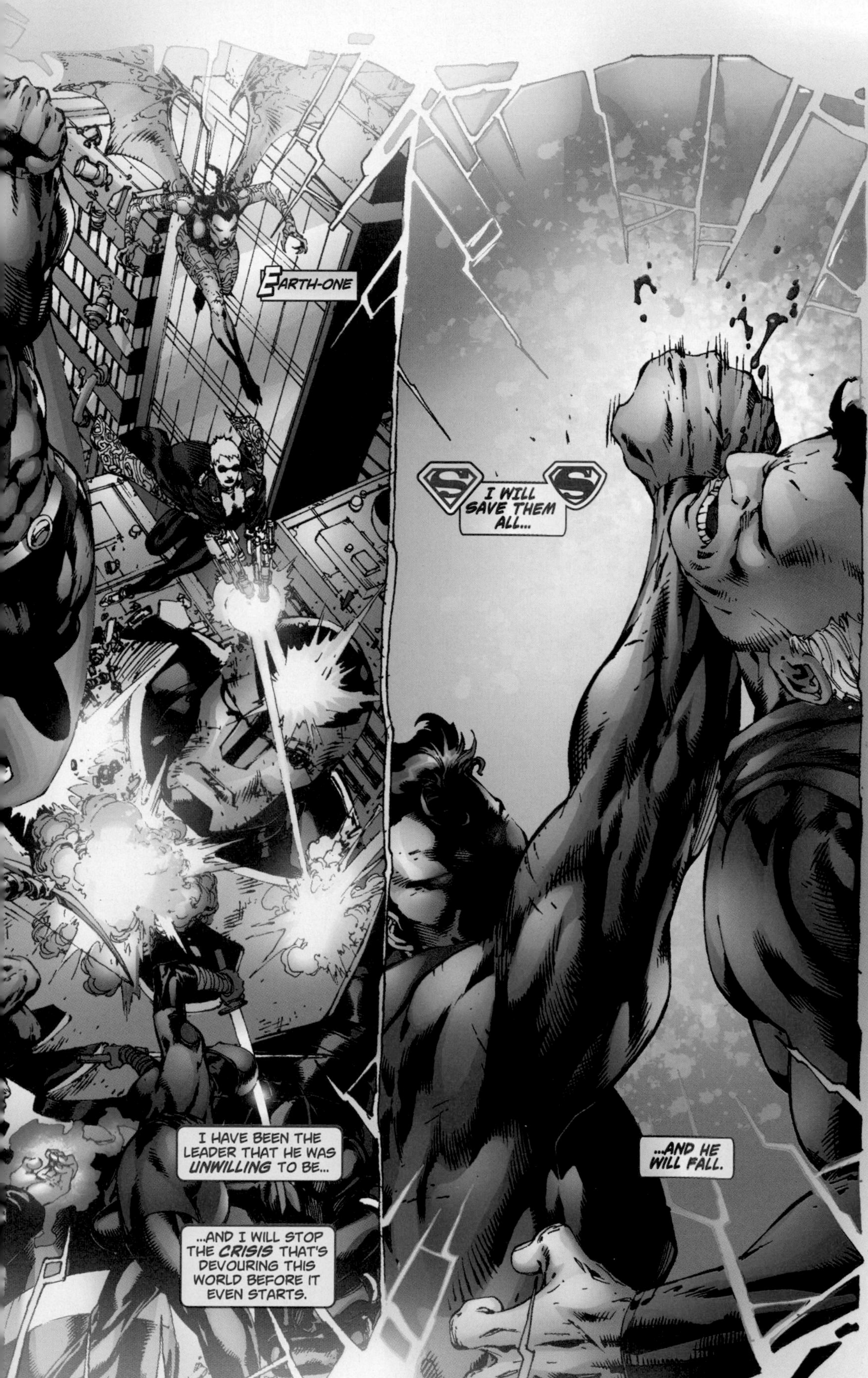
EARTH-ONE
I WILL SAVE THEM ALL...
I HAVE BEEN THE LEADER THAT HE WAS UNWILLING TO BE...
...AND I WILL STOP THE CRISIS THAT'S DEVOURING THIS WORLD BEFORE IT EVEN STARTS.
...AND HE WILL FALL.

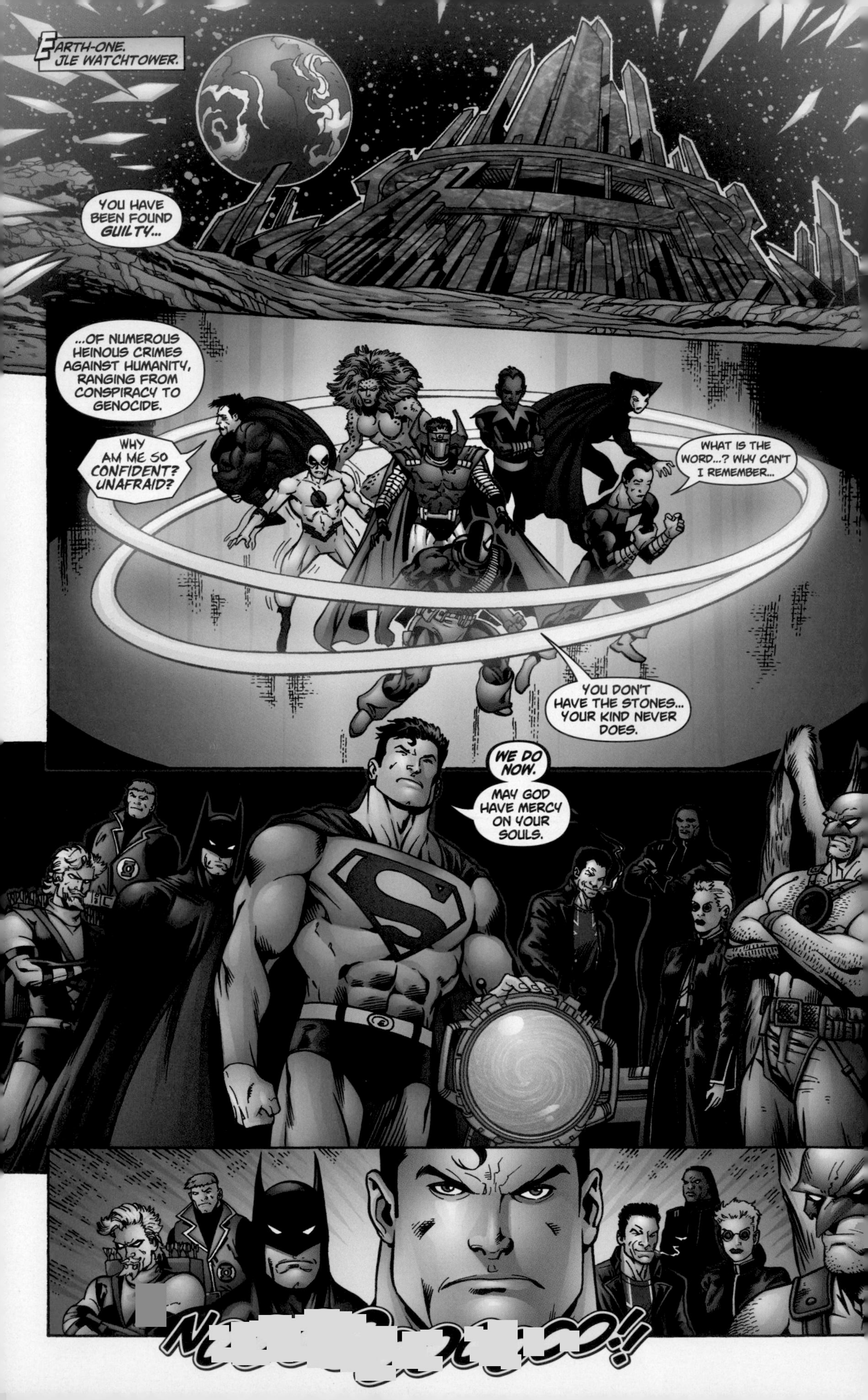
EARTH-ONE. JLE WATCHTOWER.
YOU HAVE BEEN FOUND GUILTY...
...OF NUMEROUS HEINOUS CRIMES AGAINST HUMANITY, RANGING FROM CONSPIRACY TO GENOCIDE.
WHY AM ME SO CONFIDENT? UNAFRAID?
WHAT IS THE WORD...? WHY CAN'T I REMEMBER...
YOU DON'T HAVE THE STONES... YOUR KIND NEVER DOES.
WE DO NOW.
MAY GOD HAVE MERCY ON YOUR SOULS.

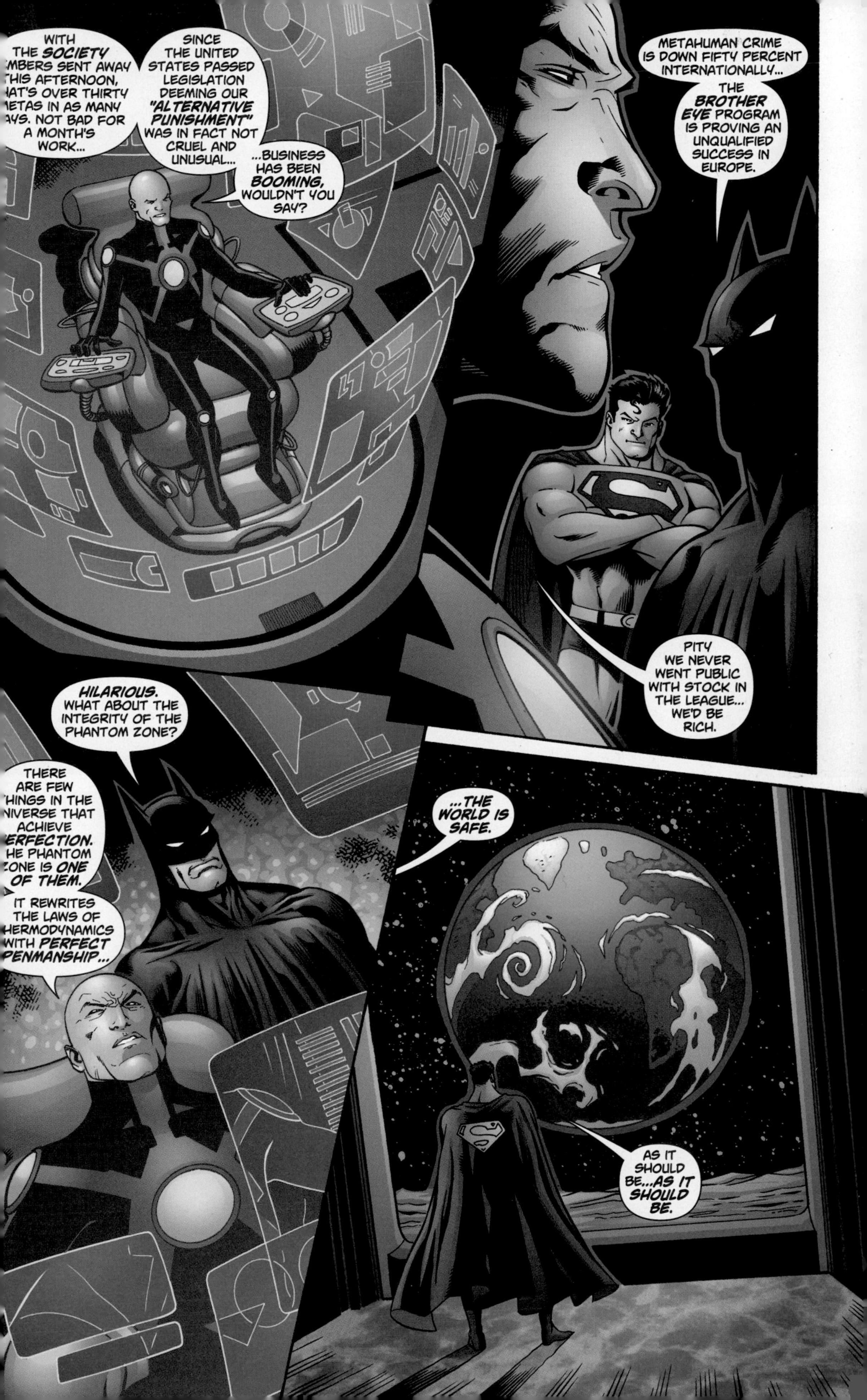
WITH THE SOCIETY MBERS SENT AWAY THIS AFTERNOON, HAT'S OVER THIRTY METAS IN AS MANY AYS. NOT BAD FOR A MONTH'S WORK...
SINCE THE UNITED STATES PASSED LEGISLATION DEEMING OUR "ALTERNATIVE PUNISHMENT" WAS IN FACT NOT CRUEL AND UNUSUAL...
...BUSINESS HAS BEEN BOOMING, WOULDN'T YOU SAY?
METAHUMAN CRIME IS DOWN FIFTY PERCENT INTERNATIONALLY...
THE BROTHER EYE PROGRAM IS PROVING AN UNQUALIFIED SUCCESS IN EUROPE.
PITY WE NEVER WENT PUBLIC WITH STOCK IN THE LEAGUE... WE'D BE RICH.
HILARIOUS. WHAT ABOUT THE INTEGRITY OF THE PHANTOM ZONE?
THERE ARE FEW HINGS IN THE NIVERSE THAT ACHIEVE ERFECTION. HE PHANTOM ONE IS ONE OF THEM.
IT REWRITES THE LAWS OF HERMODYNAMICS WITH PERFECT PENMANSHIP...
...THE WORLD IS SAFE.
AS IT SHOULD BE...AS IT SHOULD BE.

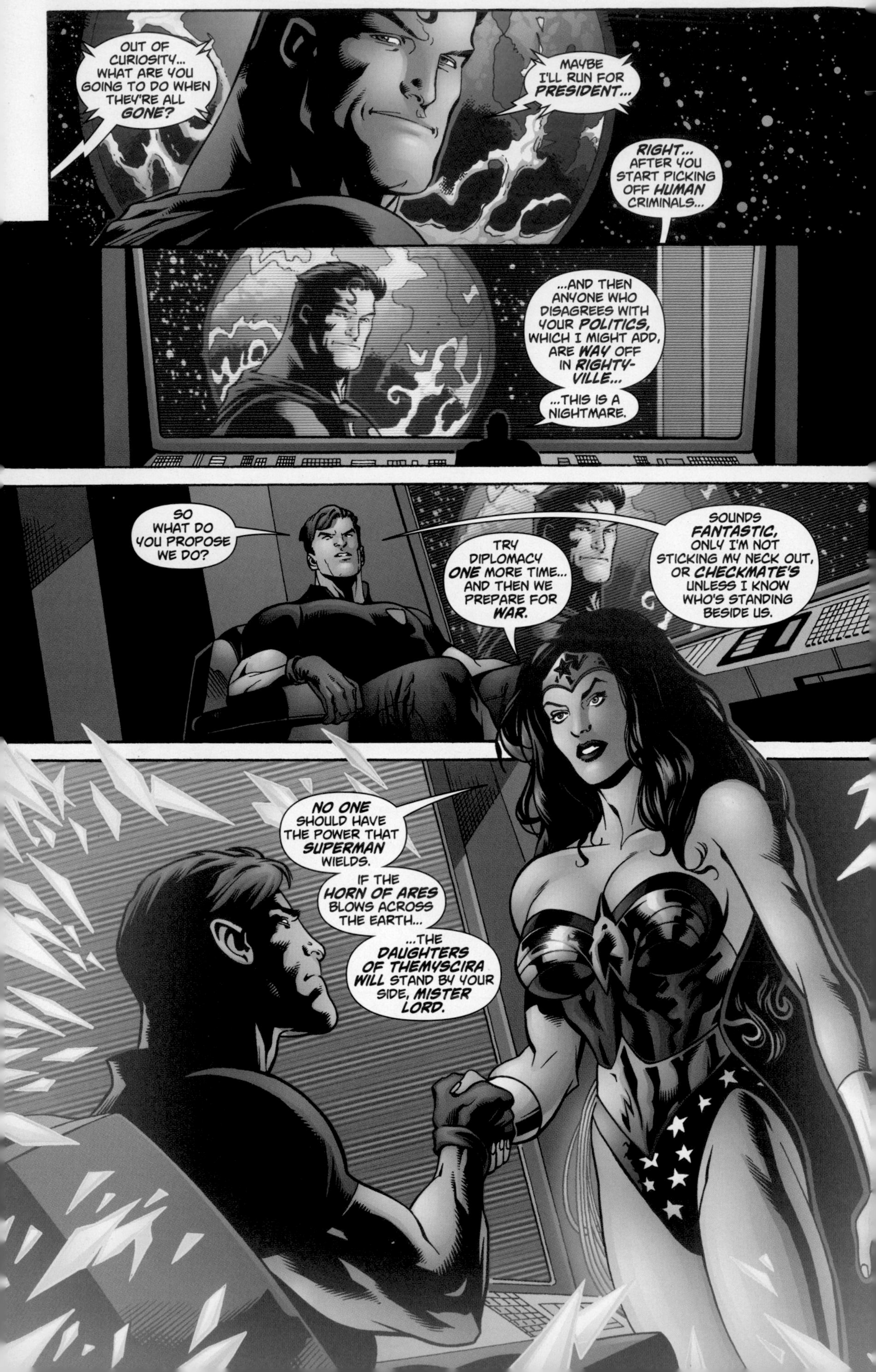
OUT OF CURIOSITY... WHAT ARE YOU GOING TO DO WHEN THEY'RE ALL GONE?
MAYBE I'LL RUN FOR PRESIDENT...
RIGHT... AFTER YOU START PICKING OFF HUMAN CRIMINALS...
...AND THEN ANYONE WHO DISAGREES WITH YOUR POLITICS, WHICH I MIGHT ADD, ARE WAY OFF IN RIGHTY-VILLE...
...THIS IS A NIGHTMARE.
SO WHAT DO YOU PROPOSE WE DO?
TRY DIPLOMACY ONE MORE TIME... AND THEN WE PREPARE FOR WAR.
SOUNDS FANTASTIC, ONLY I'M NOT STICKING MY NECK OUT, OR CHECKMATE'S UNLESS I KNOW WHO'S STANDING BESIDE US.
NO ONE SHOULD HAVE THE POWER THAT SUPERMAN WIELDS.
IF THE HORN OF ARES BLOWS ACROSS THE EARTH...
...THE DAUGHTERS OF THEMYSCIRA WILL STAND BY YOUR SIDE, MISTER LORD.

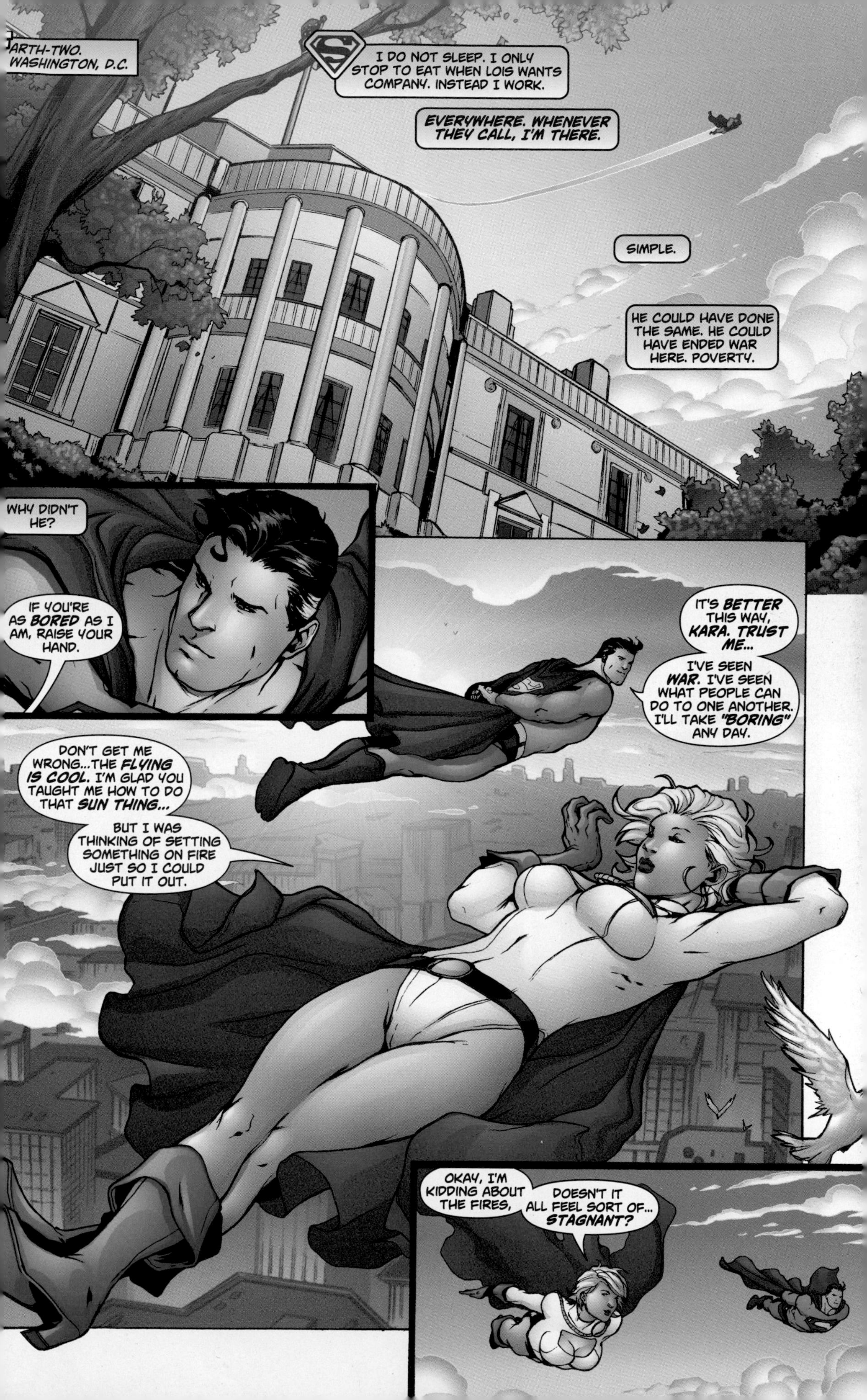

ARTH-TWO. WASHINGTON, D.C.
I DO NOT SLEEP. I ONLY STOP TO EAT WHEN LOIS WANTS COMPANY. INSTEAD I WORK.
EVERYWHERE. WHENEVER THEY CALL, I'M THERE.
SIMPLE.
HE COULD HAVE DONE THE SAME. HE COULD HAVE ENDED WAR HERE. POVERTY.
WHY DIDN'T HE?
IF YOU'RE AS BORED AS I AM, RAISE YOUR HAND.
IT'S BETTER THIS WAY, KARA. TRUST ME...
I'VE SEEN WAR. I'VE SEEN WHAT PEOPLE CAN DO TO ONE ANOTHER. I'LL TAKE "BORING" ANY DAY.
DON'T GET ME WRONG...THE FLYING IS COOL. I'M GLAD YOU TAUGHT ME HOW TO DO THAT SUN THING...
BUT I WAS THINKING OF SETTING SOMETHING ON FIRE JUST SO I COULD PUT IT OUT.
OKAY, I'M KIDDING ABOUT THE FIRES,
DOESN'T IT ALL FEEL SORT OF... STAGNANT?

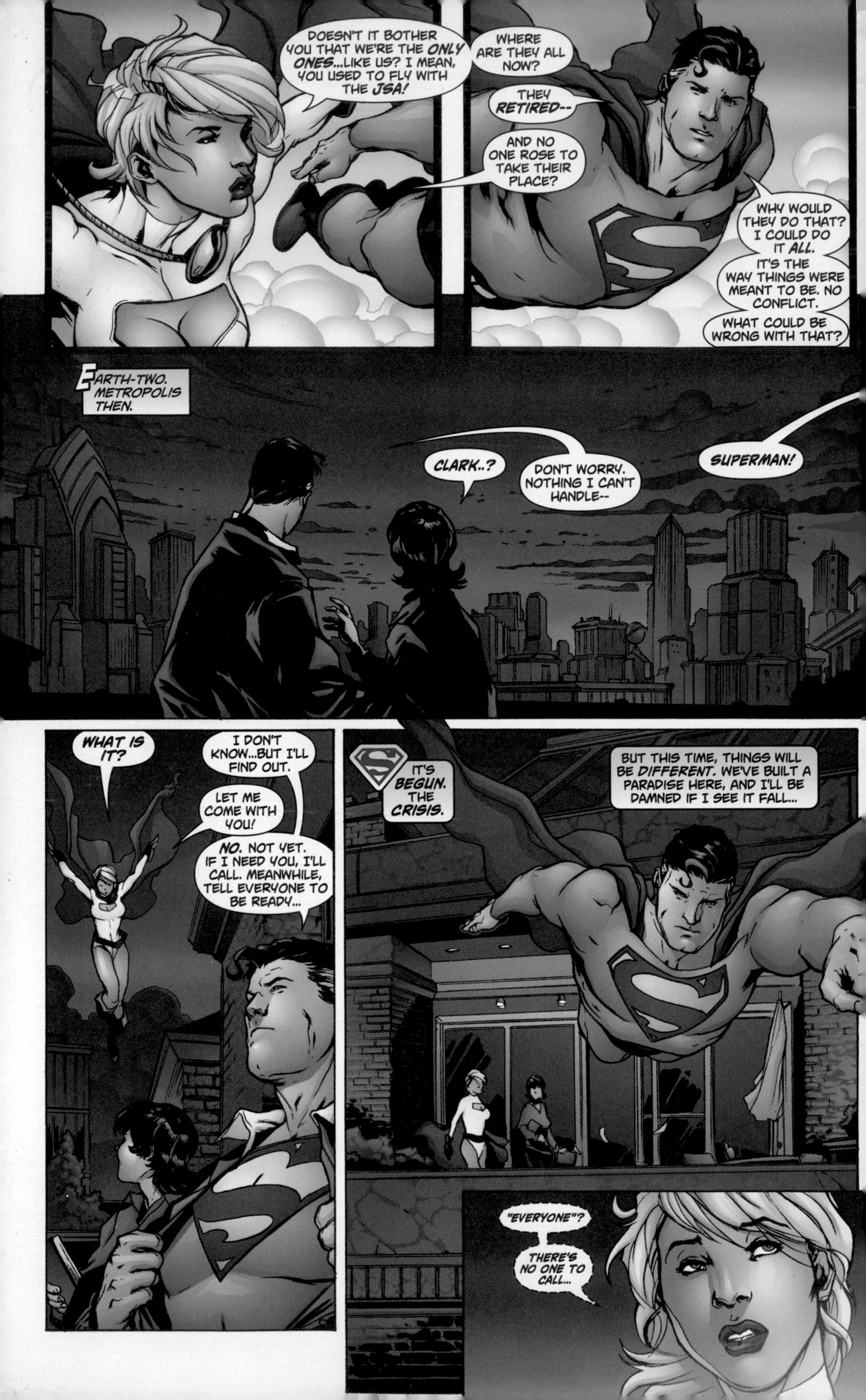
DOESN'T IT BOTHER YOU THAT WE'RE THE ONLY ONES...LIKE US? I MEAN, YOU USED TO FLY WITH THE JSA!
WHERE ARE THEY ALL NOW?
THEY RETIRED--
AND NO ONE ROSE TO TAKE THEIR PLACE?
WHY WOULD THEY DO THAT? I COULD DO IT ALL.
IT'S THE WAY THINGS WERE MEANT TO BE. NO CONFLICT.
WHAT COULD BE WRONG WITH THAT?
EARTH-TWO. METROPOLIS THEN.
CLARK..?
DON'T WORRY. NOTHING I CAN'T HANDLE--
SUPERMAN!
WHAT IS IT?
I DON'T KNOW...BUT I'LL FIND OUT.
LET ME COME WITH YOU!
NO. NOT YET. IF I NEED YOU, I'LL CALL. MEANWHILE, TELL EVERYONE TO BE READY...
IT'S BEGUN. THE CRISIS.
BUT THIS TIME, THINGS WILL BE DIFFERENT. WE'VE BUILT A PARADISE HERE, AND I'LL BE DAMNED IF I SEE IT FALL...
"EVERYONE"?
THERE'S NO ONE TO CALL...

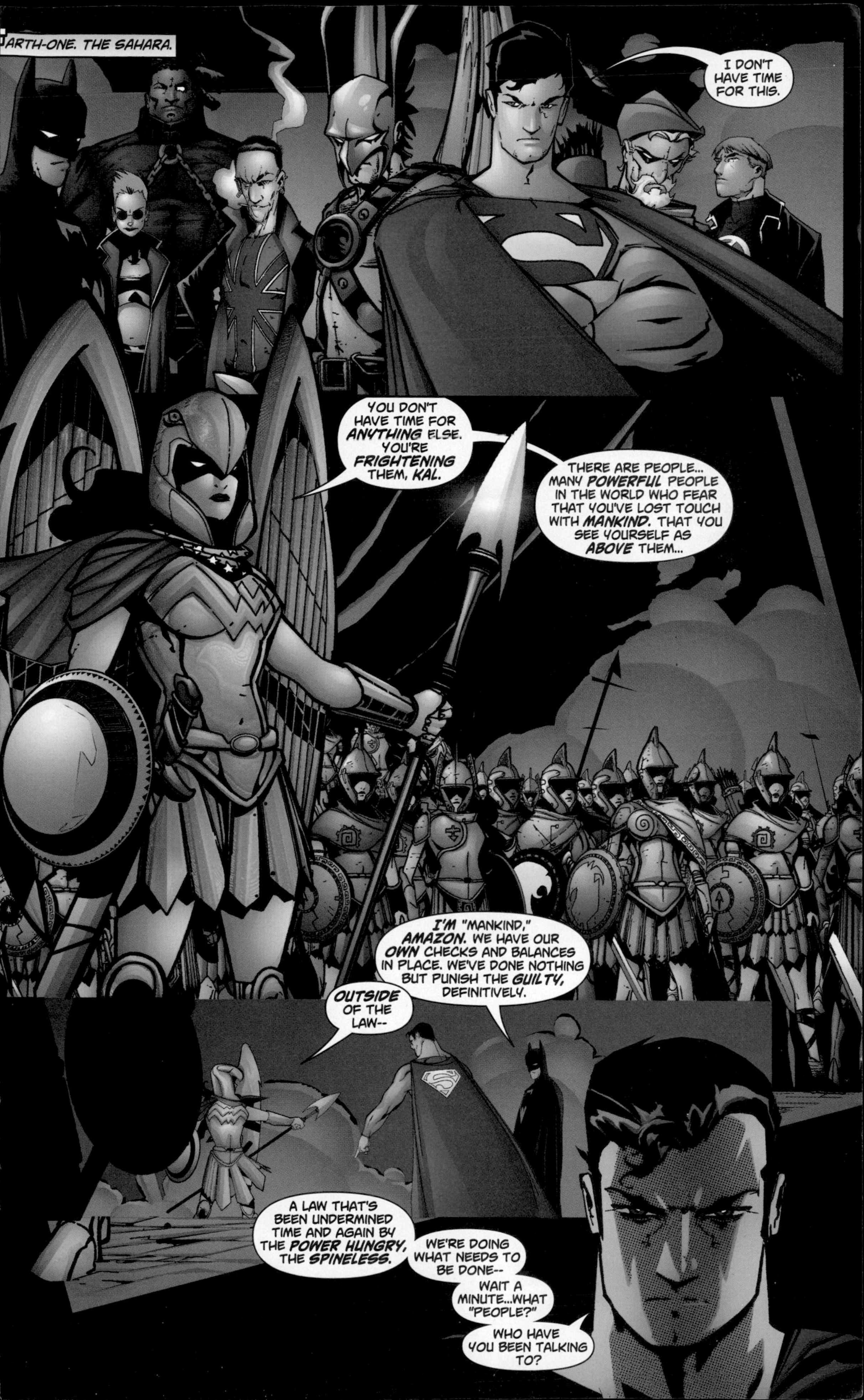

ARTH-ONE. THE SAHARA.
I DON'T HAVE TIME FOR THIS.
YOU DON'T HAVE TIME FOR ANYTHING ELSE. YOU'RE FRIGHTENING THEM, KAL.
THERE ARE PEOPLE... MANY POWERFUL PEOPLE IN THE WORLD WHO FEAR THAT YOU'VE LOST TOUCH WITH MANKIND. THAT YOU SEE YOURSELF AS ABOVE THEM...
I'M "MANKIND," AMAZON. WE HAVE OUR OWN CHECKS AND BALANCES IN PLACE. WE'VE DONE NOTHING BUT PUNISH THE GUILTY, DEFINITIVELY.
OUTSIDE OF THE LAW--
A LAW THAT'S BEEN UNDERMINED TIME AND AGAIN BY THE POWER HUNGRY, THE SPINELESS.
WE'RE DOING WHAT NEEDS TO BE DONE--
WAIT A MINUTE...WHAT "PEOPLE?"
WHO HAVE YOU BEEN TALKING TO?

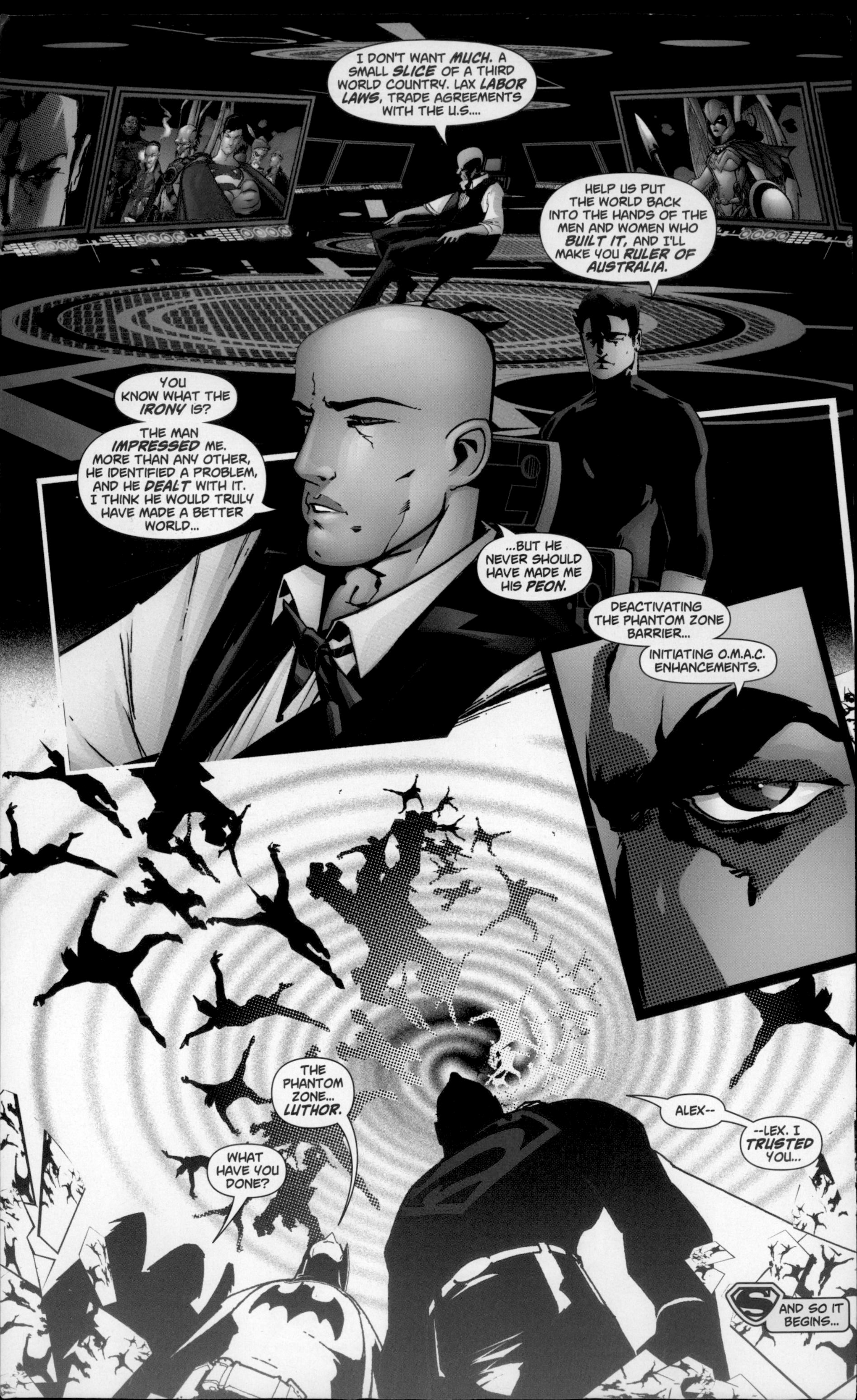

I DON'T WANT MUCH. A SMALL SLICE OF A THIRD WORLD COUNTRY. LAX LABOR LAWS, TRADE AGREEMENTS WITH THE U.S....
HELP US PUT THE WORLD BACK INTO THE HANDS OF THE MEN AND WOMEN WHO BUILT IT, AND I'LL MAKE YOU RULER OF AUSTRALIA.
YOU KNOW WHAT THE IRONY IS?
THE MAN IMPRESSED ME. MORE THAN ANY OTHER, HE IDENTIFIED A PROBLEM, AND HE DEALT WITH IT. I THINK HE WOULD TRULY HAVE MADE A BETTER WORLD...
...BUT HE NEVER SHOULD HAVE MADE ME HIS PEON.
DEACTIVATING THE PHANTOM ZONE BARRIER...
INITIATING O.M.A.C. ENHANCEMENTS.
THE PHANTOM ZONE... LUTHOR.
WHAT HAVE YOU DONE?
ALEX--
--LEX. I TRUSTED YOU...
AND SO IT BEGINS...

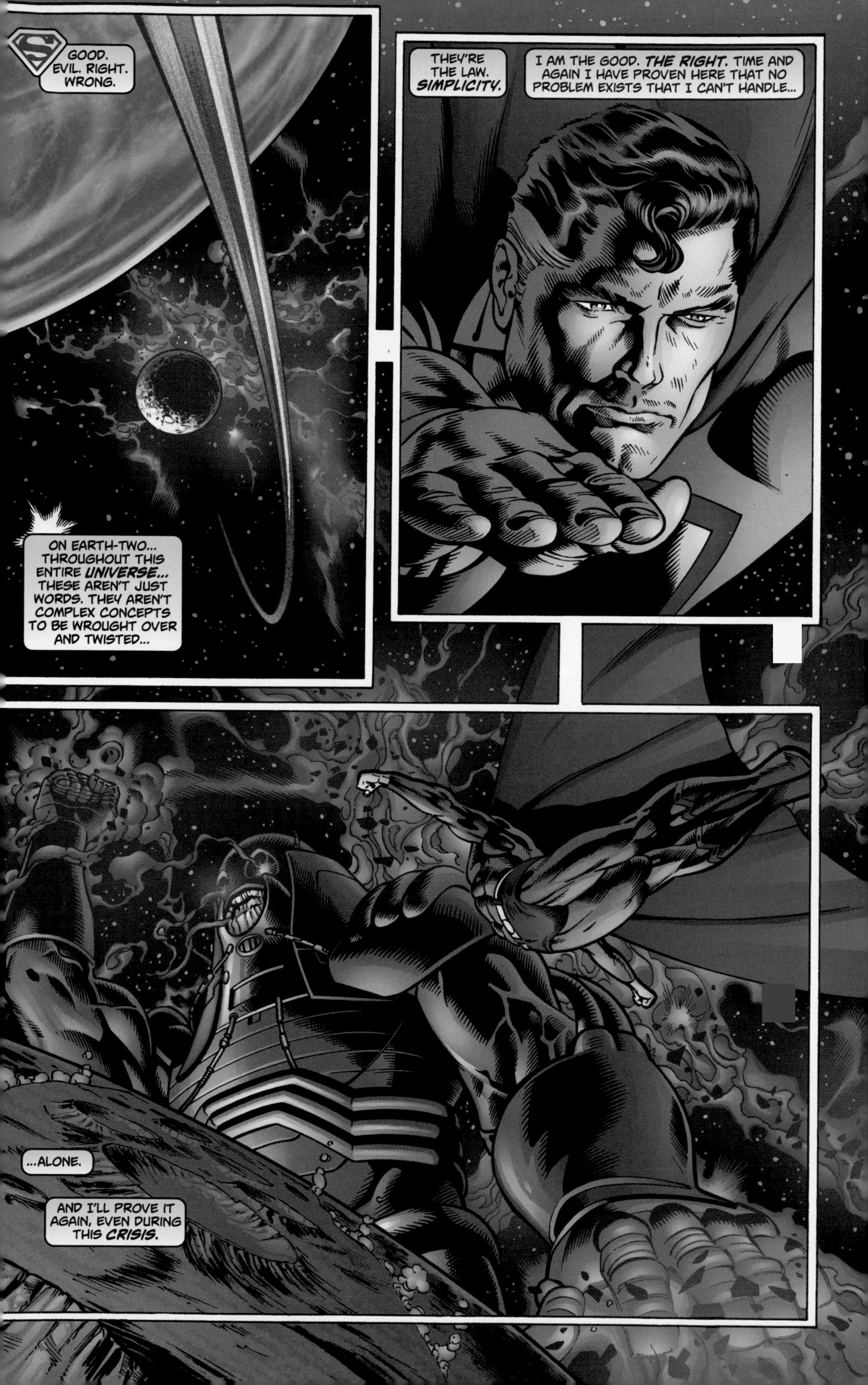
GOOD. EVIL. RIGHT. WRONG.
ON EARTH-TWO... THROUGHOUT THIS ENTIRE UNIVERSE... THESE AREN'T JUST WORDS. THEY AREN'T COMPLEX CONCEPTS TO BE WROUGHT OVER AND TWISTED...
THEY'RE THE LAW. SIMPLICITY.
I AM THE GOOD. THE RIGHT. TIME AND AGAIN I HAVE PROVEN HERE THAT NO PROBLEM EXISTS THAT I CAN'T HANDLE...
...ALONE.
AND I'LL PROVE IT AGAIN, EVEN DURING THIS CRISIS.

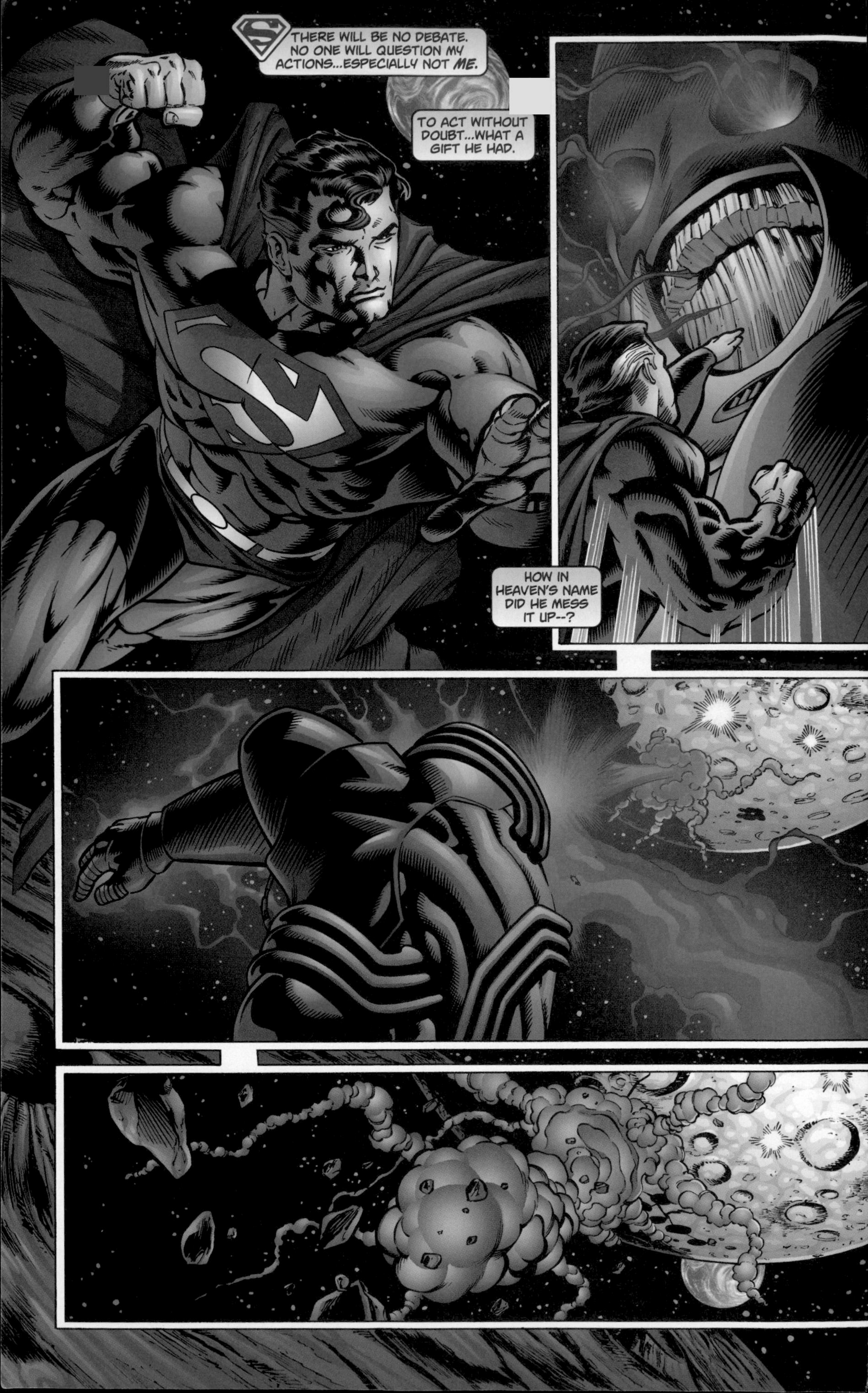
THERE WILL BE NO DEBATE. NO ONE WILL QUESTION MY ACTIONS...ESPECIALLY NOT *ME*.
TO ACT WITHOUT DOUBT...WHAT A GIFT HE HAD.
HOW IN HEAVEN'S NAME DID HE MESS IT UP--?

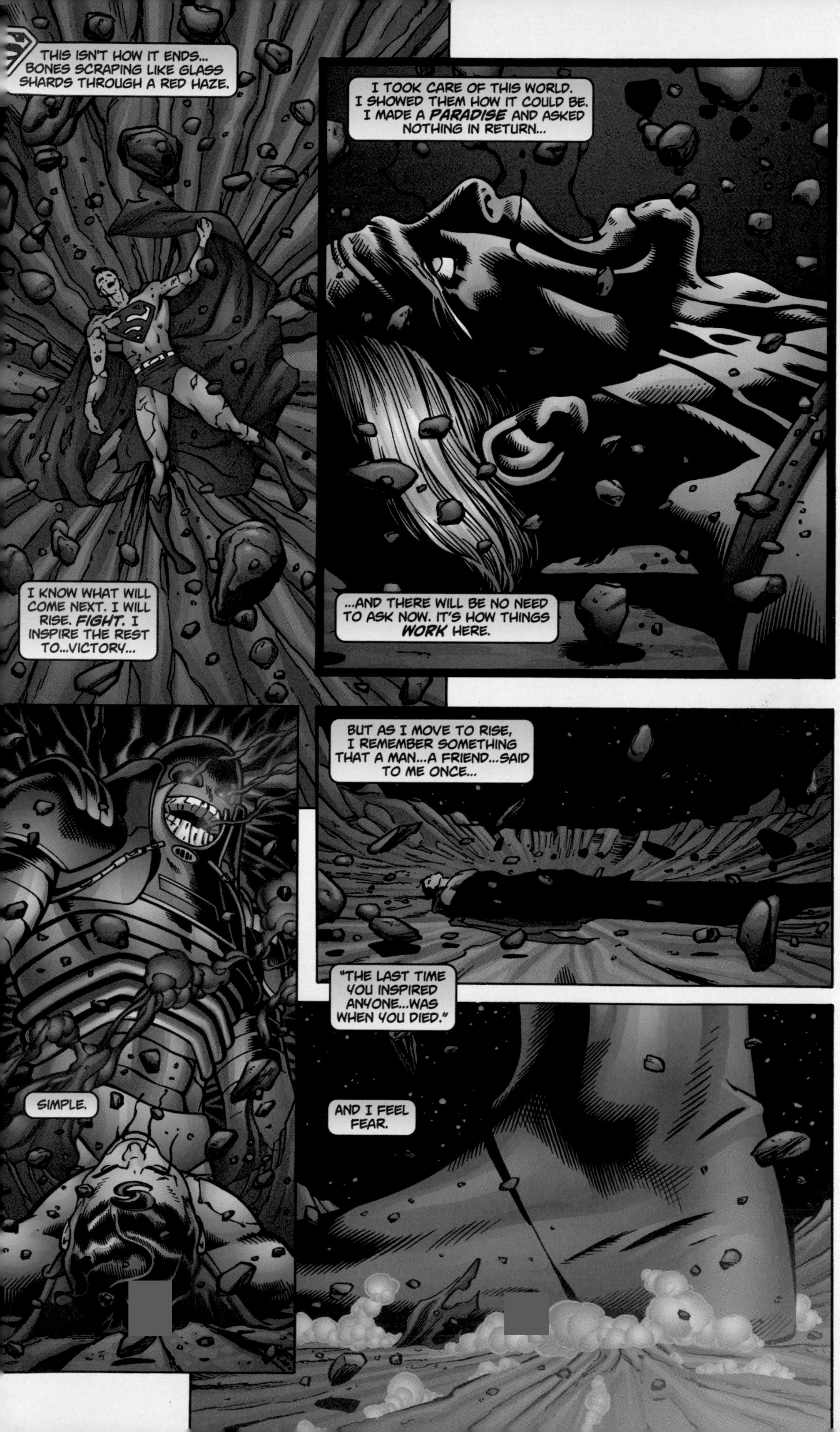
THIS ISN'T HOW IT ENDS... BONES SCRAPING LIKE GLASS SHARDS THROUGH A RED HAZE.
I TOOK CARE OF THIS WORLD. I SHOWED THEM HOW IT COULD BE. I MADE A *PARADISE* AND ASKED NOTHING IN RETURN...
I KNOW WHAT WILL COME NEXT. I WILL RISE. *FIGHT.* I INSPIRE THE REST TO...VICTORY...
...AND THERE WILL BE NO NEED TO ASK NOW. IT'S HOW THINGS *WORK* HERE.
BUT AS I MOVE TO RISE, I REMEMBER SOMETHING THAT A MAN...A FRIEND...SAID TO ME ONCE...
"THE LAST TIME YOU INSPIRED ANYONE...WAS WHEN YOU DIED."
SIMPLE.
AND I FEEL FEAR.

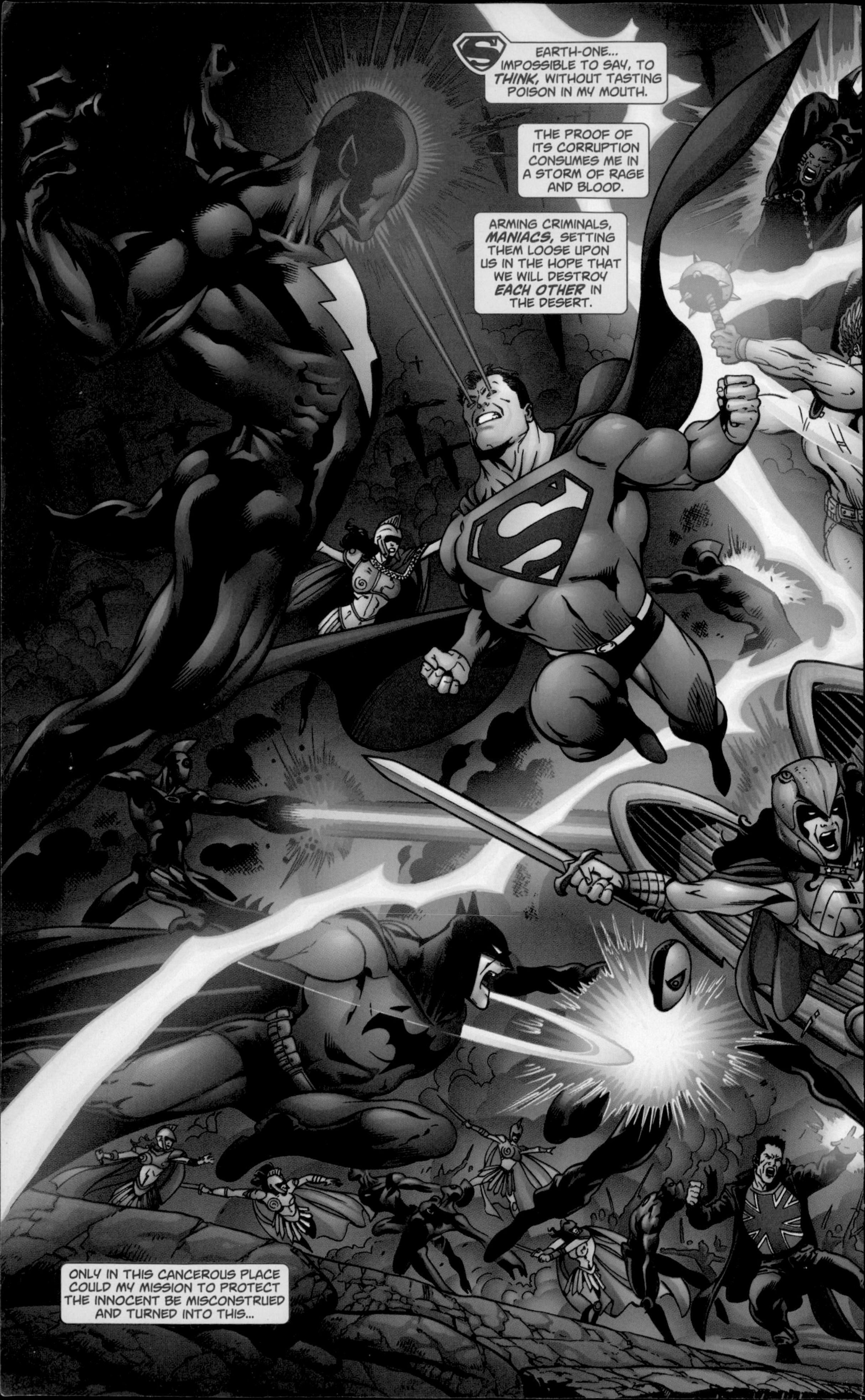
EARTH-ONE... IMPOSSIBLE TO SAY, TO THINK, WITHOUT TASTING POISON IN MY MOUTH.
THE PROOF OF ITS CORRUPTION CONSUMES ME IN A STORM OF RAGE AND BLOOD.
ARMING CRIMINALS, MANIACS, SETTING THEM LOOSE UPON US IN THE HOPE THAT WE WILL DESTROY EACH OTHER IN THE DESERT.
ONLY IN THIS CANCEROUS PLACE COULD MY MISSION TO PROTECT THE INNOCENT BE MISCONSTRUED AND TURNED INTO THIS...

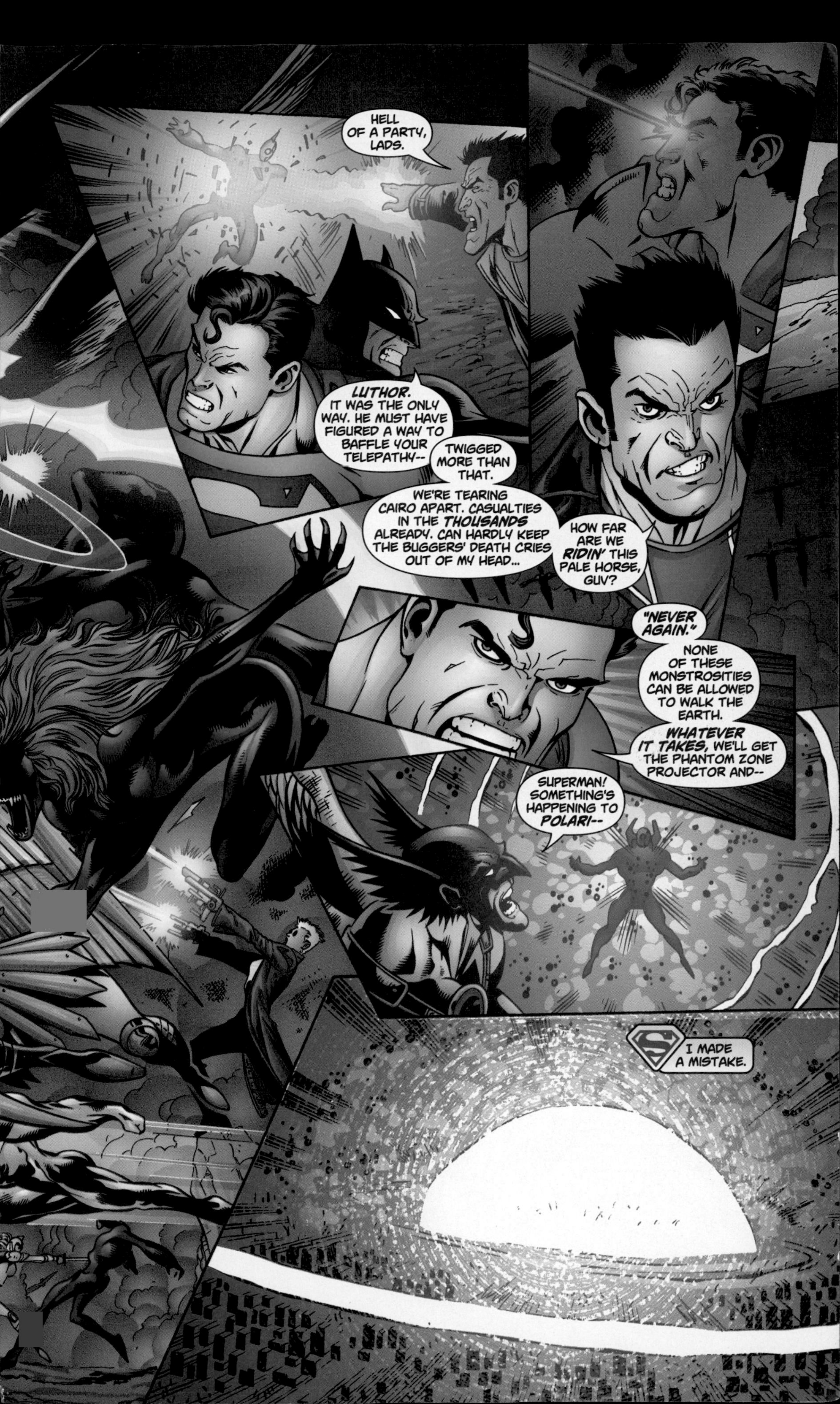
HELL OF A PARTY, LADS.
LUTHOR. IT WAS THE ONLY WAY. HE MUST HAVE FIGURED A WAY TO BAFFLE YOUR TELEPATHY--
TWIGGED MORE THAN THAT.
WE'RE TEARING CAIRO APART. CASUALTIES IN THE THOUSANDS ALREADY. CAN HARDLY KEEP THE BUGGERS' DEATH CRIES OUT OF MY HEAD...
HOW FAR ARE WE RIDIN' THIS PALE HORSE, GUV?
"NEVER AGAIN."
NONE OF THESE MONSTROSITIES CAN BE ALLOWED TO WALK THE EARTH.
WHATEVER IT TAKES, WE'LL GET THE PHANTOM ZONE PROJECTOR AND--
SUPERMAN! SOMETHING'S HAPPENING TO POLARI--
I MADE A MISTAKE.

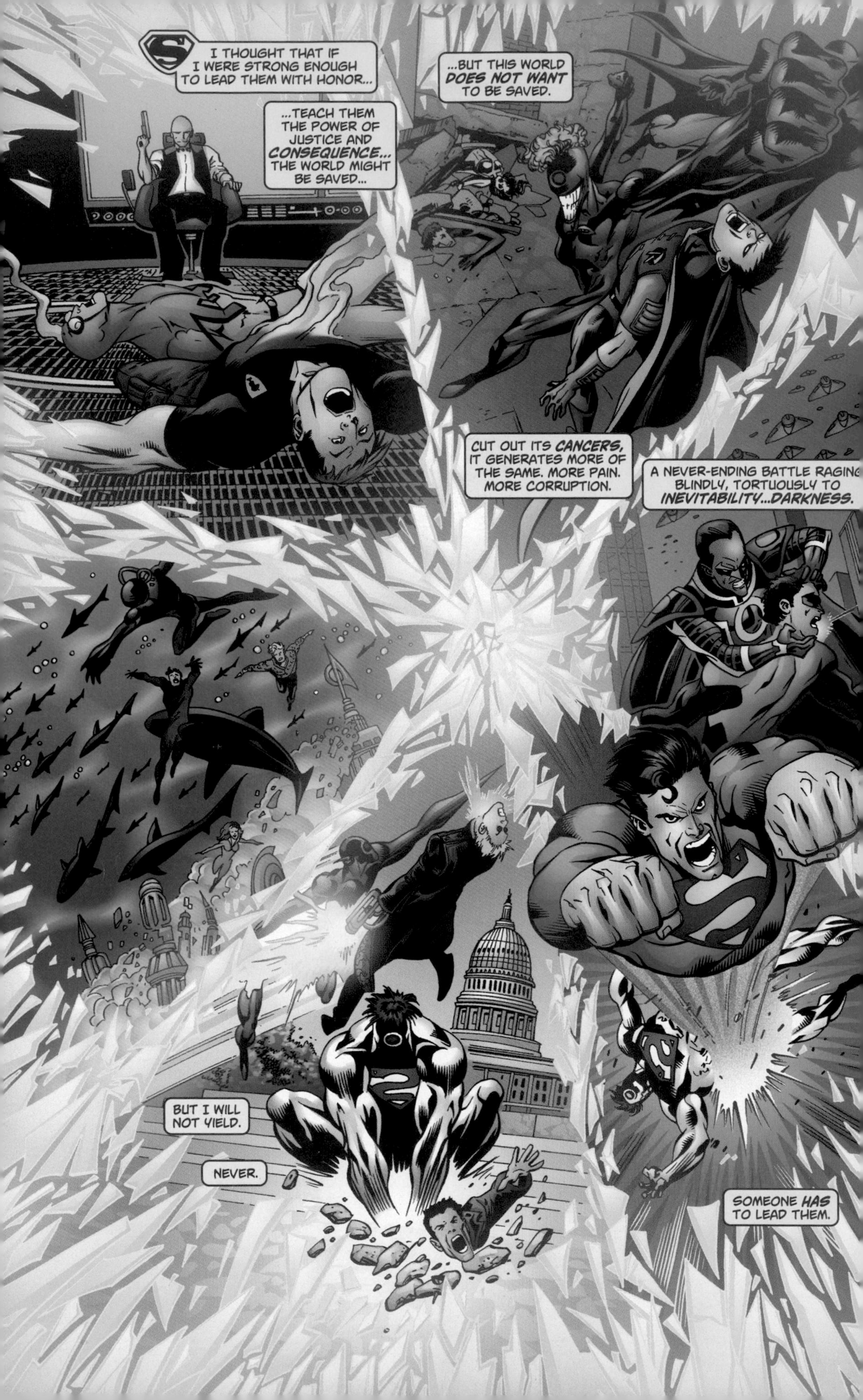
I THOUGHT THAT IF I WERE STRONG ENOUGH TO LEAD THEM WITH HONOR...
...TEACH THEM THE POWER OF JUSTICE AND CONSEQUENCE... THE WORLD MIGHT BE SAVED...
...BUT THIS WORLD DOES NOT WANT TO BE SAVED.
CUT OUT ITS CANCERS, IT GENERATES MORE OF THE SAME. MORE PAIN. MORE CORRUPTION.
A NEVER-ENDING BATTLE RAGING BLINDLY, TORTUOUSLY TO INEVITABILITY...DARKNESS.
BUT I WILL NOT YIELD.
NEVER.
SOMEONE HAS TO LEAD THEM.

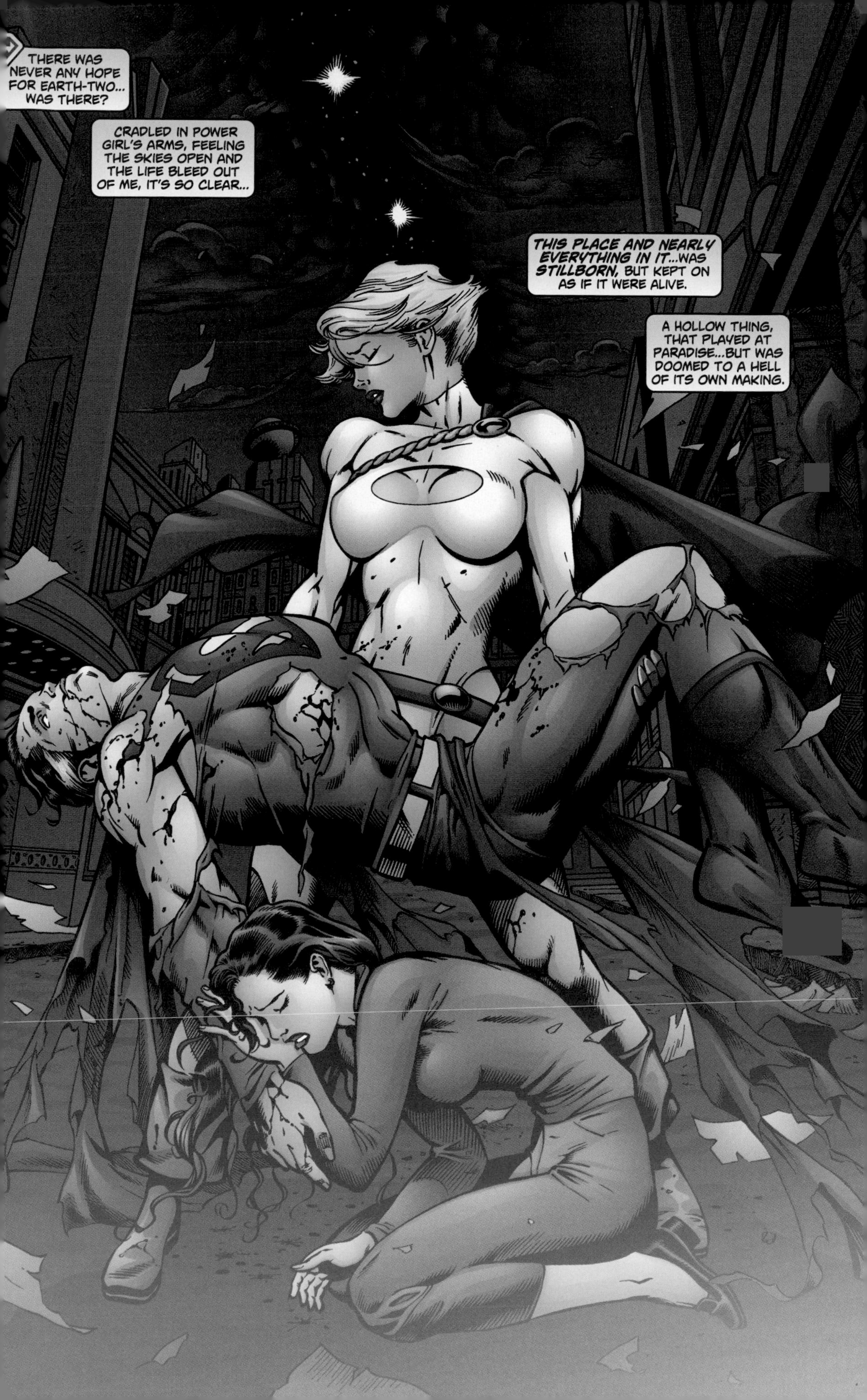
THERE WAS NEVER ANY HOPE FOR EARTH-TWO... WAS THERE?
CRADLED IN POWER GIRL'S ARMS, FEELING THE SKIES OPEN AND THE LIFE BLEED OUT OF ME, IT'S SO CLEAR...
THIS PLACE AND NEARLY EVERYTHING IN IT...WAS STILLBORN, BUT KEPT ON AS IF IT WERE ALIVE.
A HOLLOW THING, THAT PLAYED AT PARADISE...BUT WAS DOOMED TO A HELL OF ITS OWN MAKING.

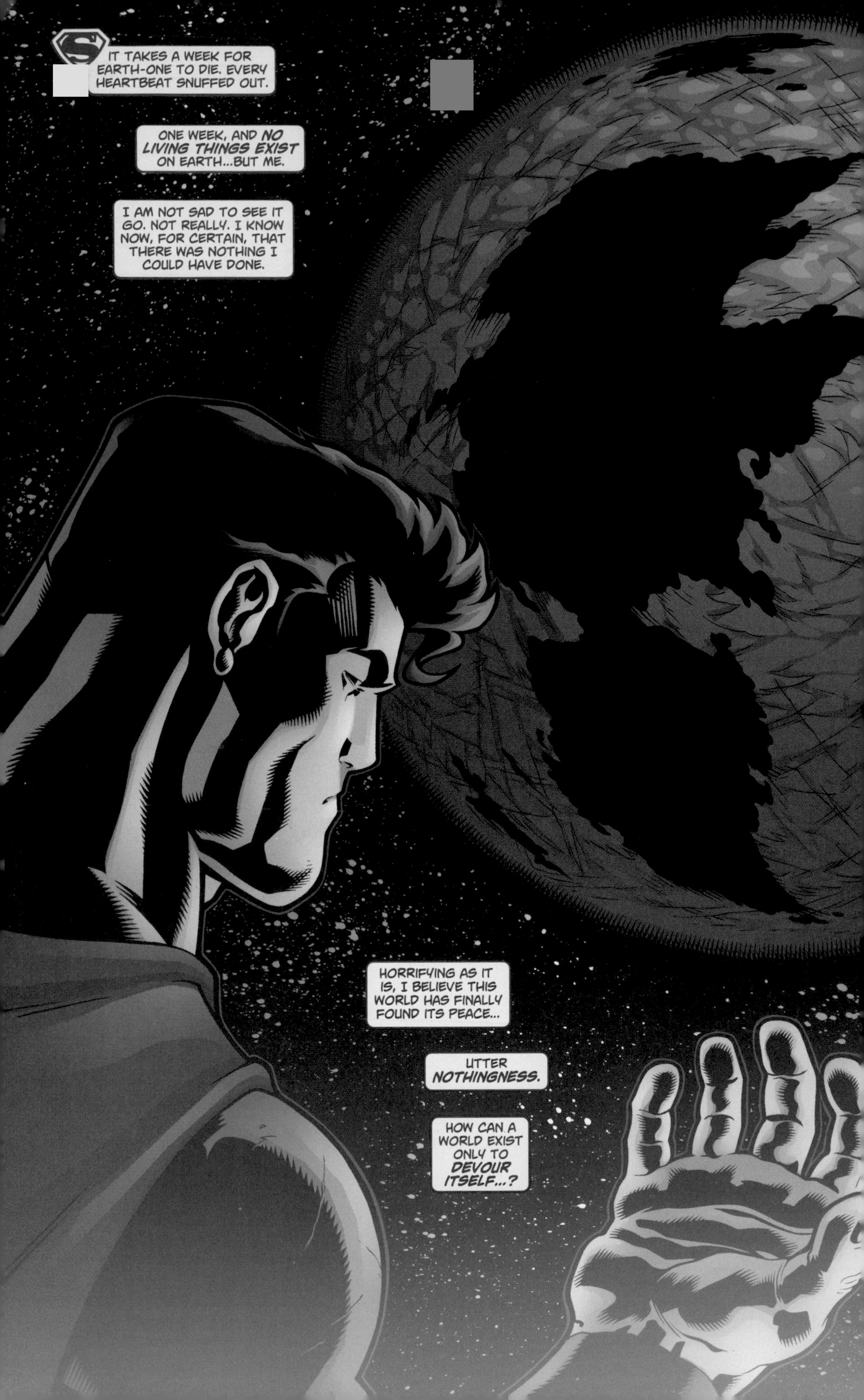
IT TAKES A WEEK FOR EARTH-ONE TO DIE. EVERY HEARTBEAT SNUFFED OUT.
ONE WEEK, AND NO LIVING THINGS EXIST ON EARTH...BUT ME.
I AM NOT SAD TO SEE IT GO. NOT REALLY. I KNOW NOW, FOR CERTAIN, THAT THERE WAS NOTHING I COULD HAVE DONE.
HORRIFYING AS IT IS, I BELIEVE THIS WORLD HAS FINALLY FOUND ITS PEACE...
UTTER NOTHINGNESS.
HOW CAN A WORLD EXIST ONLY TO DEVOUR ITSELF...?

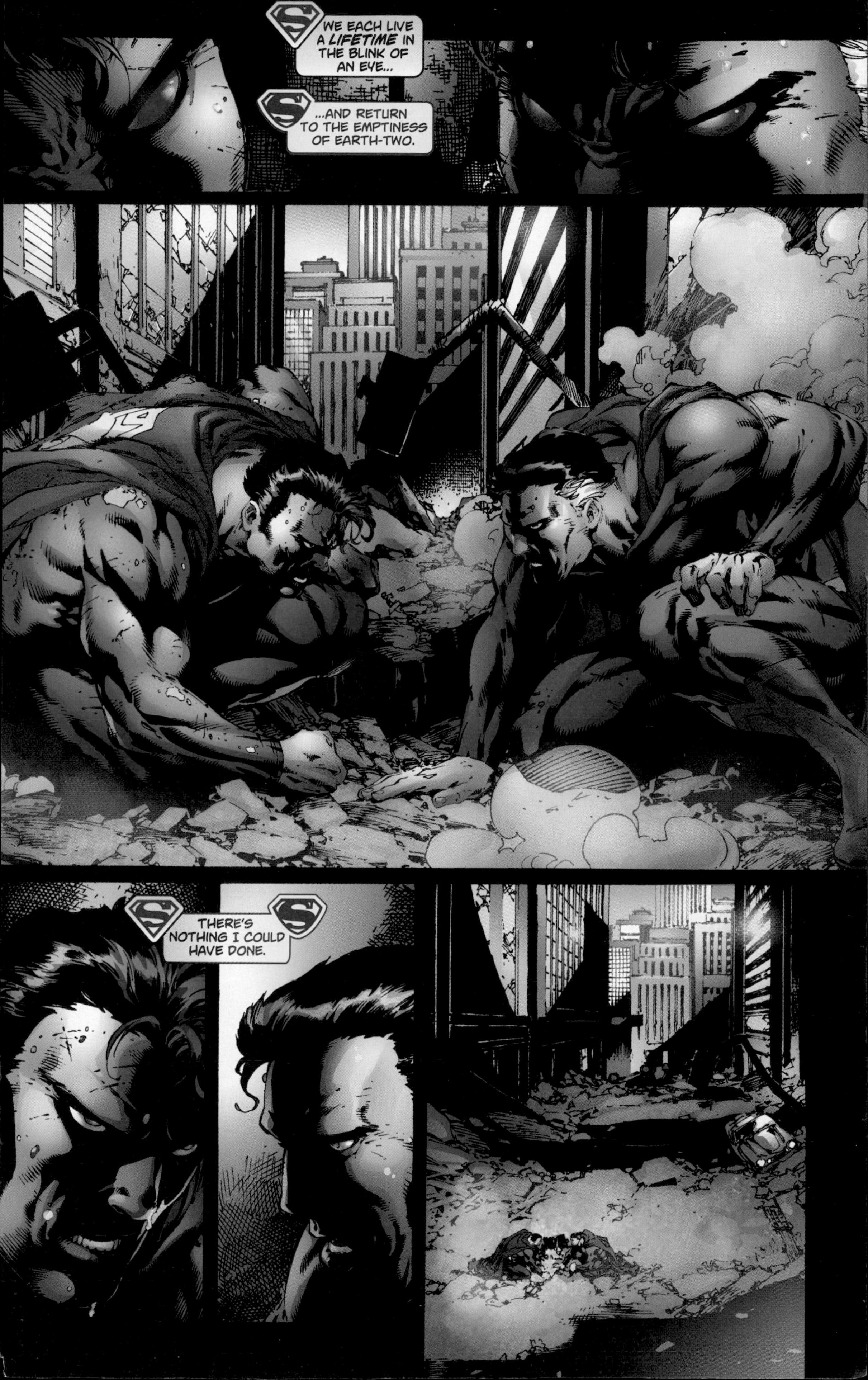
WE EACH LIVE A LIFETIME IN THE BLINK OF AN EYE...
...AND RETURN TO THE EMPTINESS OF EARTH-TWO.
THERE'S NOTHING I COULD HAVE DONE.

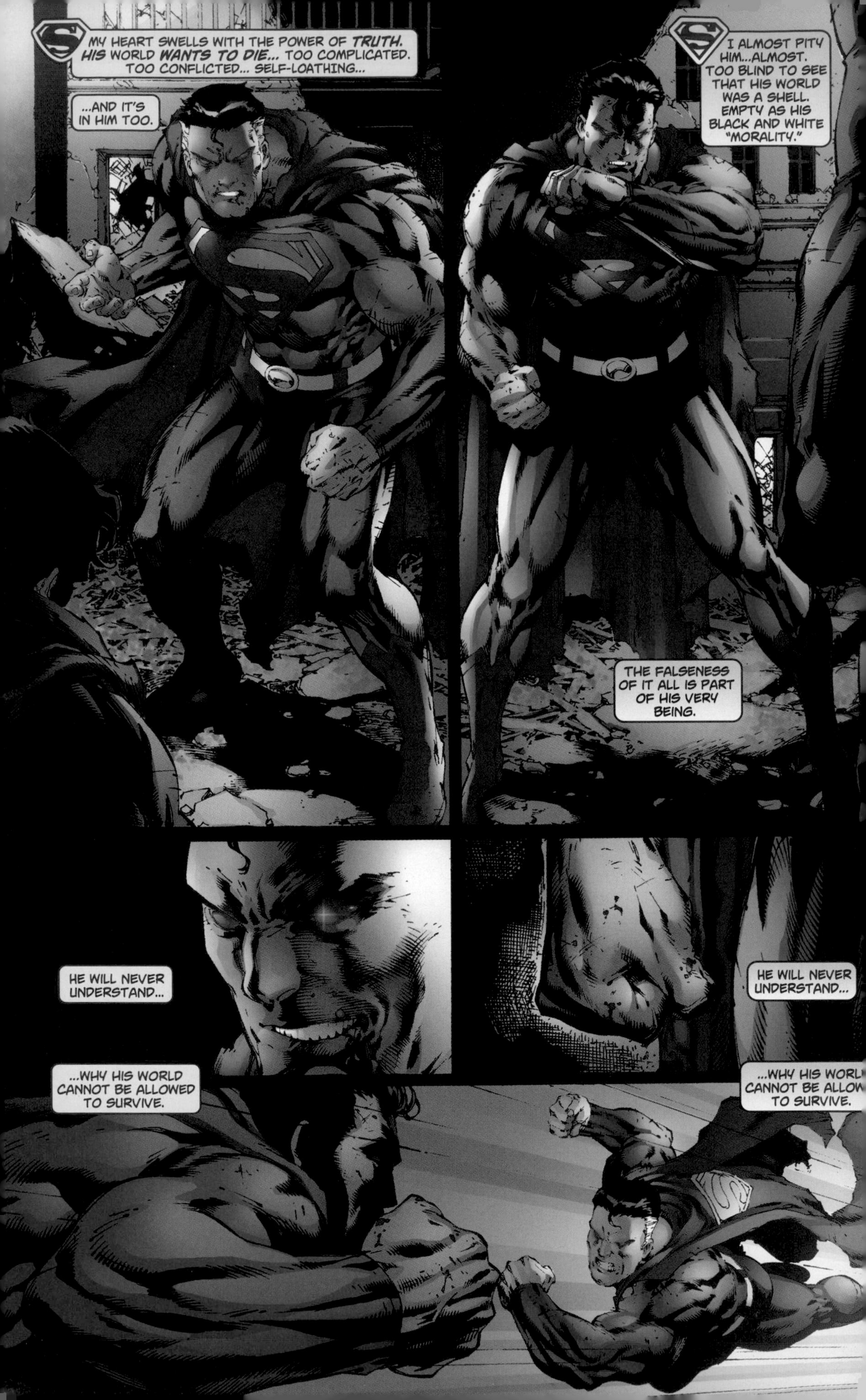

MY HEART SWELLS WITH THE POWER OF TRUTH. HIS WORLD WANTS TO DIE... TOO COMPLICATED. TOO CONFLICTED... SELF-LOATHING...
...AND IT'S IN HIM TOO.
I ALMOST PITY HIM...ALMOST. TOO BLIND TO SEE THAT HIS WORLD WAS A SHELL. EMPTY AS HIS BLACK AND WHITE "MORALITY."
THE FALSENESS OF IT ALL IS PART OF HIS VERY BEING.
HE WILL NEVER UNDERSTAND...
HE WILL NEVER UNDERSTAND...
...WHY HIS WORLD CANNOT BE ALLOWED TO SURVIVE.
...WHY HIS WORL CANNOT BE ALLOW TO SURVIVE.

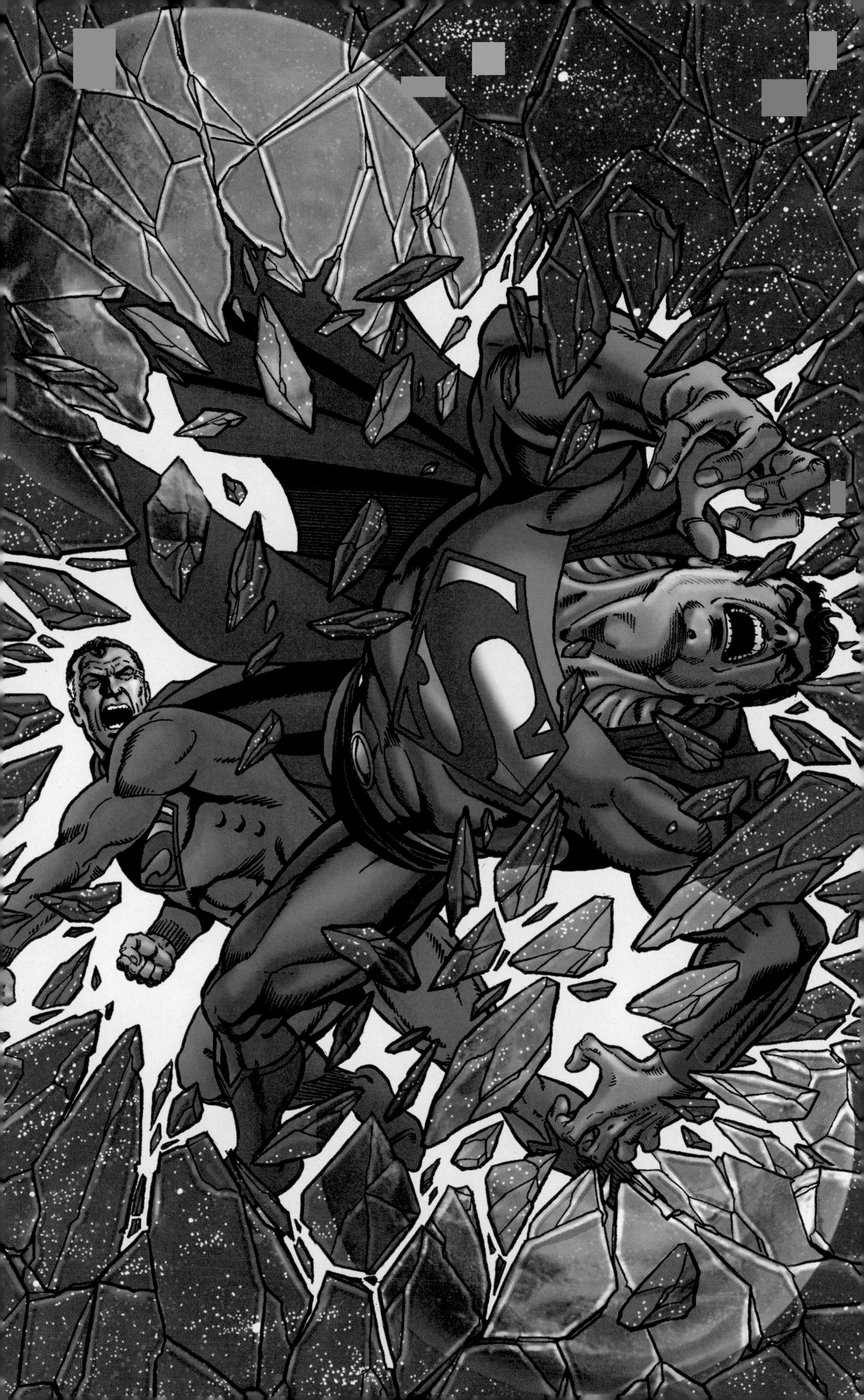

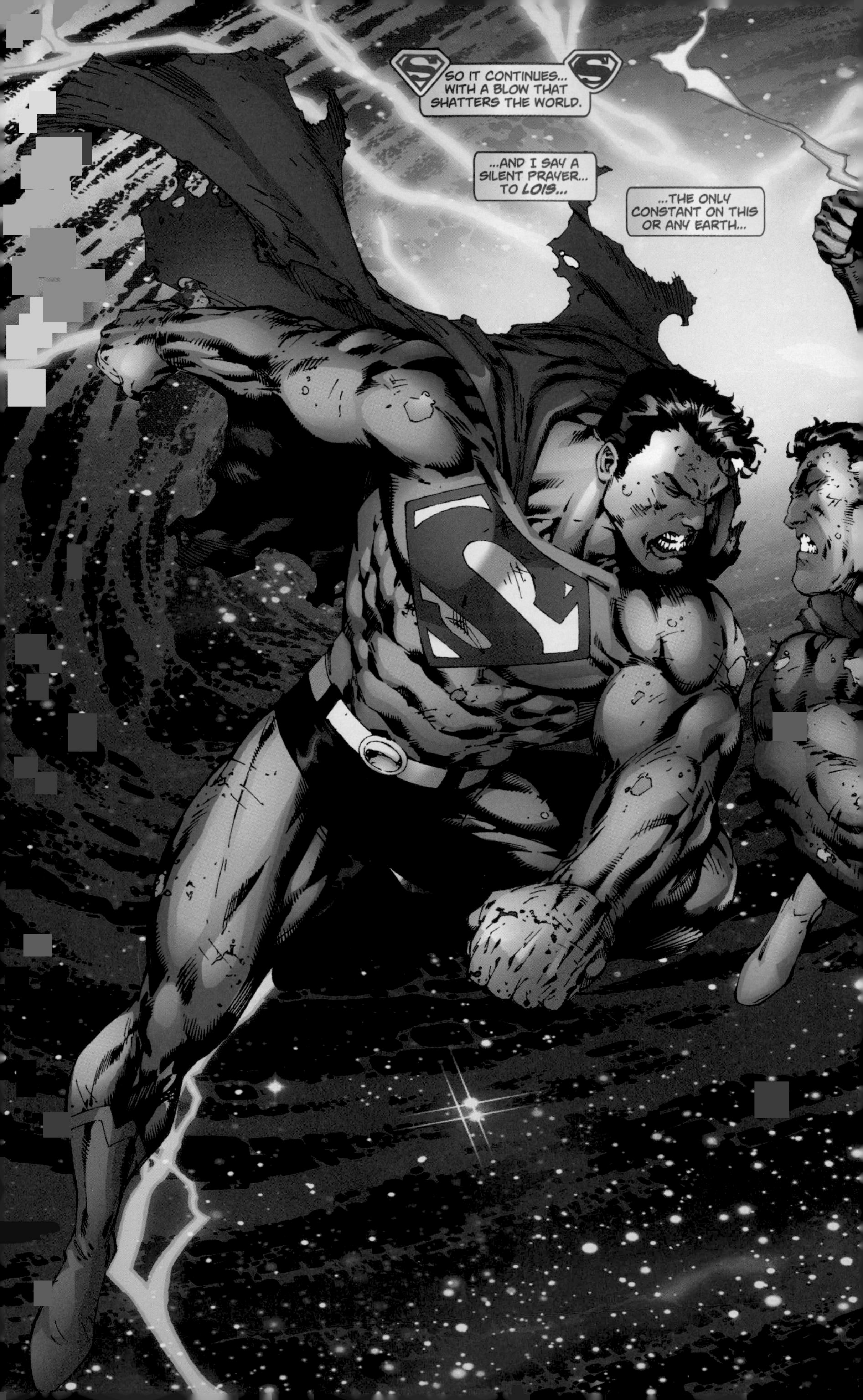
SO IT CONTINUES... WITH A BLOW THAT SHATTERS THE WORLD.
...AND I SAY A SILENT PRAYER... TO LOIS...
...THE ONLY CONSTANT ON THIS OR ANY EARTH...

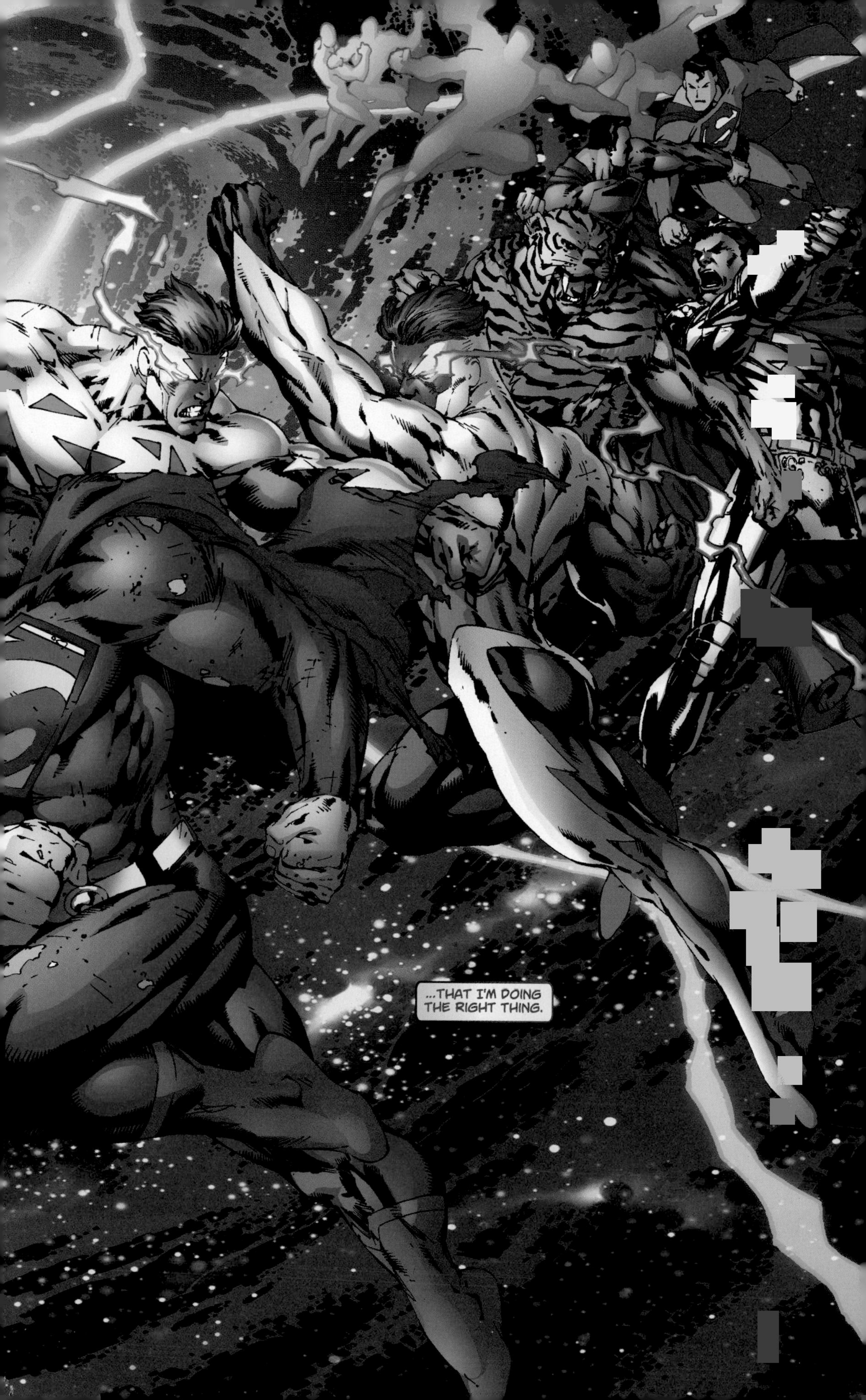
...THAT I'M DOING THE RIGHT THING.

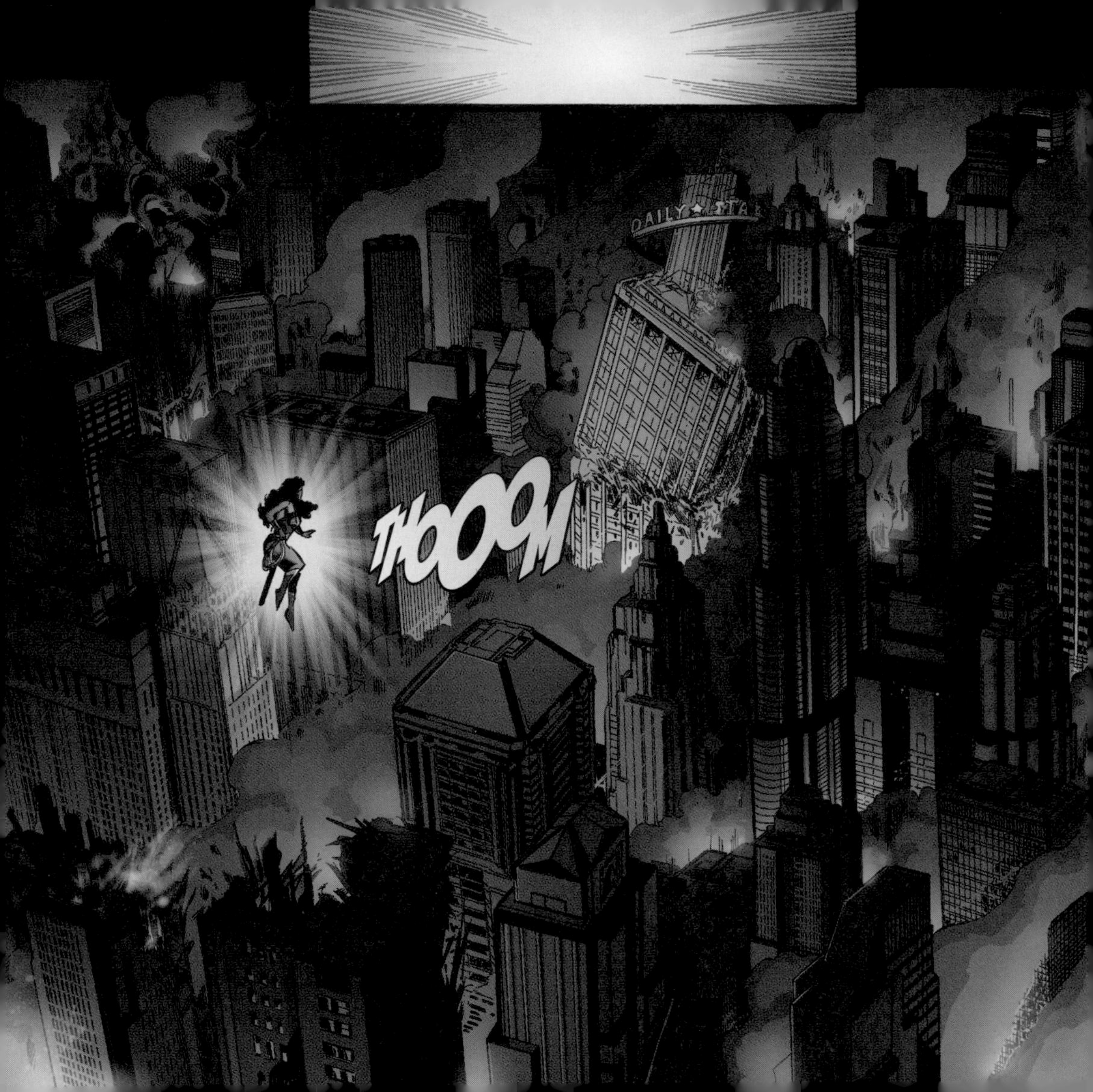
DAILY STAR
THOOOM

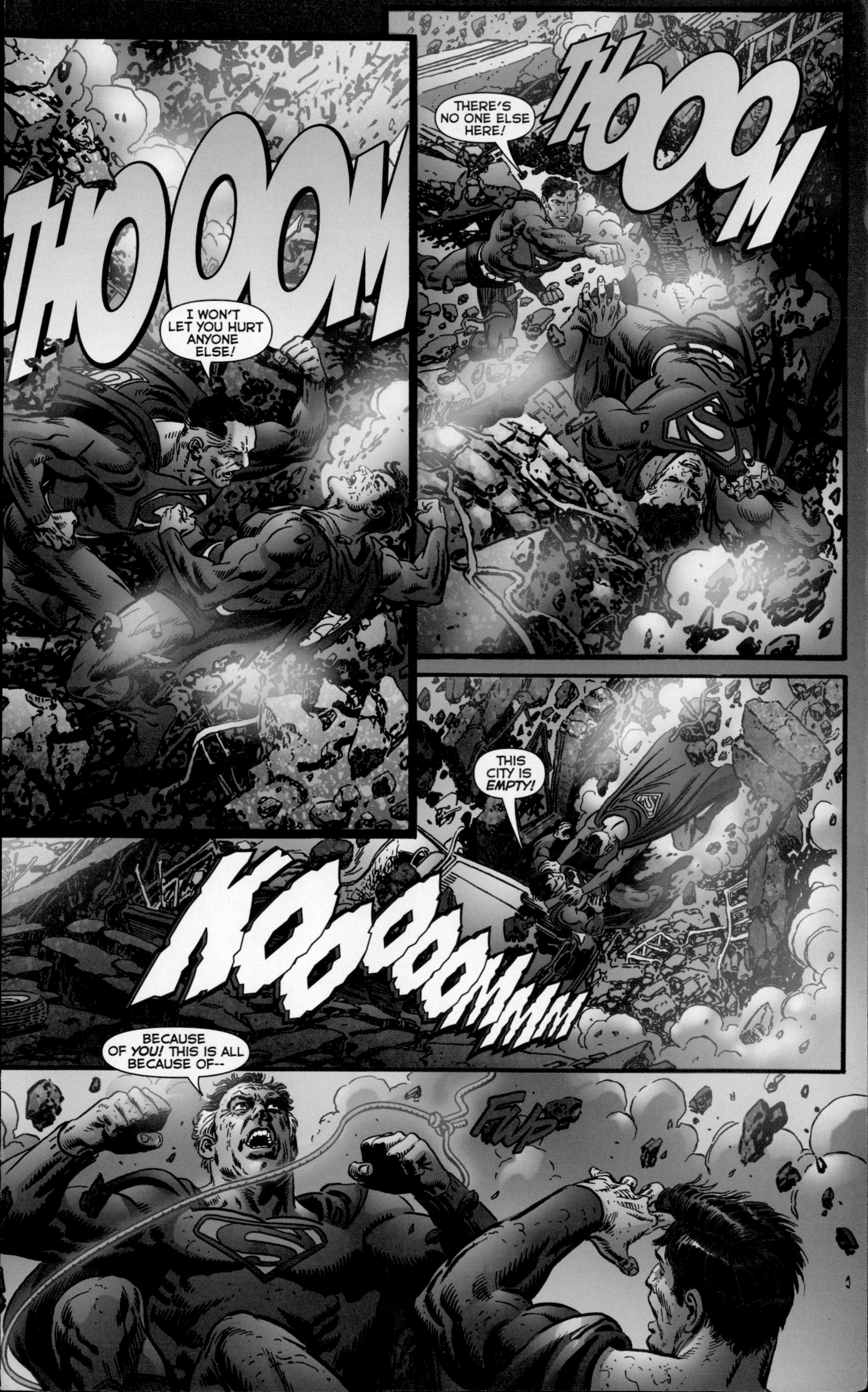
THOOOM
I WON'T LET YOU HURT ANYONE ELSE!
THERE'S NO ONE ELSE HERE!
THOOOM
THIS CITY IS *EMPTY!*
KOOOOOMMMM
BECAUSE OF *YOU!* THIS IS ALL BECAUSE OF--

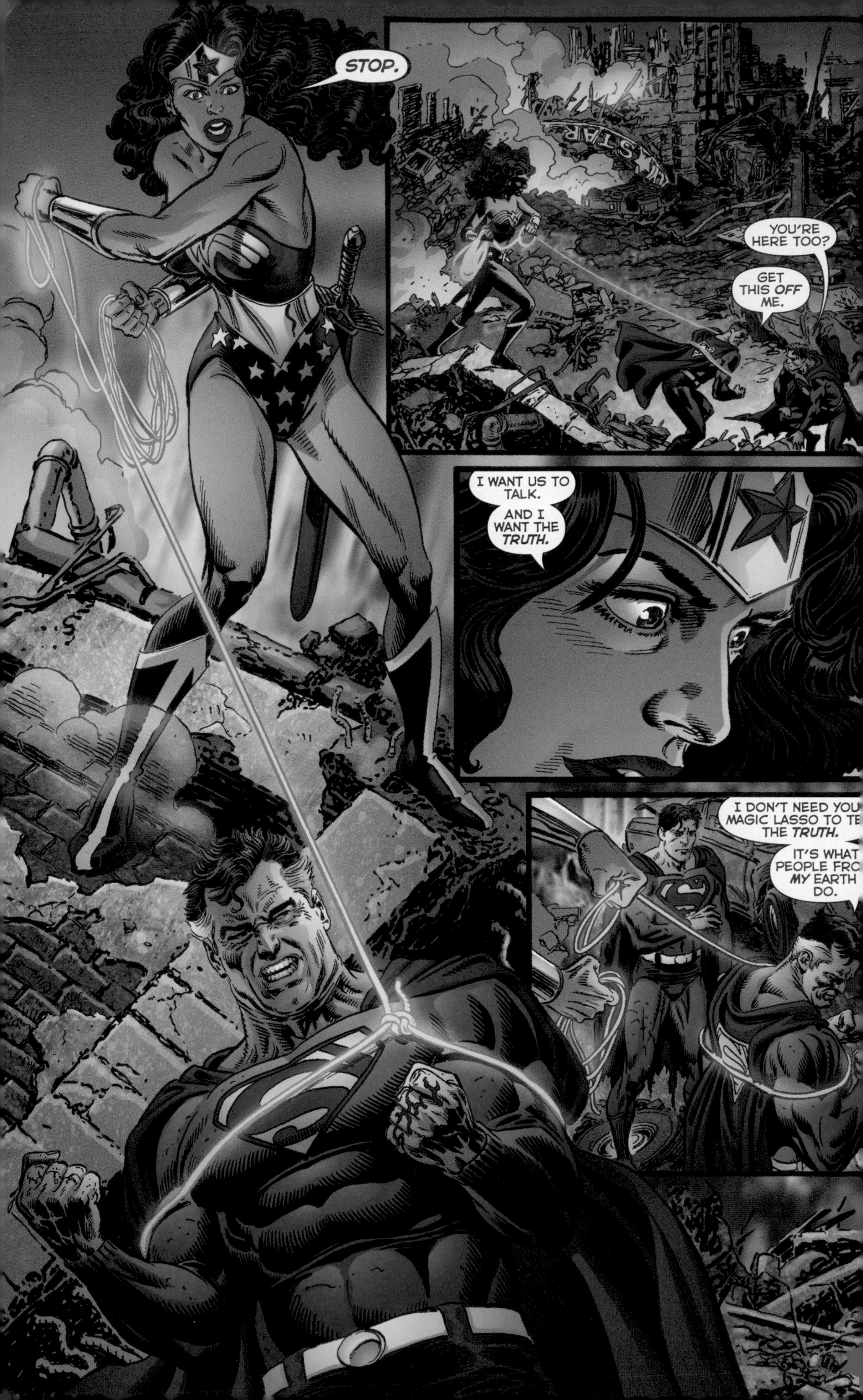
STOP.
YOU'RE HERE TOO?
GET THIS OFF ME.
I WANT US TO TALK.
AND I WANT THE TRUTH.
I DON'T NEED YOU MAGIC LASSO TO TE THE TRUTH.
IT'S WHAT PEOPLE FRO MY EARTH DO.

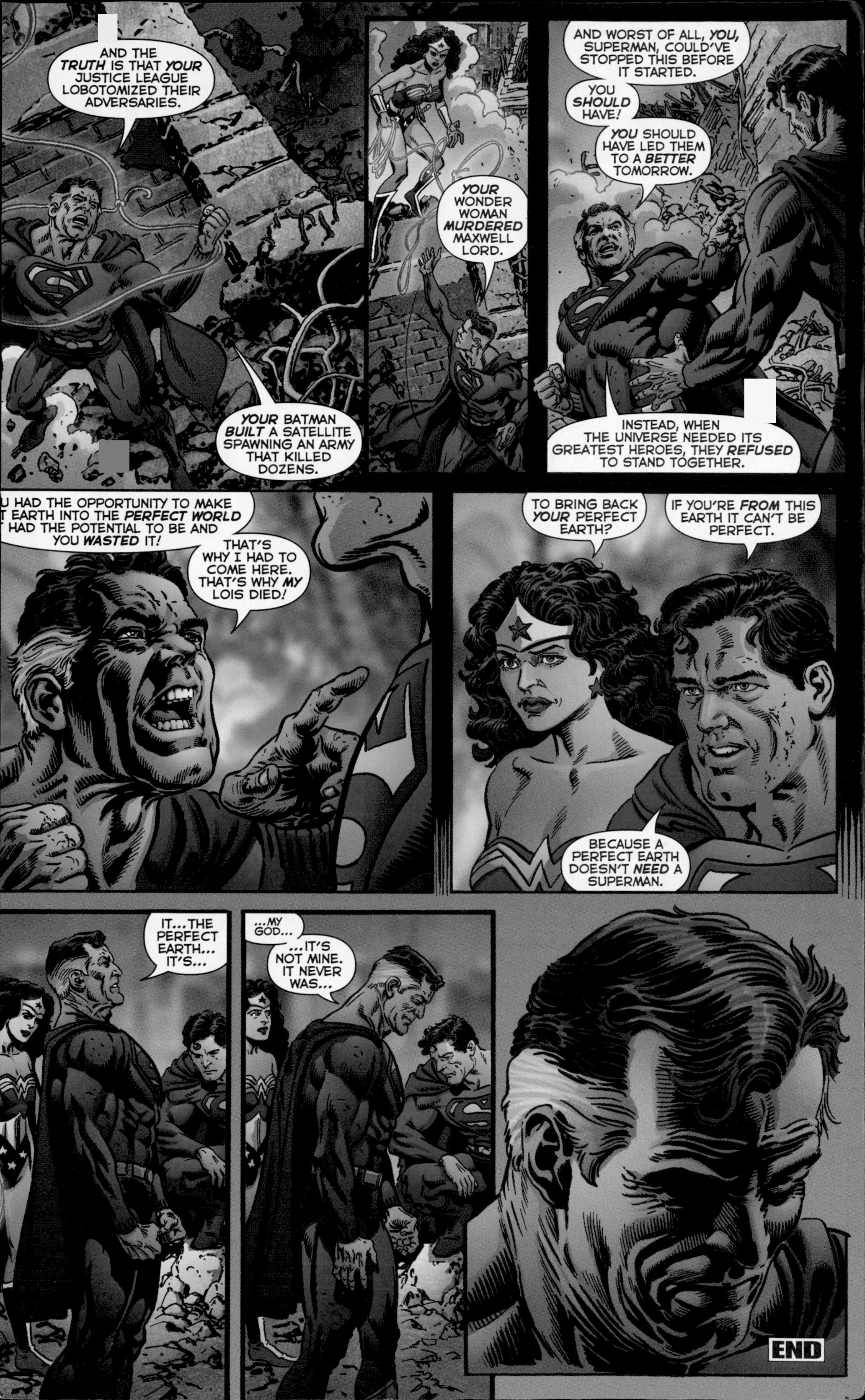
AND THE TRUTH IS THAT YOUR JUSTICE LEAGUE LOBOTOMIZED THEIR ADVERSARIES.
YOUR BATMAN BUILT A SATELLITE SPAWNING AN ARMY THAT KILLED DOZENS.
YOUR WONDER WOMAN MURDERED MAXWELL LORD.
AND WORST OF ALL, YOU, SUPERMAN, COULD'VE STOPPED THIS BEFORE IT STARTED.
YOU SHOULD HAVE!
YOU SHOULD HAVE LED THEM TO A BETTER TOMORROW.
INSTEAD, WHEN THE UNIVERSE NEEDED ITS GREATEST HEROES, THEY REFUSED TO STAND TOGETHER.
U HAD THE OPPORTUNITY TO MAKE T EARTH INTO THE PERFECT WORLD T HAD THE POTENTIAL TO BE AND YOU WASTED IT!
THAT'S WHY I HAD TO COME HERE. THAT'S WHY MY LOIS DIED!
TO BRING BACK YOUR PERFECT EARTH?
IF YOU'RE FROM THIS EARTH IT CAN'T BE PERFECT.
BECAUSE A PERFECT EARTH DOESN'T NEED A SUPERMAN.
IT... THE PERFECT EARTH... IT'S...
...MY GOD...
...IT'S NOT MINE. IT NEVER WAS...
END

SUPERMAN
EARTH-TWO

First Appearance: **ACTION COMICS #1 (June, 1938)**
Real Name: **Kal-L**
Secret Identity: **Clark Kent**
Occupation: **Reporter/Editor**
Relatives: **John & Mary (Parents)**
Ht: **6'2"** Wt: **222 lbs.**
Eyes: **Blue** Hair: **Black**
Base of Operations: **Metropolis**

When famed scientist Jor-L discovered that both age and groundquakes would soon destroy his homeworld of Krypton, he and his wife, Lora, placed their infant son, Kal-L, into a hastily prepared rocket and launched it into the heavens.

The tiny ship hurtled toward Earth, landing on the outskirts of the farming community of Smallville. John and Mary Kent, who had pined for a child of their own, found the infant and adopted him, naming him Clark.

On Earth, Clark's Kryptonian superhuman abilities were magnified by the planet's lighter gravity. By the time he reached adulthood, radio documentaries of the era heralded him "Faster than a speeding bullet! More powerful than a locomotive! Able to leap tall buildings in a single bound!"

After John and Mary's deaths, Clark moved to Metropolis, where he wrote a story on the first Superman sighting, when the hero stopped a public lynching. Impressed by the young man's tenacity and skill, Daily Star editor George Taylor quickly snapped him up as a reporter.

Clark met his match in intrepid reporter Lois Lane and, even in the face of Superman's heroic glamour, his passion for the truth eventually won her heart.

The two were married for forty-seven years when the Anti-Monitor succeeded in destroying the vast majority of the multiverse. Superman and an array of heroes and villains defeated the Anti-Monitor even as the remaining Earths collapsed into one.

Superman, Lois, Alex Luthor and Superboy-Prime watched as the deadly wake of the Anti-Monitor's destruction headed straight for them, but Alex made a desperate choice, opening a dimensional tunnel into another realm, a newfound Heaven.

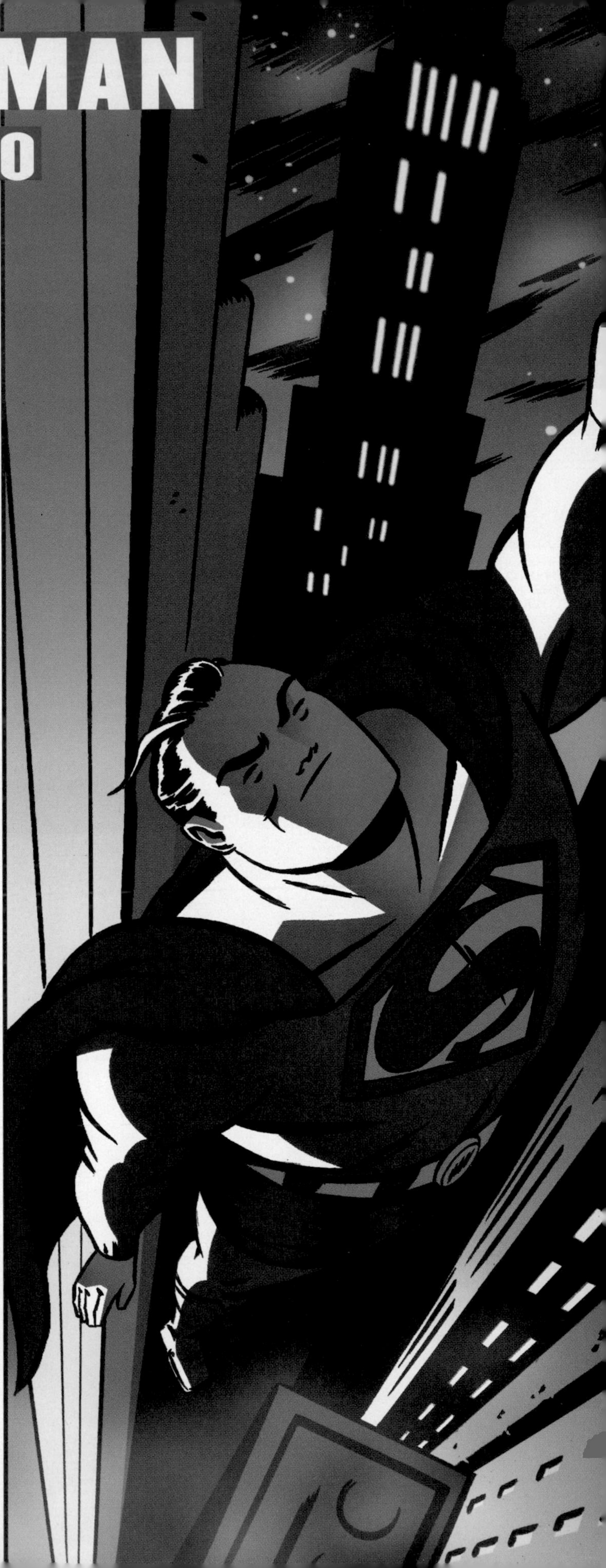

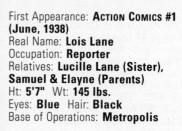

LOIS LANE
EARTH-TWO

First Appearance: **ACTION COMICS #1 (June, 1938)**
Real Name: **Lois Lane**
Occupation: **Reporter**
Relatives: **Lucille Lane (Sister), Samuel & Elayne (Parents)**
Ht: **5'7"** Wt: **145 lbs.**
Eyes: **Blue** Hair: **Black**
Base of Operations: **Metropolis**

Lois and her sister were born in Cleveland, Ohio, daughters of United States Marine Colonel Samuel L. Lane. The fast-paced life of moving from base to base sparked Lois's fertile imagination, every country a new source of danger and adventure.

Enthralled even at the earliest age by the combination, Lois sought them out wherever she went, sneaking away from home to explore local towns, pursuing and evading thieves and slavers.

The thrill of the hunt led her directly to a job at the Metropolis Daily Star, the leading newspaper in the city, where she demanded the most dangerous overseas assignments, reporting on the massive war breaking out across Europe. Her personal observations and incisive interviews not only led to her name becoming larger than life (she was thrown out of Germany on the orders of Hitler himself!), but, more important, they were the driving force behind convincing America to enter the war.

Once back in America, Lois met the two men who would forever change her life: mild-mannered reporter Clark Kent and the superhuman Superman. Lois was instantly and inexorably drawn to Superman's power and charisma, but she soon found her true match in Clark, who proved to be neither as unsophisticated nor clumsy as he had once seemed.

Lois continued working for the Daily Star until her mid-sixties, when the Crisis on Infinite Earths began. Before Earth-Two disappeared from existence, Lois was rescued by Earth-Three's Alex Luthor, who reunited her with her husband in an alternate dimension.

ALEX LUTHOR
EARTH-THREE

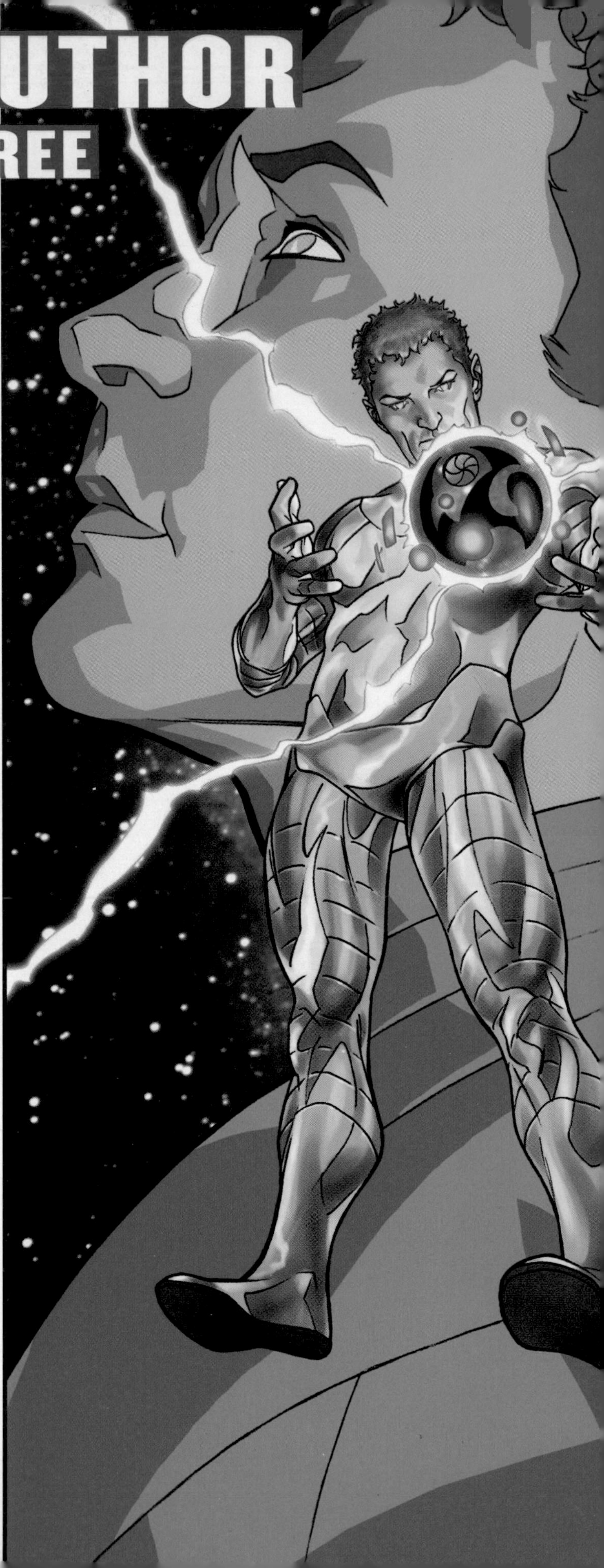

First Appearance: **CRISIS ON INFINITE EARTHS #1 (January, 1985)**
Real Name: **Alex Luthor**
Occupation: **None**
Relatives: **Alexander & Lois Lane Luthor (Parents)**
Ht: **5'11"** Wt: **164 lbs.**
Eyes: **Blue** Hair: **Red**
Base of Operations: **Limbo**

On the world known as Earth-Three, evil usually triumphed over good, a trend that culminated in the brutal rule of super-villains over every nation.

The most famous non-powered citizens were former reporter Lois Lane and her husband, the brilliant scientist Alexander Luthor, who used his genius in the constant struggle against the tyranny of their rulers, becoming Earth-Three's sole super-hero.

Alexander detected the Crisis long before the skies on Earth-Three turned red, and, knowing their world was coming to an abrupt and absolute end, he placed their newborn son, Alex, into a dimensional capsule, sending it rocketing along the edges of the multiverse to what they prayed was safety. That safety was in the orbit of Earth-One, where he was found by the being known as the Monitor.

But something had happened to Alex as he bridged the dimensions: matter and antimatter manifested within him simultaneously. Instead of instantly destroying everything around him, it nurtured him, and he aged at an incredible rate. Within hours, he went from newborn to teenager.

Therefore, it was an older Alex Luthor who joined the Monitor and the unlikely alliance of heroes and villains who had gathered to destroy the Anti-Monitor.

Alex saved who he could from the collapsing multiverse. When the shock wave of the Anti-Monitor's destruction ripped toward him and fellow survivors Superman, Lois Lane and Superboy-Prime, Alex used his matter/antimatter powers to transport them to another dimension, where things were perfect, for a time.

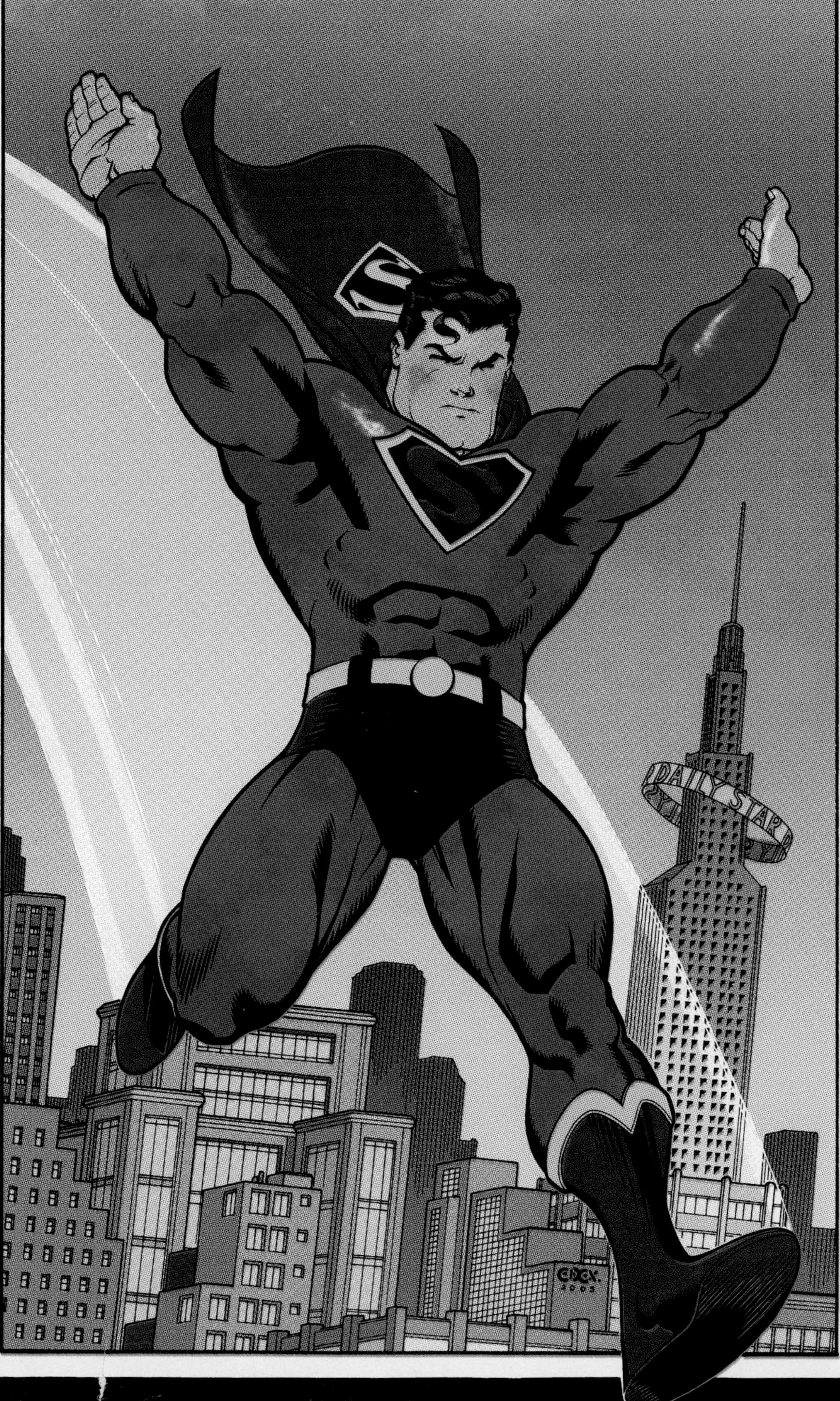
DAILY STAR
SUPERMAN 226 BY ED McGUINNESS, DEXTER VINES AND DAVE McCAIG

INFINITE CRISIS SECRET FILES AND ORIGINS 2006
BY IVAN REIS, MARC CAMPOS AND DAVE McCAIG

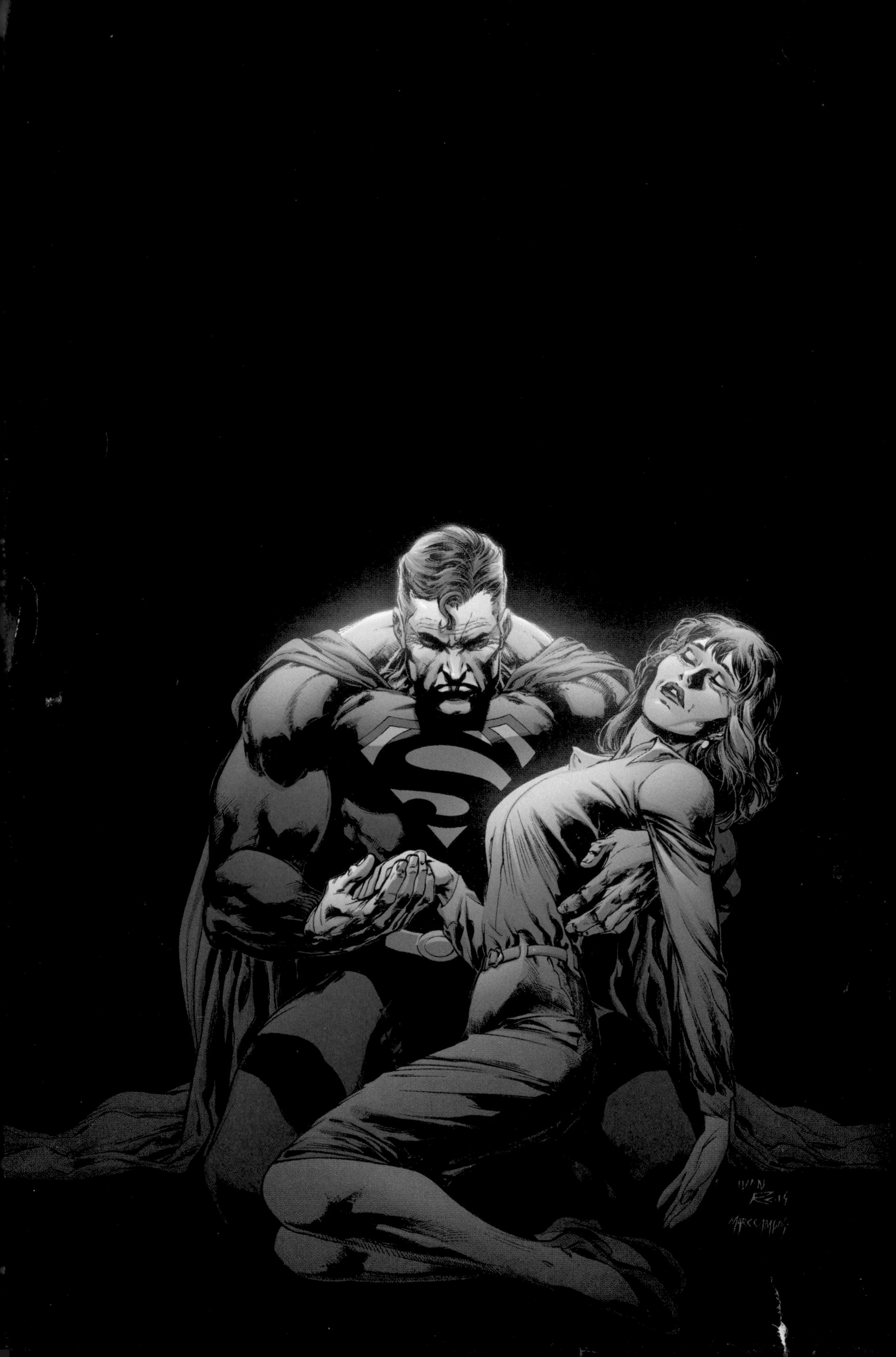

ACTION COMICS 836 BY MARK SCHULTZ AND DAVE McCAIG

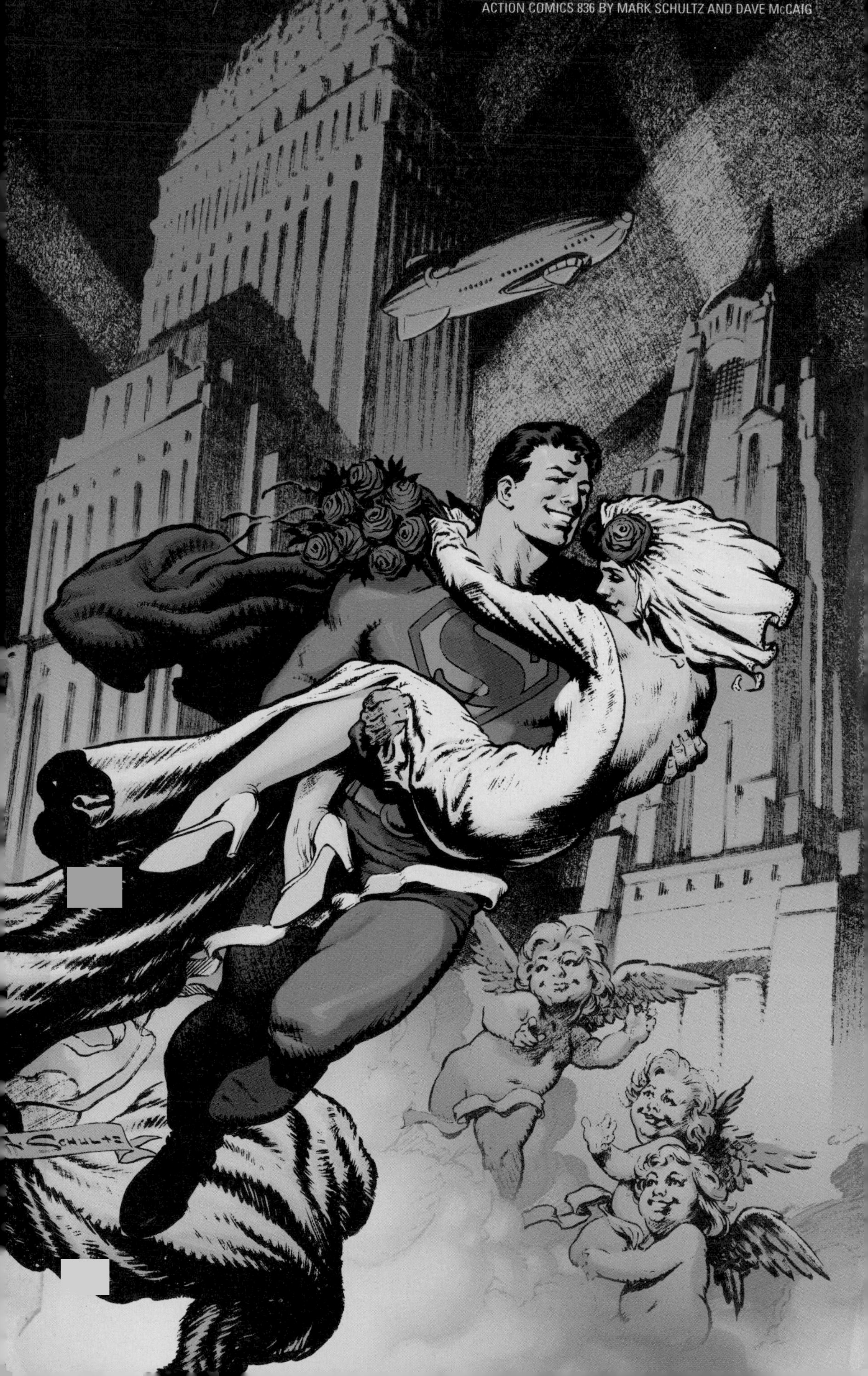
SCHULTZ

ADVENTURES OF SUPERMAN 649
BY IVAN REIS, MARC CAMPOS AND DAVE McCAIG

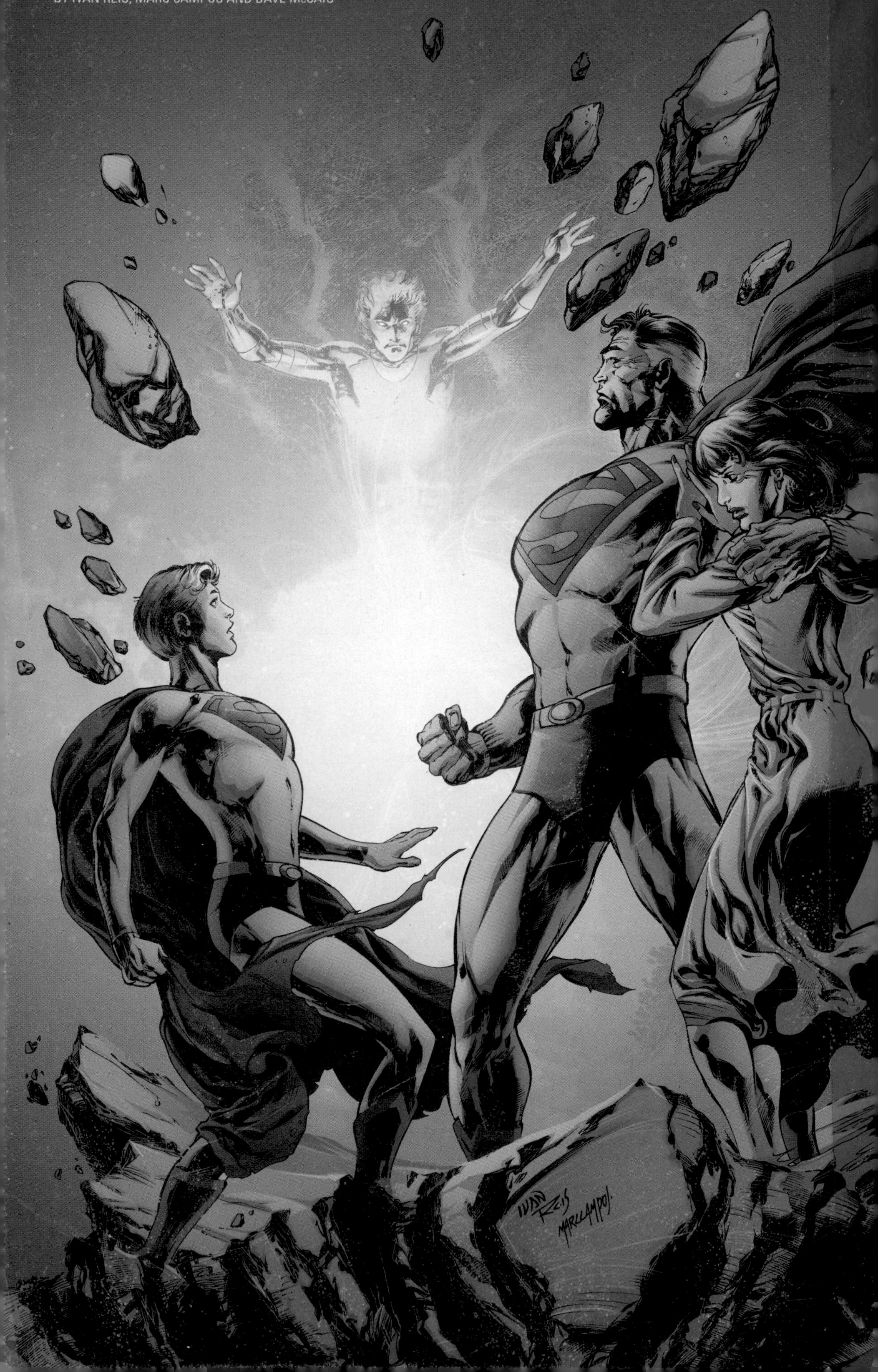
IVAN REIS
MARCCAMPOS.